COLOR HARMONY
for ARTISTS

COLOR HARMONY *for* ARTISTS

How to Transform Inspiration into Beautiful Watercolor Palettes and Paintings

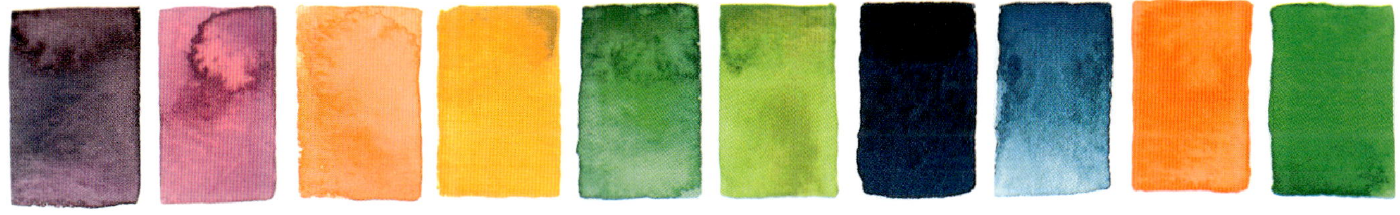

ANA VICTORIA CALDERÓN

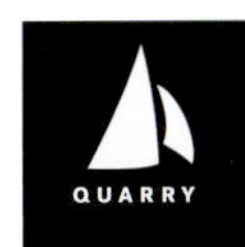

Quarto.com

First Published in 2020 by Quarry Books, an imprint of The Quarto Group,
100 Cummings Center, Suite 265-D, Beverly, MA 01915, USA.
T (978) 282-9590 F (978) 283-2742

EEA Representation, WTS Tax d.o.o.,
Žanova ulica 3, 4000 Kranj, Slovenia.
www.wts-tax.si

Quarry Books titles are also available at discount for retail, wholesale, promotional, and bulk purchase. For
details, contact the Special Sales Manager by email at specialsales@quarto.com or by mail at The Quarto Group,
Attn: Special Sales Manager, 100 Cummings Center, Suite 265-D, Beverly, MA 01915, USA.

10

ISBN: 978-1-63159-771-8

Digital edition published in 2020

Library of Congress Cataloging-in-Publication Data is available

Design: Allison Meierding
Page Layout: Megan Jones Design
Artwork courtesy of Ana Victoria Calderón
Photography: Shutterstock; except for page 8 & 144, Ana Victoria Calderón

Printed in Huizhou City, Guangdong, China TT012026

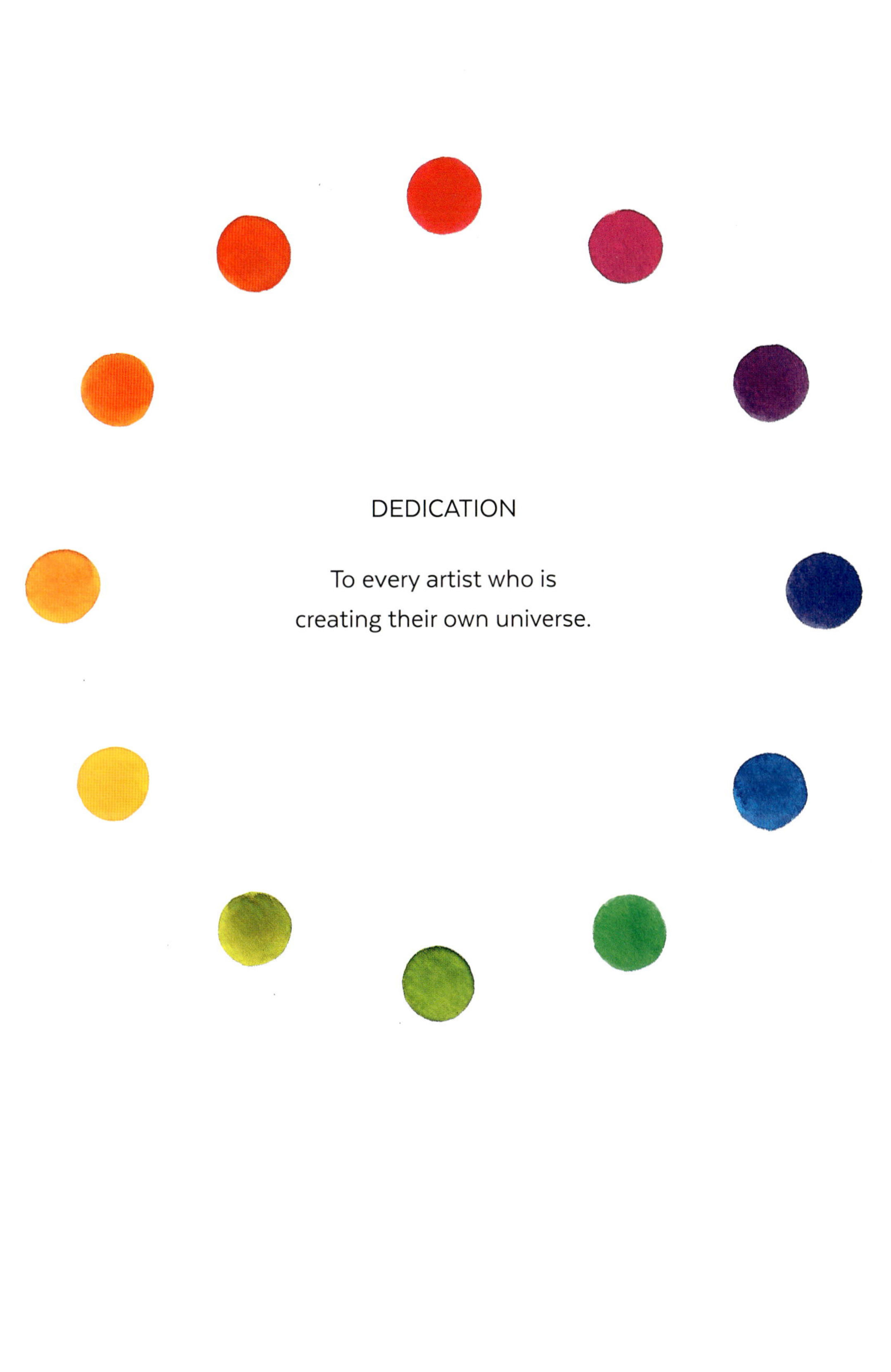

DEDICATION

To every artist who is
creating their own universe.

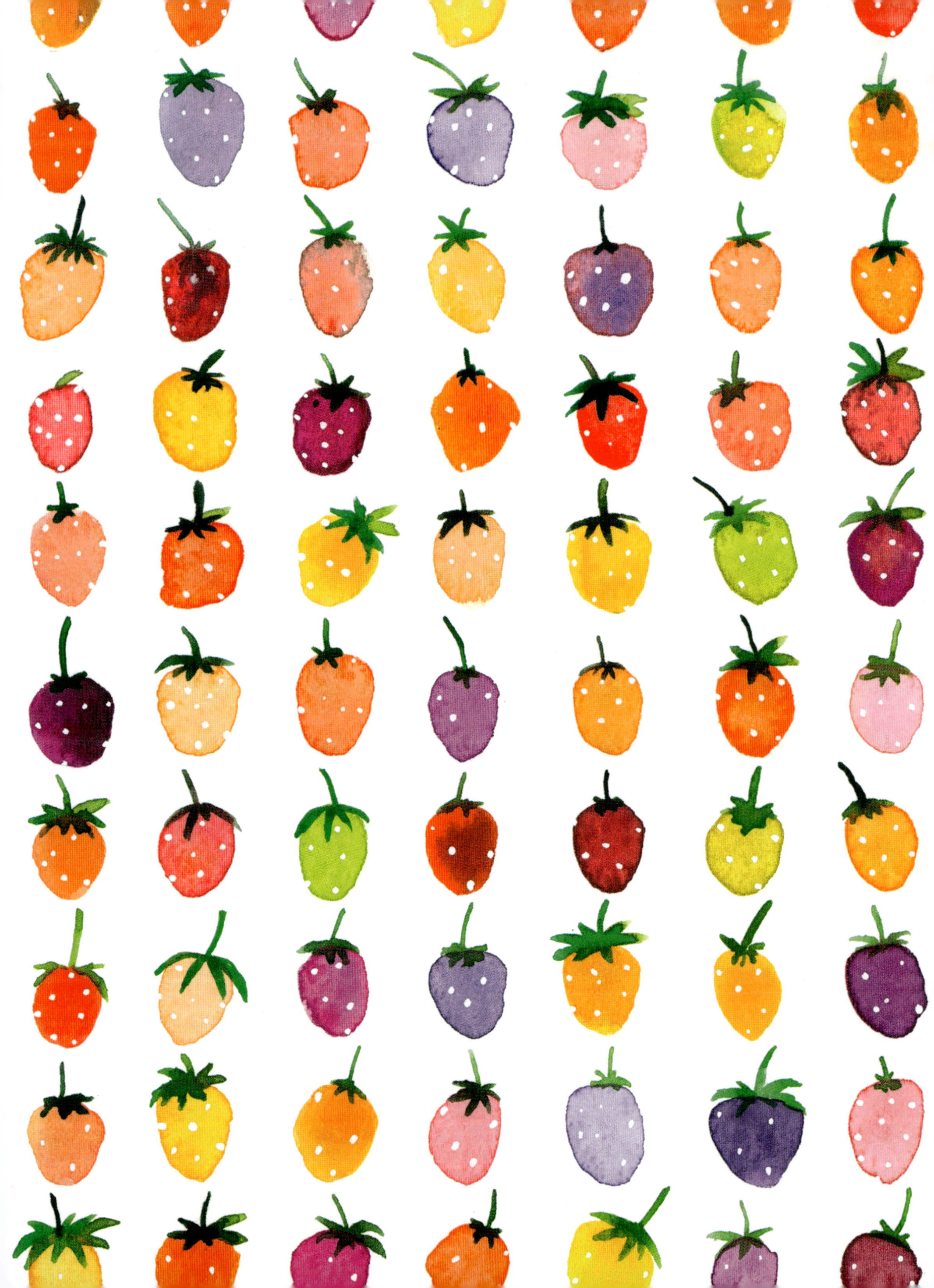

Contents

Capturing moods and playing with textures in beautiful swatches of watercolor mixes that reflect a variety of visual inspirations

Preface

Back in 2016, my sister, Maggie, and I found ourselves visiting Sedona, Arizona, for a few days after a conference we attended nearby. We decided to visit this mystical spot because we had heard all kinds of fun stories about crystal shops and energy vortexes. All this was true, but what I was not prepared for were the breathtaking landscapes made up of red sandstone geological formations, glowing in the reflection of the orange sky. It's the kind of visual that you can see in pictures yet is magnified times a hundred when you are in its presence.

All of this was even more impactful for me because, despite being born near the Rocky Mountains, I have spent most of my life in the tropics. So my everyday color palette had always been deeply inspired by the bright turquoise Caribbean Sea and Cancun's lush jungle vegetation and flora. Finding myself in this new deep red, warm, and earthy color theme was invigorating—and sparked an idea.

During our time in Sedona I took pictures on my phone of special spots we visited on hikes—cactus patches, stones, my bare feet at the top of a vortex, and the glowing sky. I made sure to edit them while I was still in each location so as to capture the true vibrance and hues of what I was witnessing.

When I got back home from this trip, I printed out the pictures and began swatching color boards and painting textures or mini-landscapes inspired by each photo. When I would see the photo next to each color palette and minipainting, I got this pure feeling of satisfaction, and I also realized how powerful taking inspiration from nature and new life experiences are for an artist's growth.

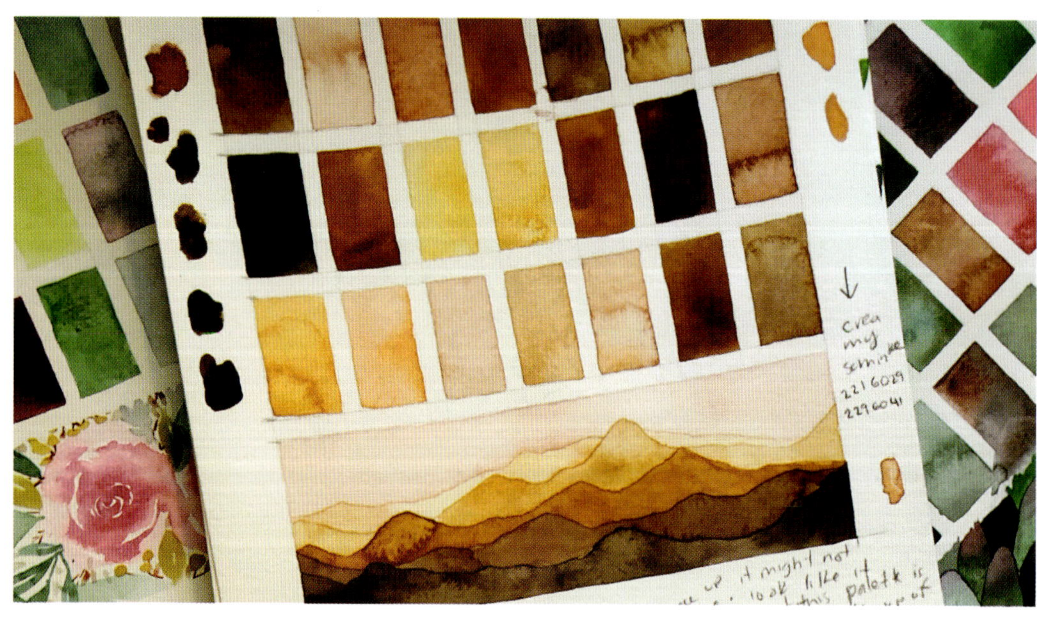

I wanted to pass on this message to my students who come to the creative retreats I host, so I decided to turn it into a field painting workshop. Whether it be in the Mayan Jungle, Sicily, or Morocco, the surrounding areas are new for everyone, and I knew this activity was an incredible way for students to begin picking up ideas for new paintings and settle in to their new environment while familiarizing themselves with the local color palette. I now begin every retreat with this activity, and I find it sets the tone for a beautiful week of making art.

Now that I look back at this Arizona trip, I recognize a turning point in my personal art. Finding myself surrounded by this special color theme and landscape, I can truly see how I integrated that life experience into my personal color palette and subject matter from that moment on.

The idea for this book was initially inspired in this one creative activity while in Sedona, but why stop there? What if we take this swatching exercise and use it as a tool to stimulate the creative process and break out into new painting themes? Even the most accomplished artists can sometimes feel they have fallen into a creative rut or that their art begins to look repetitive. I know that, personally, I have felt this way many times, and this simple creative tool can help one relax as an artist and ease into new ideas and subject matters.

In this book, we selected a series of themes to draw inspiration from, ranging from cities, to time periods, art movements, humans, floral arrangements, landscapes, and skies. I demonstrate how using color mixing as a tool can set the mood for your creative process, and taking small elements from a photograph can spark ideas for complete pieces of art. A rock formation may inspire you to paint a texture you can later integrate into a larger landscape you're thinking about. Or the style of ocean waves in ancient Thai paintings can inspire you to paint a composition of your own using this one element as a starting point. I always encourage taking elements as inspiration while staying true to your signature drawing style and aesthetic. The idea is to create your own unique universe by mixing what you see in the lustrous world with pictures from your imagination.

Having basic color knowledge definitely helps, and we cover this. But in the end, I think it really comes down to connecting with your emotions and intuition. This is what gives art spirit.

Think of this book as a tool: whenever you see an image that strikes your attention, there is something there. Hold on to that and begin painting!

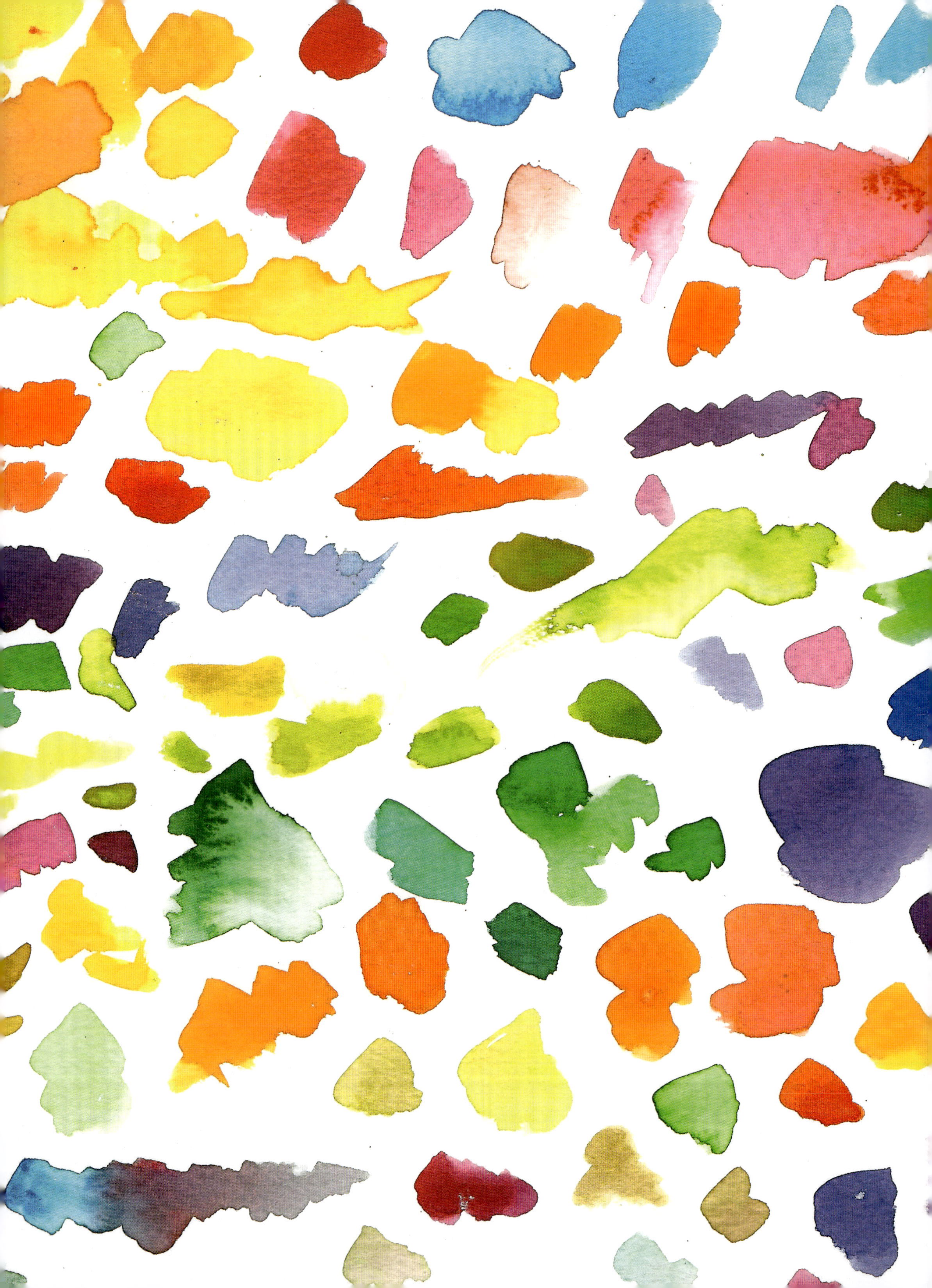

Hands-On
Color Theory

The Color Wheel

To understand how to mix color, I suggest you familiarize yourself with the color wheel, then use your feelings and intuition. We've all seen this rainbow-style wheel chart, either in school or on the back of art-supply packaging, and it's likely you know the basics: red, yellow, and blue are the three primary colors.

Mixing any of these two together will make secondary colors: red and yellow make orange, yellow and blue make green, and blue and red make violet.

Finally, to make tertiary colors, simply mix a primary with a secondary color: green and blue make turquoise (or green-blue). The tertiary colors are, in fact, usually named with the colors of both hues mixed together: red-orange, orange-yellow, yellow-green, green-blue, blue-violet, and violet-red.

I painted an example of a color wheel here. The dots indicate each color, and in the spirit of watercolor and color mixing, I created a gradient pie with a slice of each color blending into its complementary color—in other words, its opposite. This is one of the most important concepts in the color wheel, along with a few other harmony schemes.

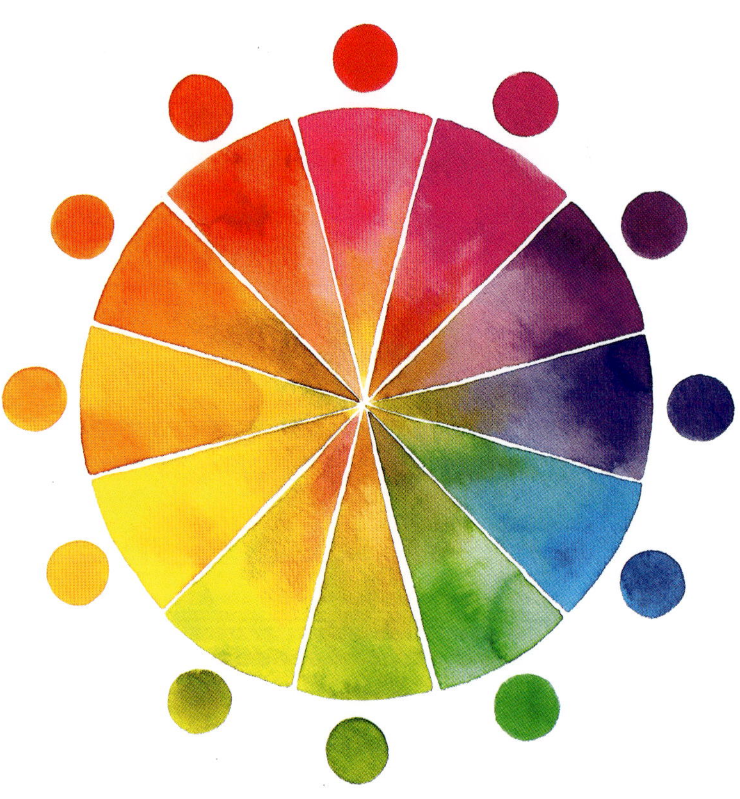

Color Harmonies

There are many harmony schemes around the color wheel that vary depending on the medium and application. While the basic color theory concepts are similar in interior design as they are in watercolor, there are a few variations and specific aspects to watercolor because of the medium's nature. Here's a selection of the standout harmony schemes relevant to this book.

MONOCHROMATIC

In color theory, **monochrome** usually refers to the same hue with a variation in tints, tones, and shades. In some cases, monochromatic schemes involve adding black, white, and gray to a specific hue, but in this case, in the spirit of watercolor, I like to keep hues pure. One of the most appealing aspects of working with watercolor is the variety in values that can be achieved by mixing different amounts of water into an individual pigment. So in this case, when I refer to monochrome, it will most likely be a base color with different amounts of water. See how in this example the color blue is watered down to create a monochromatic harmony with varying opacity and transparency in the paint.

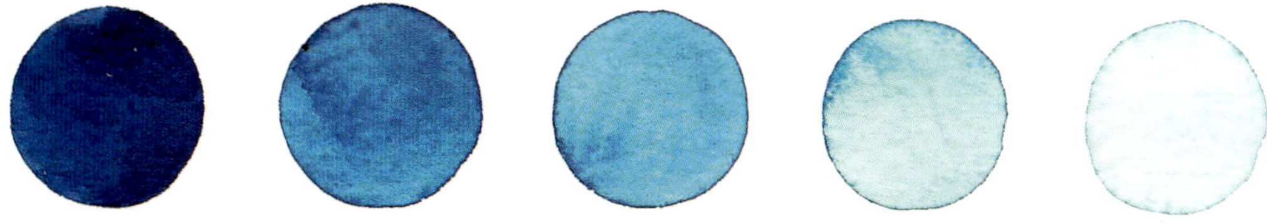

A monochromatic color scheme in blue.

ANALOGOUS

Analogous colors are extremely pleasing to the eye because they're the combination of colors that are next to each other on the wheel. There's little contrast, they match, and they're comforting. An example of this type of harmony is red-violet, violet, blue-violet, and blue. Another classic example would be yellow, yellow-green, green, and green-blue. This scheme is often found in nature, plants, or sunsets.

COMPLEMENTARY

Let's go back to complementary colors, using the example shown on page 15 in orange and blue. It's easy to see that these colors are on opposite sides of the color wheel. This basically means that there's no blue in orange and no orange in blue. In my opinion, this is the most important concept in color theory: Not only does each color complement the other (one makes the other pop by creating contrast), but in mixing color with paint, complementary colors are often used as tools to desaturate or darken a certain hue.

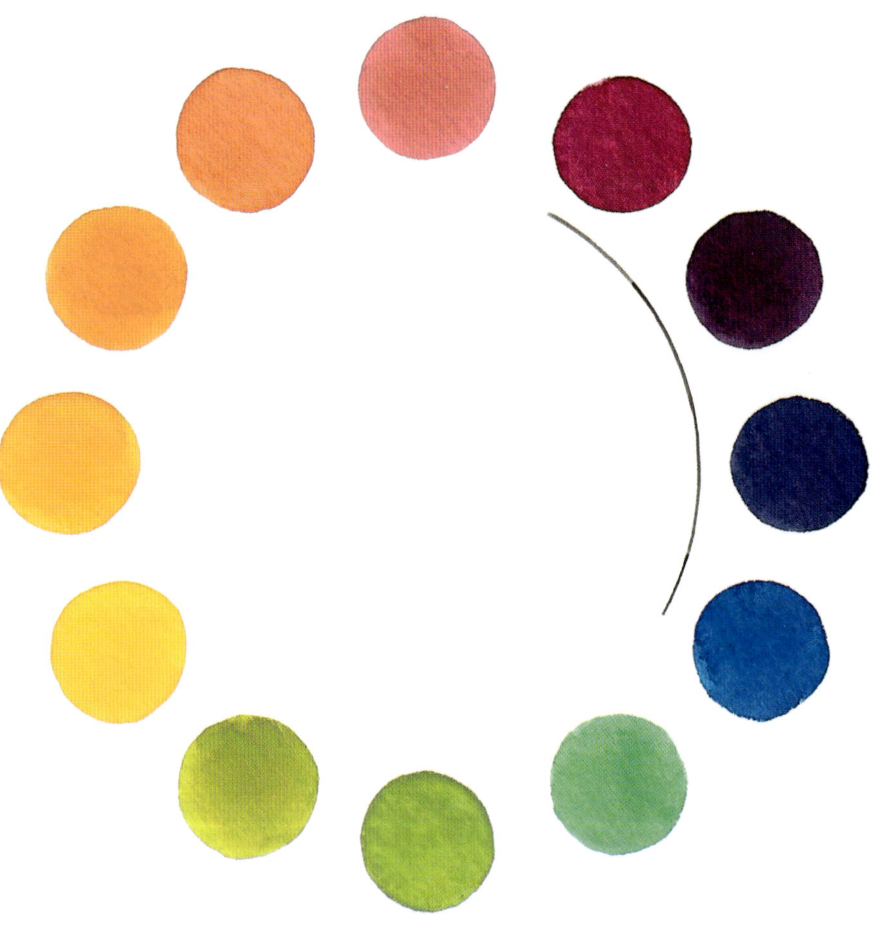

An analogous color scheme.

For example, yellow and violet are complementaries, as are green and red. Let's say you have a bright yellow in your color palette, but what you really want is a deeper mustard yellow. The not-so-obvious choice to make this color would be to add a tiny bit of violet. This will deepen the yellow without removing vibrance from your mix—the way, say, adding a bit of brown or black into your yellow would.

What if you want to make a brick red? If you only have primary colors in your palette, simply add a touch of green to your red and the color will immediately transform into a deep, dark red.

Learning to mix color this way will result in beautiful, organic colors with undertones that will give your art a secret complementary touch. I'll mention complementaries many times throughout this book because, in addition to being a basic concept in color theory, they're also fundamental to color mixing.

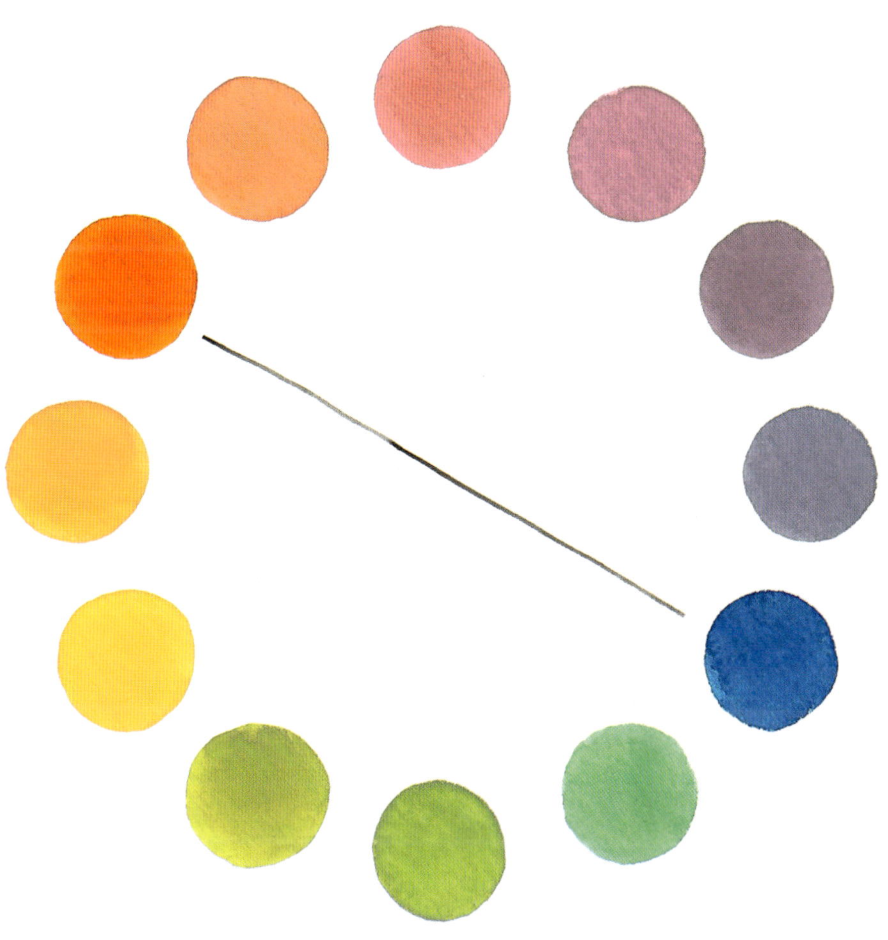

A complementary color scheme.

SPLIT-COMPLEMENTARY

This variation of complementary
harmony takes one color as a base
and two colors from the opposite
side of the wheel that are next to the
complementary. For example, if green
and red are complementaries, the split-
complementary would be red, yellow-
green, and green-blue. Another example
is yellow, red-violet, and violet-blue. This
color scheme is high in contrast like classic
complementaries, but has less tension;
the two splits are similar to each other and
the complementary is different, but not
the complete opposite, as with
regular complementaries.

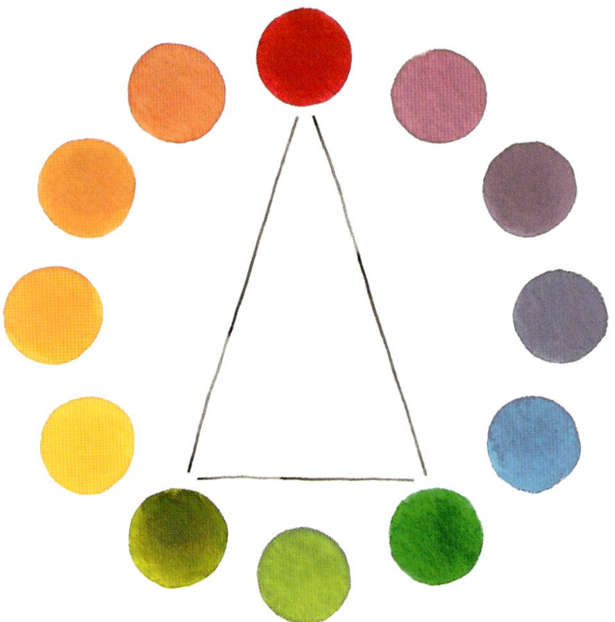

A split-complementary color scheme.

TRIADIC

This type of harmony uses three hues that
are evenly spaced around the color wheel.
It's common for artists using this scheme
to take one of the hues as a dominant
color and accent with the other two. For
example, yellow-orange as the main color
would have red and blue-green as the
accent colors. This is the most varied type
of color scheme because of the way the
colors are selected evenly around
the wheel.

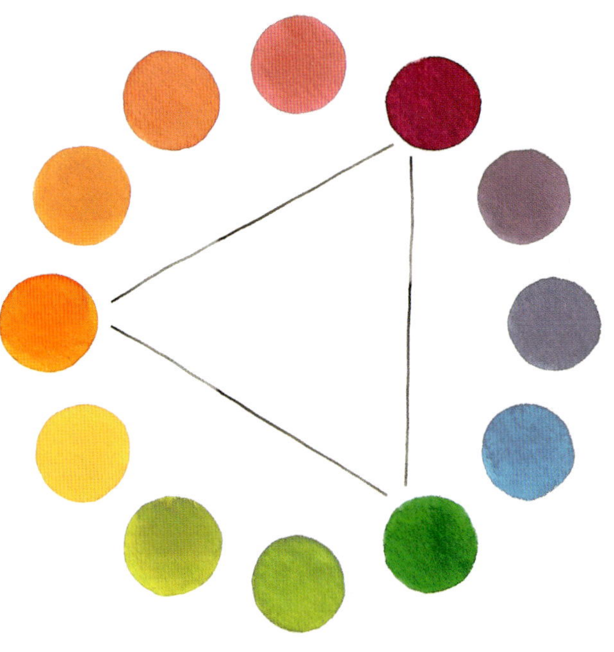

A triadic color scheme.

TETRADIC

This scheme is quite colorful and mixes warms and cools (see page 18). It takes two split-complementaries from each side to mix four different colors. In this example I selected red-orange and violet-red to be combined with the opposing blue-green and yellow-green. There is contrast but also quite a bit of ease. The range is wider and the two pairs are harmonious while creating contrast with the opposites, forming a rectangle within the wheel.

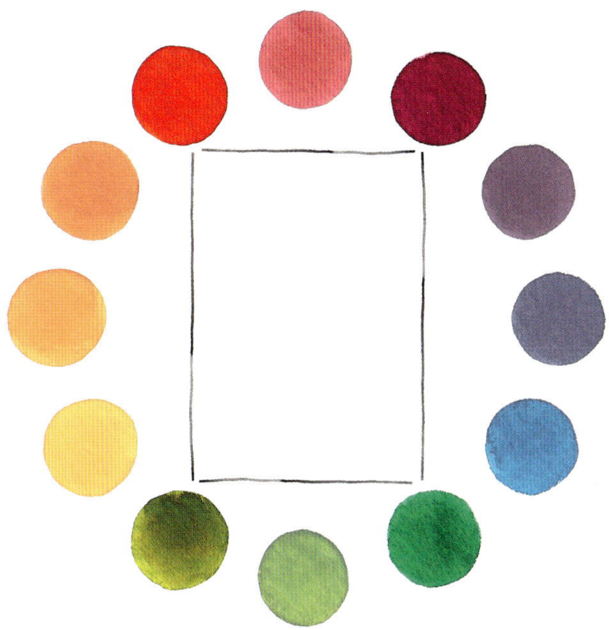

A tetradic color scheme.

Color & Temperature

If we split the color wheel down the middle, one side comprises **cool tones** (blue, violet, and green) and the other side **warm tones** (red, orange, and yellow).

Note that greens and violets can go either way, depending on the amount of yellow or red in each.

Greens. If in the mixture the yellow overpowers the blue, then it will be a warm green, such as a moss green; if the blue overpowers the yellow, then it will be a cool green, like a turquoise or teal.

Violets. If red overpowers the mixture, the result is a warm violet like a mauve or red wine color; if blue is stronger, the color will lean toward a deep indigo.

Although **neutrals** such as grays and browns aren't typically included in a wheel-based color chart, I show them here to make the point that they can usually be mixed in with your warm or cool swatches without altering the predominant mood too much.

EVEN NEUTRALS HAVE TEMPERATURE

Although so-called neutral grays and browns can often work well with both warm and cool palettes, they can, in fact, be categorized as either warm or cool. Even a black can be warmer or cooler, depending on the content of its pigment.

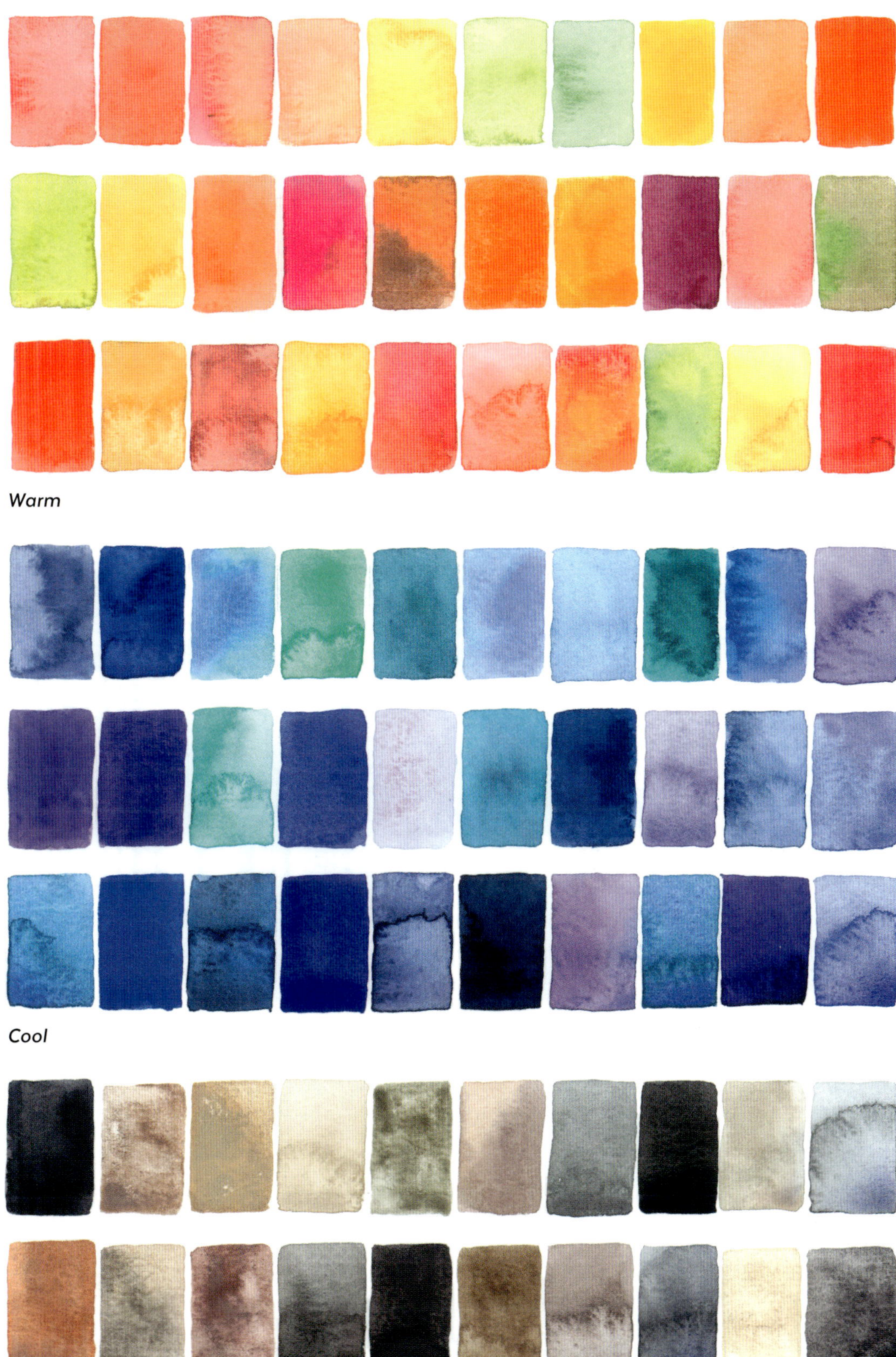

Warm

Cool

Neutral

Warm & Cool Variations

If you're an artist or feel particularly sensitive to color, you already know that color can profoundly impact the mood of an artwork or design piece. Color is deeply connected to human psychology, memory, and feelings.

I like to share the following experiment at every color class I teach. I learned it from one of my teachers in college and found it to be extremely powerful and instructive.

1. Begin with a drawing of anything you like: a nature scene, animals, the sun or moon, a human figure, a character—it's up to you. I chose a floral composition.

2. Either transfer or redraw the drawing twice, on two different pieces of watercolor paper. Paint one drawing exclusively in warm tones, the other entirely in cool ones. Be restrictive, making sure to swatch your colors before painting to confirm which are warm and which are cool.

Note that although you're painting exactly the same piece, different feelings will arise in response to each version. When you're done, you'll see a drastic difference in their "moods": Even the time of day and climate can feel different, depending on the temperature of your color mixes.

For example, I experienced two very different sensations when I viewed my paintings (see opposite). One isn't better than the other; they're simply different. Try this out and you'll be amazed by the power of color!

USING COLOR AS A CREATIVE TOOL

Color might even inspire you to try something new. I painted my warm palette first, then my cool one. While painting my cool florals, I decided to make the background dark blue, and my intuition told me to add a few sparkly stars. Just using that color inspired me to add a specific detail. It's a small but important example of how color can guide us.

Keep in mind that the feelings I got from my experiment don't necessarily have to match yours; it's about getting in touch with how the use of color alters our artwork and can affect our—and our viewers'—response to it. Color is indeed a powerful tool, and using it to develop palettes that suit and enhance the subjects at hand and influence a viewer's emotions is a beautiful and wildly interesting part of painting.

I used this drawing to explore emotional responses to warm and cool palettes. (See page 140 for a full-size version.)

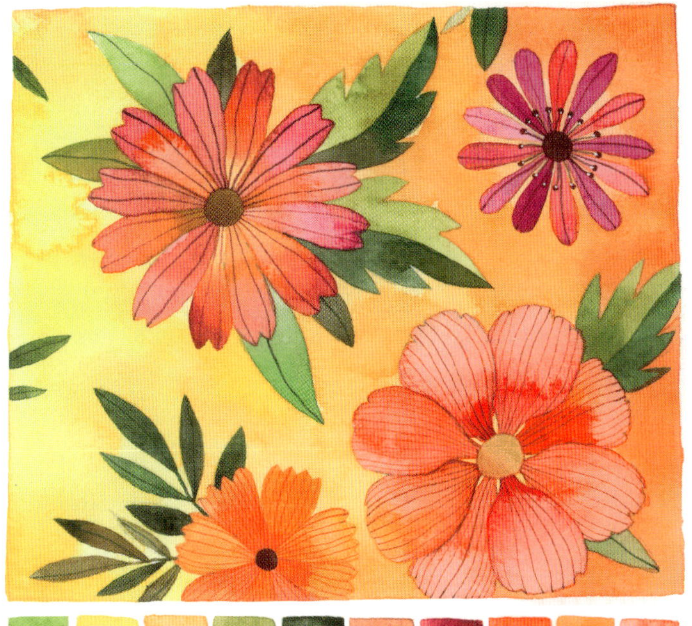

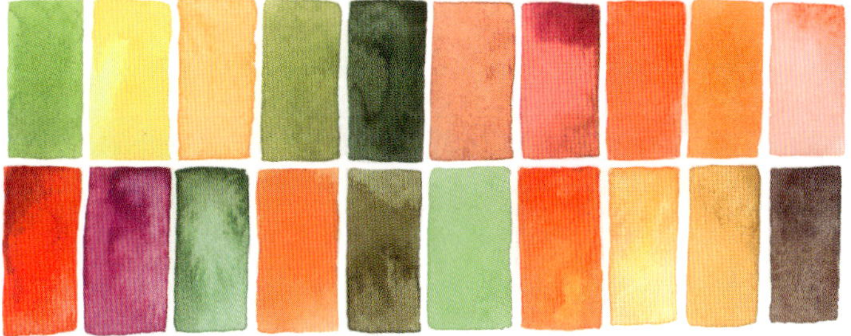

My **warm** painting aroused these descriptions and feelings:

Happy
Joyful
Hot
Tropical
Inviting
Celebratory
Movement
Excitement
Daylight
Morning
Sunshine
Humid

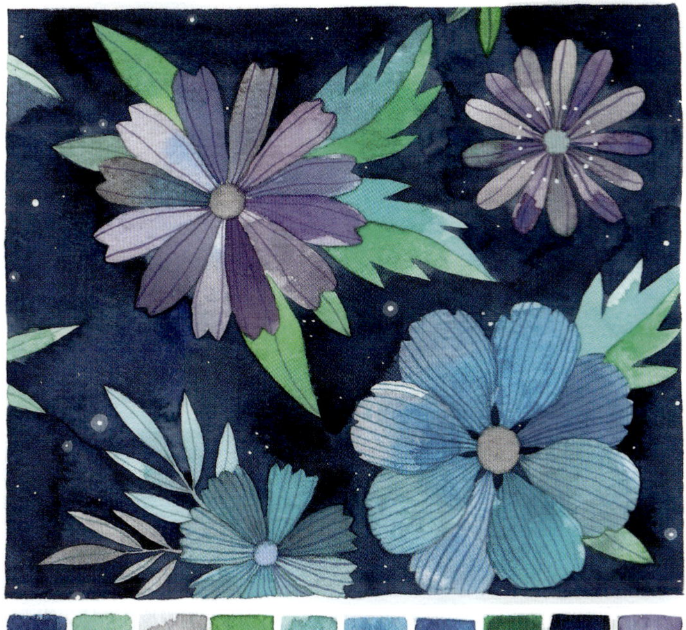

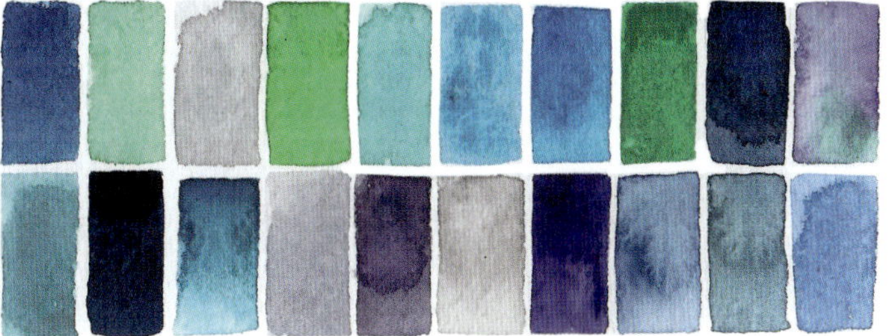

My **cool** painting evoked these impressions:

Distance
Mystery
Chilly
Night
Sadness
Contemplation
Calm
Somnolence
Meditative
Gloomy
Rest
Tranquility

Watercolor Paints for Swatching

A big part of color mixing is experimenting with paints you own or take the opportunity to try so you can discover your personal favorites. Throughout this book I'll share a few tips that mention specific colors and why I like them. Having said that, I wholeheartedly encourage every artist to come up with a collection of favorite pigments from what you may already have on hand.

You don't need to have any of these paints in your personal collection to create amazing color palettes and paintings. Discovering your favorites through experimentation is such a special part of making art. Here's my list of pigments that I find particularly special and one of a kind.

PAN WATERCOLORS

I use watercolor pan sets as a base. Pan sets usually come with a mixing palette built into the box and that is exactly where I do most of my mixing. I add some of my favorite tube and liquid watercolors into this pan set to create my own unique colors. The three major pan sets I use regularly are by Winsor & Newtown, Schmincke, and Sennelier.

Winsor & Newton was the first large pan set I acquired, and until this day I haven't found another brand's Yellow Ochre pigment that I enjoy as much. *My personal palette has a lot of earthy tones in the mix, and this is just the perfect texture and balance between bright and deep.*

Schmincke was the second large pan set I invested in, and I've used this set almost daily for the past five years. It's super-high quality and also has some noteworthy colors:

Venetian Red. Their browns in general are fantastic, but this brick-like color with hints of orange is perfectly opaque and bright.

Jaune Brilliant Dark. A creamy opaque watercolor, light yellow. I don't paint human figures, but I've been told it's amazing for skin tones.

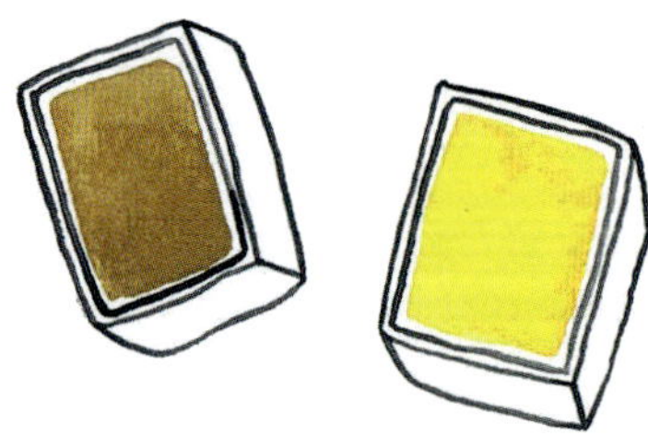

And finally, my latest large pan set is from the French brand Sennelier. The quality is similar to Schmincke—they're both outstanding—but each brand has certain pigments that I prefer:

Dioxazine Purple. An intense, bright pure purple.

Pyrrole Orange. A bright and bold orange; a great pigment for mixing warm tones.

Brown Pink. The name is kind of a mystery for this specific desaturated olive green, which I find lovely and unique to this brand.

Yellow Deep. My favorite warm yellow, the pigment is so bright and sunny.

Cobalt Violet Light Hue. Highly luminous and brilliant, a great warm violet to have in a pan set.

Opera Rose. A bright pink that's great for mixing with blues for brilliant violets.

Emerald Green. A cool and brilliant bright green.

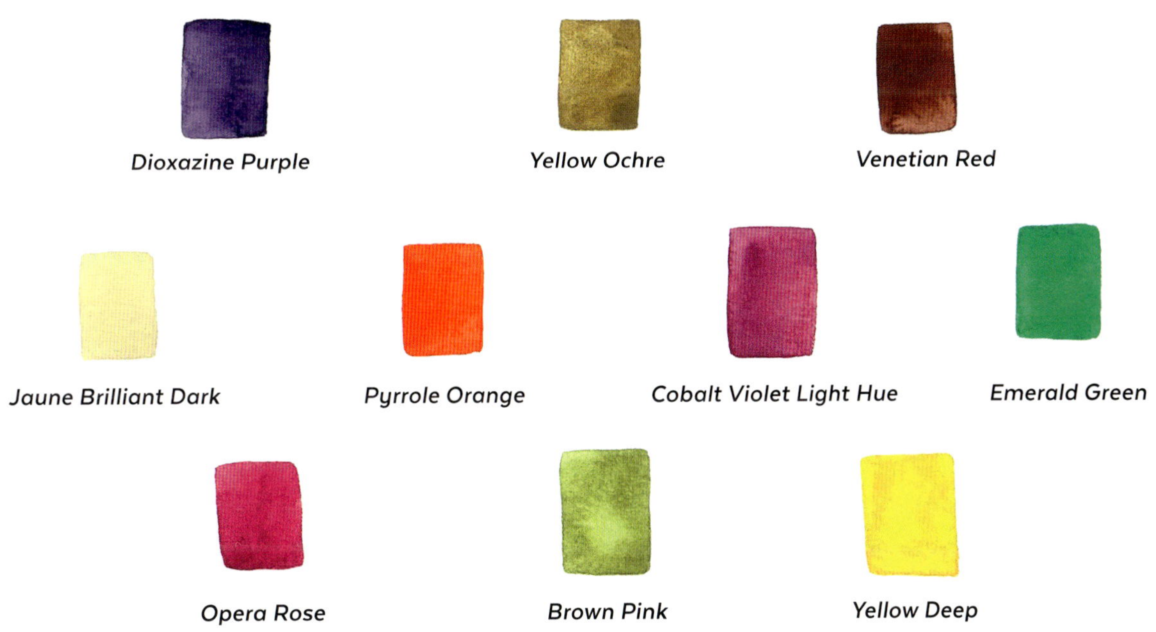

Dioxazine Purple *Yellow Ochre* *Venetian Red*

Jaune Brilliant Dark *Pyrrole Orange* *Cobalt Violet Light Hue* *Emerald Green*

Opera Rose *Brown Pink* *Yellow Deep*

TUBE WATERCOLORS

I have a special place in my heart for each one of these paints for different reasons.
A majority of the tubes I keep buying are by Holbein. This brand has some very distinct
pigments and tends to have some really nice opaque watercolors that can be handy.
My preferred Holbein tubes include:

Opera. A bright neon pink. I've tried a few different brands of this pigment and found
Holbein to have the most punch and a creamier texture.

Shell Pink. A pastel pink, slightly opaque, similar to a gouache paint.

Lavender. Opaque watercolor that works great as a periwinkle when mixed with
a peacock blue.

Lilac. A pastel-like, light purple I've not found in other brands.

Leaf Green. A bright, bold, almost neonlike yellow-green.

Pyrrole Red. A really nice warm red.

Viridian Hue. A bright forest green, vibrant, that works as a great base for mixing a large
range of greens.

Daniel Smith is another brand that I enjoy specifically in tube form. It has all kinds
of natural pigments with some great texture and granulation. My preferences:

Cobalt Blue. This is a classic primary blue that works great for mixing and creating
a variety of cool tones.

Quinacridone. Also called deep gold, I like its vibrance and earthy granulation.
A perfect rusty orange.

Payne's Gray. This is a great alternative to black; also works great for nighttime
sky paintings.

Ivory Black. Yes, there are different shades of black! This particular black is warm
and semitransparent.

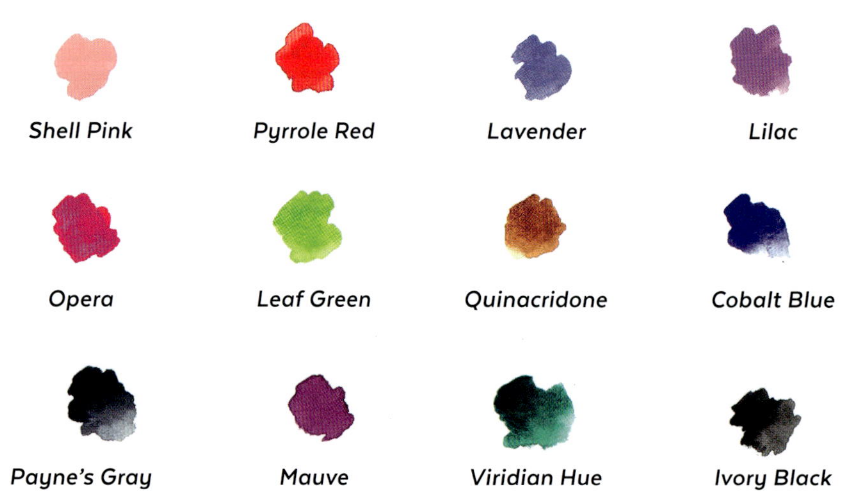

Shell Pink	Pyrrole Red	Lavender	Lilac
Opera	Leaf Green	Quinacridone	Cobalt Blue
Payne's Gray	Mauve	Viridian Hue	Ivory Black

I don't have a large collection of Winsor & Newton tubes because I have one of their large pan sets with most of the colors I use. But there is one pigment that I specifically enjoy using in tube form:

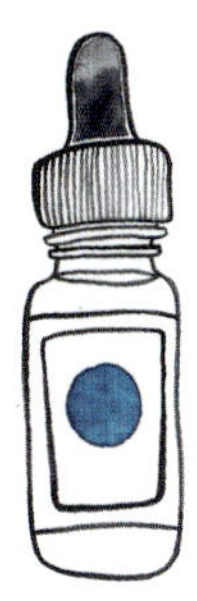

Mauve. A rich, warm, vibrant violet color.

LIQUID WATERCOLORS

Of all the brands I've tried, Dr. Ph. Martin's is perfectly bright and a great addition to my pan sets. In other words, these paints are so bright that I rarely use them on their own. Instead, I mix in touches of liquid watercolors with my pan and tube mixes to make my own one-of-a-kind color combinations.

These colors are so bright, and in some cases even neon or fluorescent, because they're dye-based instead of pigment-based. I most enjoy the Radiant Concentrated line of Dr. Ph. Martin's. The colors that I find to be most special are:

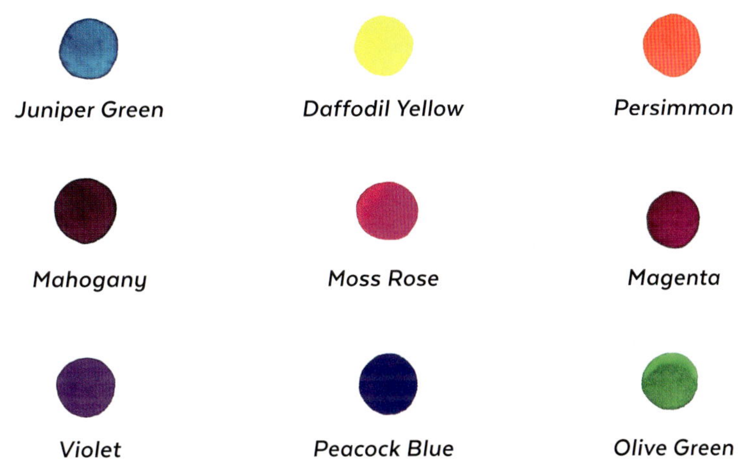

I like all of these colors for the same reason: they're extremely bright and vibrant.

A NOTE ABOUT WHITE GOUACHE

There will be a few occasions when I suggest adding hints of white gouache to your mixes, specifically when making pastel tones. This is a great trick if you're looking for more of a chalky consistency instead of a transparent wash. Holbein works great, but brand doesn't really matter.

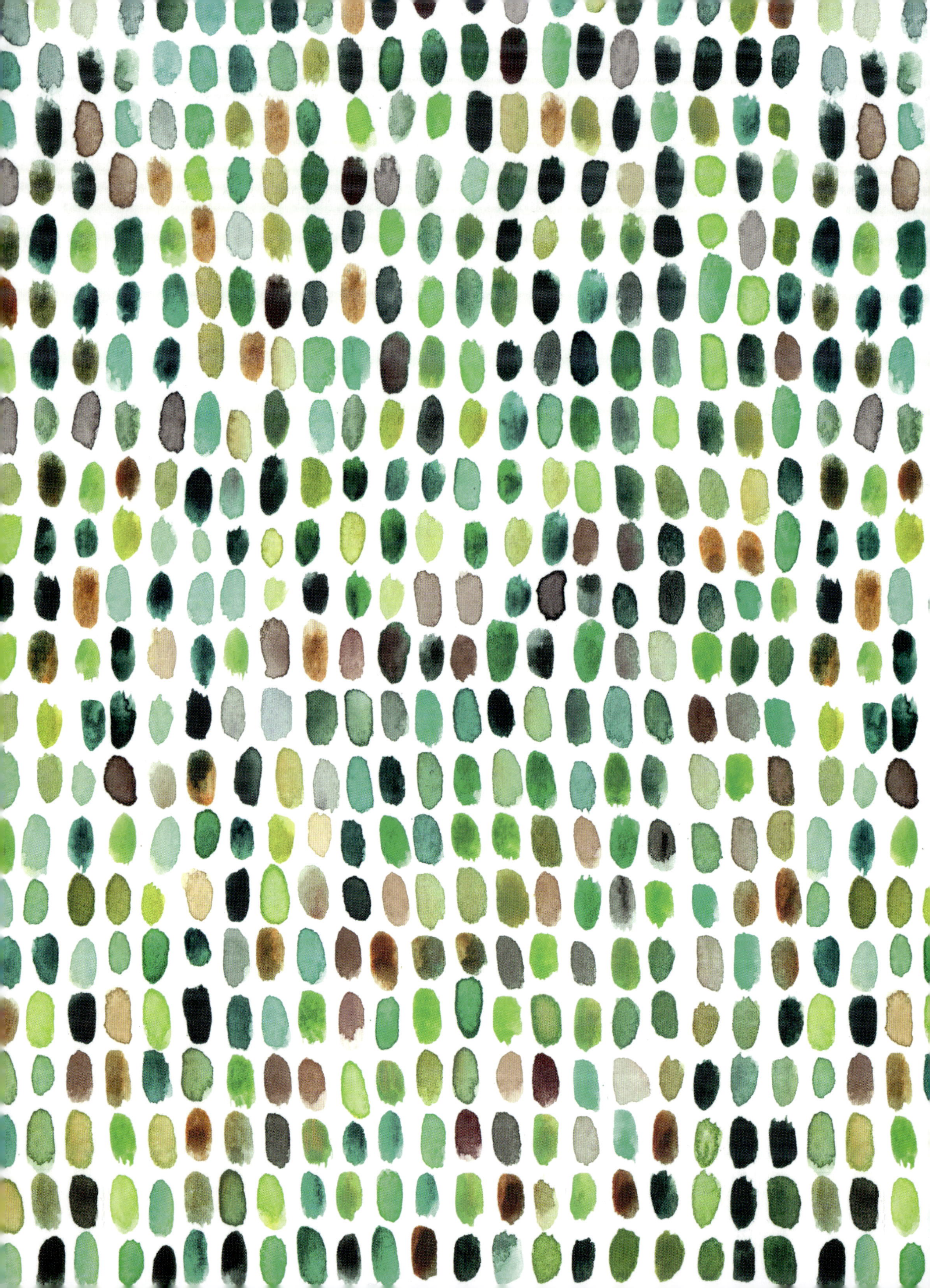

Inspired
Palettes

Austere De Stijl

When studying art history in college, De Stijl always stood out for me because it was so distinctive. De Stijl, which translates to "The Style," was a Dutch art and architecture movement founded in 1917. Also known as Neoplasticism, the approach has many strict rules, including using only vertical and horizontal lines and rectangular shapes in black, white, gray, and primary colors (red, blue, and yellow).

For this palette's primaries, use your purest pigments. For instance, a neutral blue like cobalt or royal blue is a better fit than an indigo or navy (both of which lean toward violet) or a turquoise (which tends toward green).

For the texture swatch, I decided to create my own De Stijl composition.

TECHNIQUE NOTES Swatching this movement is challenging because of its many restrictions. Although I limited myself to black and the three primaries, I followed watercolor's lead and swatched those colors in different values by modifying the amount of water in each swatch to create some visual variation. Note that this is the only palette in the book where the colors aren't mixed together.

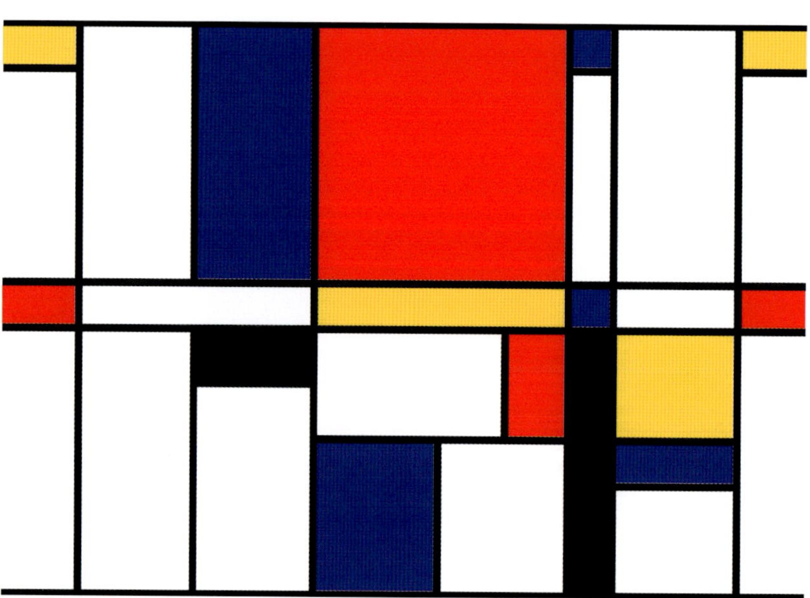

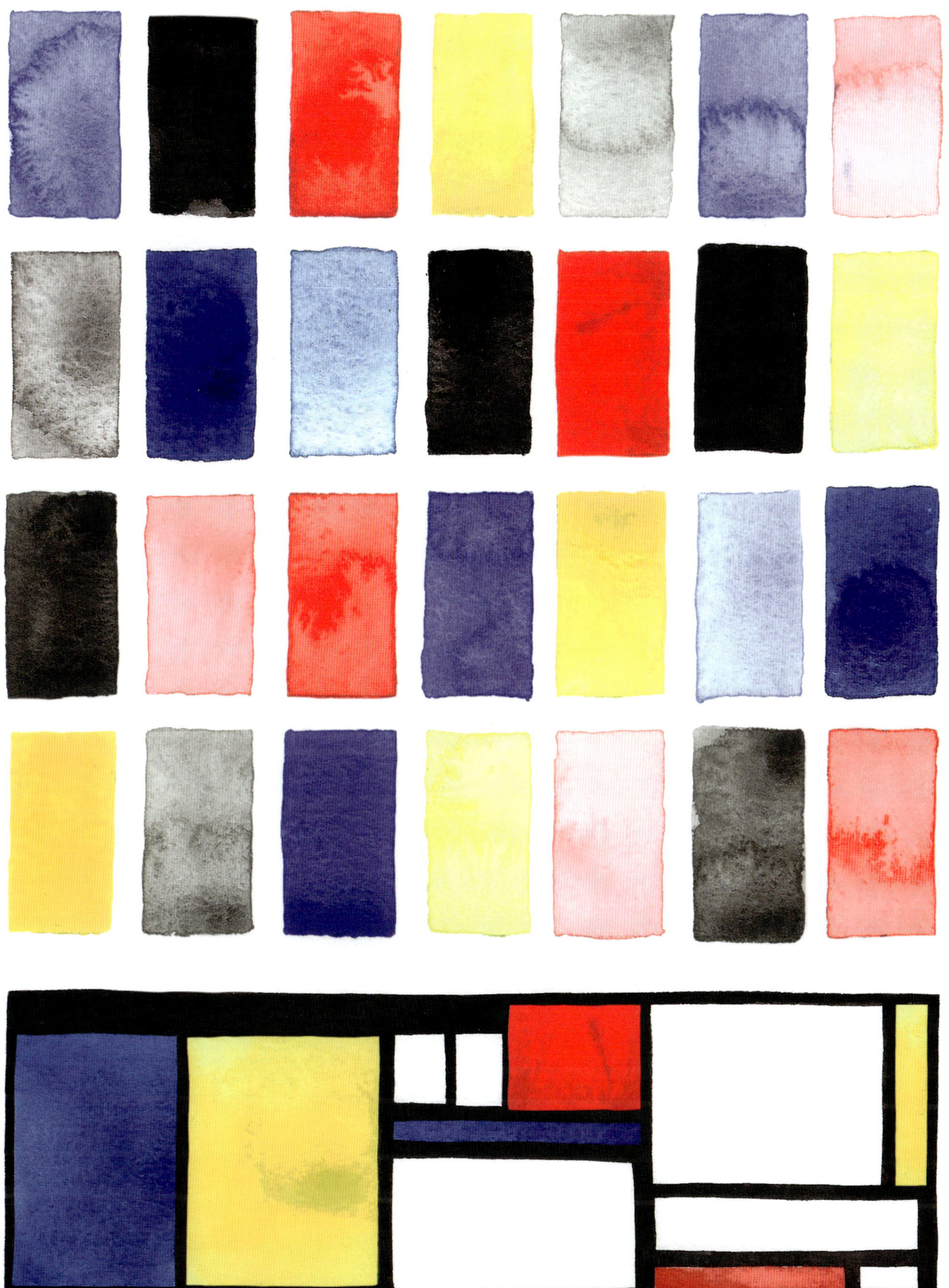

Shimmering Impresionism

Nineteenth-century Impressionism, originally centered in Paris, is famous for a specific style of brushstroke that is repetitive, relatively small, and uses lighter tones of paint to allude to the effects of reflected light.

The movement's name comes from Claude Monet's *Impression, Sunrise,* painted in 1892, when an art critic in France published a satirical review of the style. Hence the name "Impressionism." Another inspiring painting is Monet's *Vétheuil in Summer,* 1880. In this scene from the Seine River, the shimmering effect of repetitive brushstrokes on water demonstrates the importance Monet placed on representing light accurately.

In honor of this movement, I experimented with mixing color by laying out numerous short brushstrokes. The direction and value of each stroke is incredibly important to create enough contrast.

COLOR NOTES This palette is soft, romantic, and slightly muted. The painting mainly depicts a cool vibe with light greens and blues as accents and details of lovely peachy tones. To create the perfect peach, water down an orange mix or add a touch of white gouache to give it a creamy appearance.

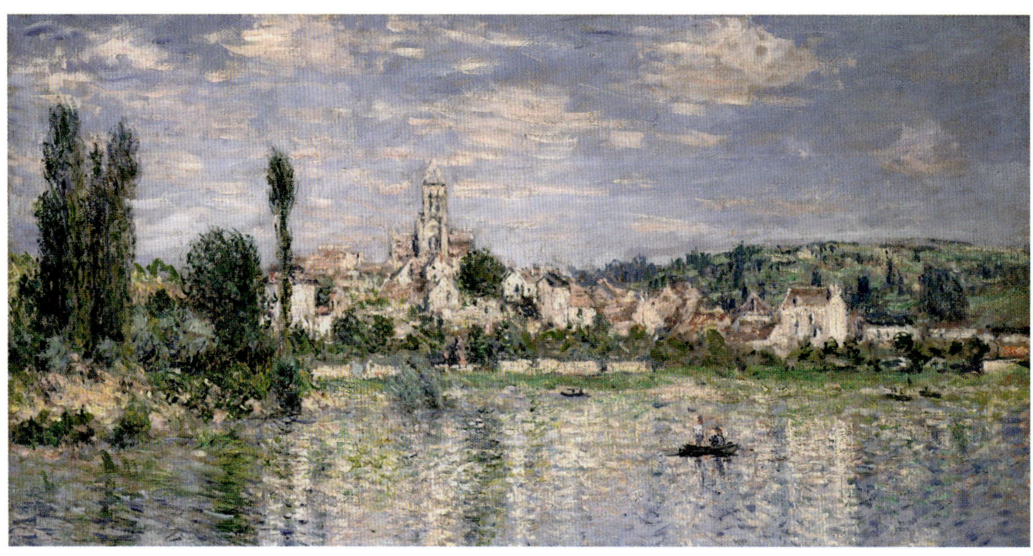

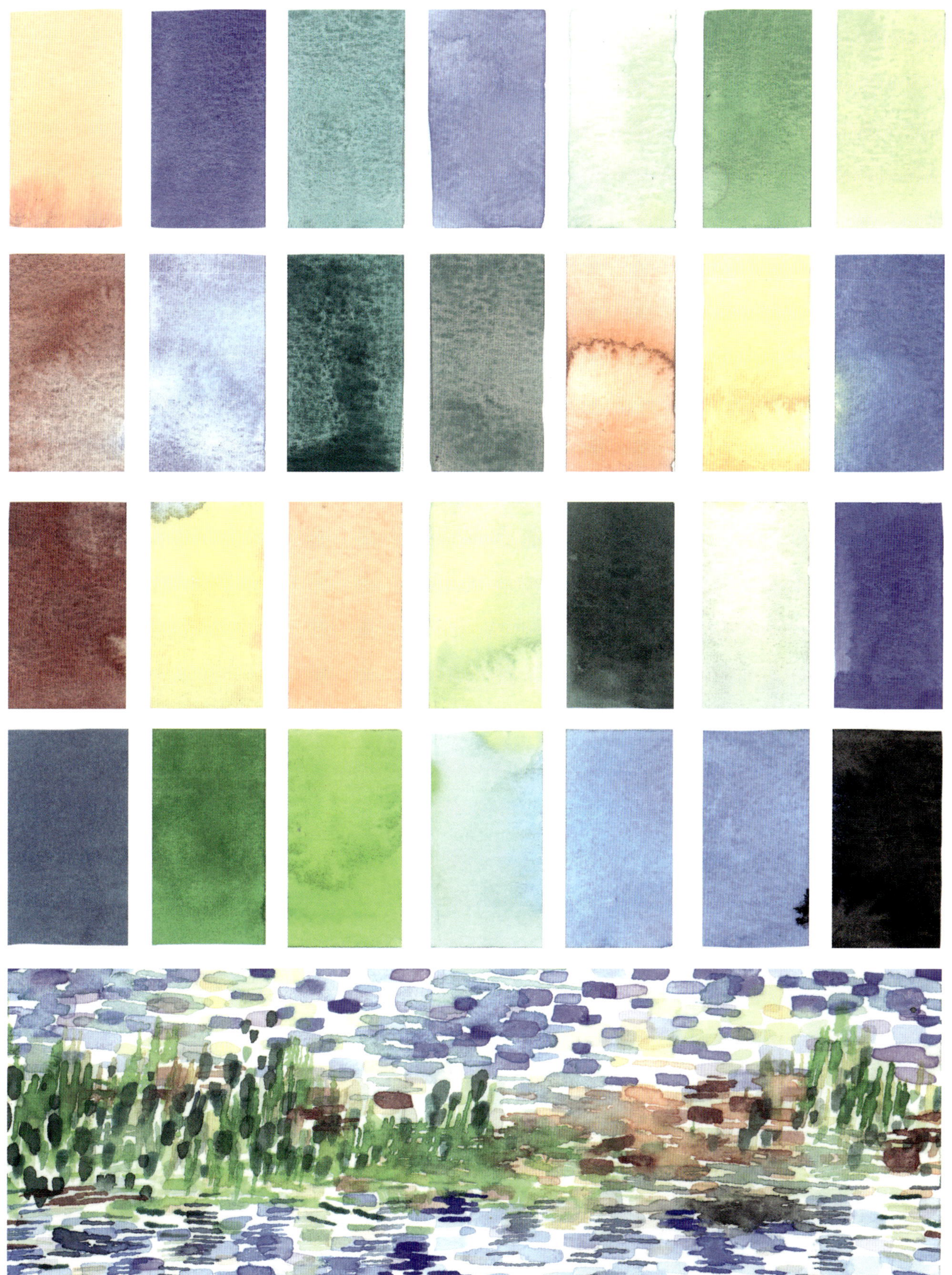

31

Swirling Art Nouveau

Art Nouveau arose when European art was heavily academic. The movement drew inspiration from such styles as two-dimensional Japanese woodblock prints, Rococo curves, and Celtic motifs. Organic yet structured, applications of this style moved beyond the canvas and fine art to poster art, stained glass, architecture, metal art, jewelry, ceramics, textiles, and wallpapers, to name a few. It's an important ancestor to what we know as graphic design. The movement also paved the way for Art Deco and Modernism.

I'm pretty sure this is my favorite movement, specifically pieces by artists like Gustav Klimt and Alphonse Mucha. Our reference design is Mucha's *The Arts: Poetry*, 1898.

The color palette is muted and soft, and an exemplary use of split-complementary color harmony. Orange tones make perfect contrast with the various blue and green shades, plus a touch of neutrals. I used complementaries in the color mixing process, adding a touch of blue to the orange mix to dull the bright and sunny feel and gain a rusty aspect.

COLOR NOTES I always turn to Holbein's Jaune Brilliant when I want a perfect cream color. Remember, you don't need the exact paints I use. I'm just mentioning some of my favorites. You can use white gouache as a base and add minimal touches of orange and yellow until you find the hue you're looking for. I also created many olive greens and made a perfect mint by adding equal amounts of emerald green and white gouache.

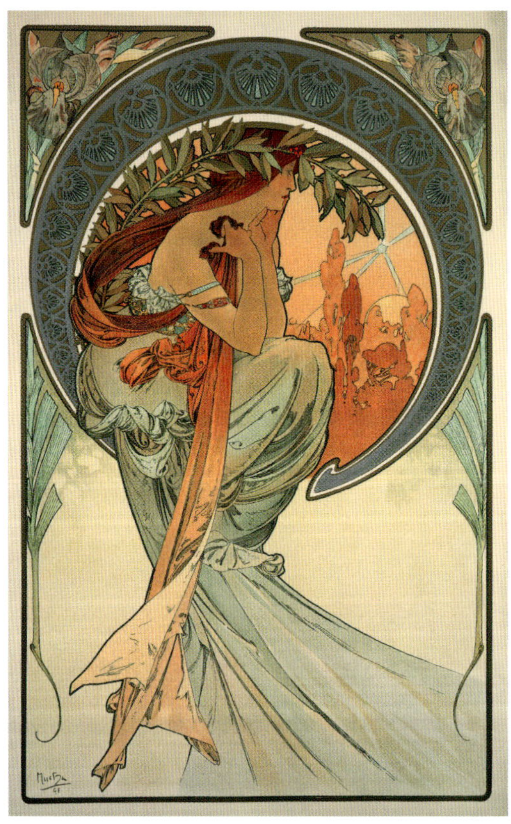

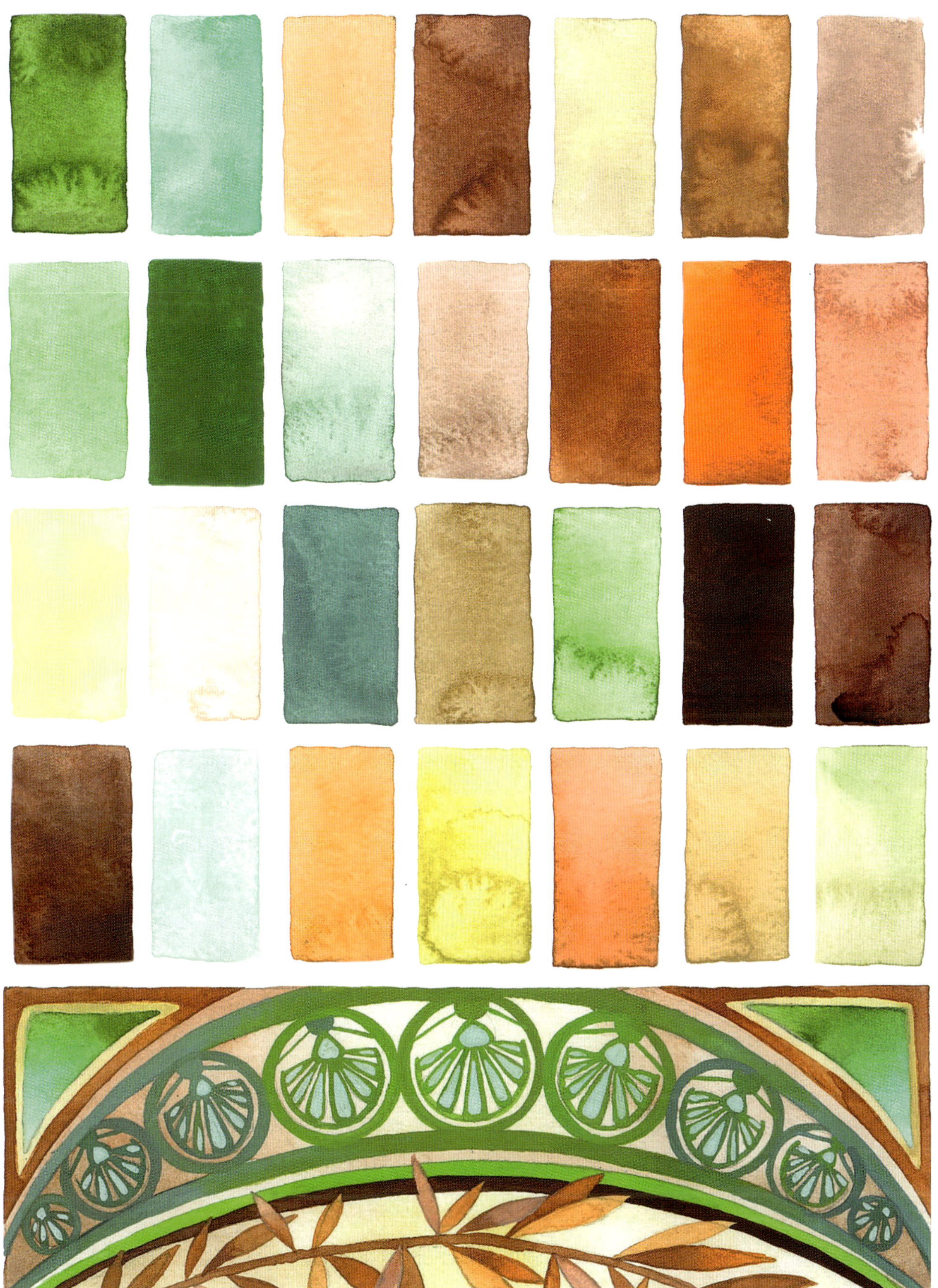

33

Pop Art Pow

Pop Art began in the 1950s, mainly in the United Kingdom and the United States. The movement emphasized everyday elements, advertising, comic books, and mass culture of the time, usually with an ironic tone.

Some of the best-known artists of this movement are Roy Lichtenstein, famous for large comic book–like paintings with a sense of parody, and Andy Warhol, who depicted thirty-two Campbell's soup cans and numerous variations of Marilyn Monroe's face screen printed in bold colors. This screen-print collection inspired the image demonstrated here. I chose bold and bright colors with pastel accents for contrast. There isn't necessarily any blending in this method of screen printing, just separation of ink on different areas of the surface.

For the inspiration board, I thought it would be fun to paint an element that I always use in my personal art: a crescent moon. What shapes do you want to paint in this repeat style?

COLOR NOTES The bright red is Holbein's Pyrrole Red with a dab of Dr. Ph. Martin's Persimmon for that extra brightness. I wanted a real warm red, like in the picture, so this works nicely. I also turned to Opera Pink for that bright pink pigment and added a touch of white gouache for pastel pink variations. I also enjoyed working with Schmincke's Lemon Yellow to create my base yellow and oranges. Most pan sets include a lemon yellow, so it's widely available.

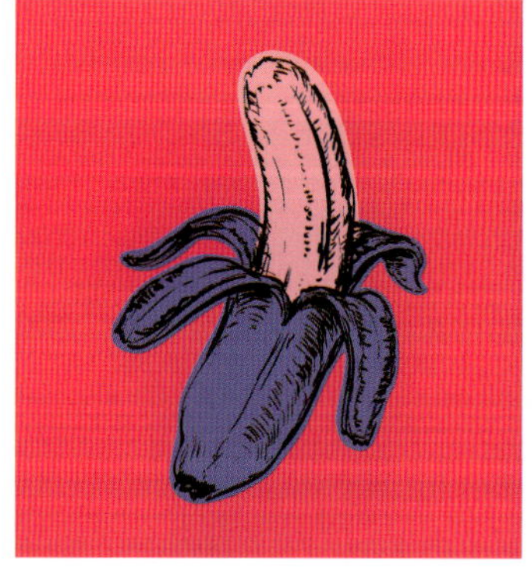 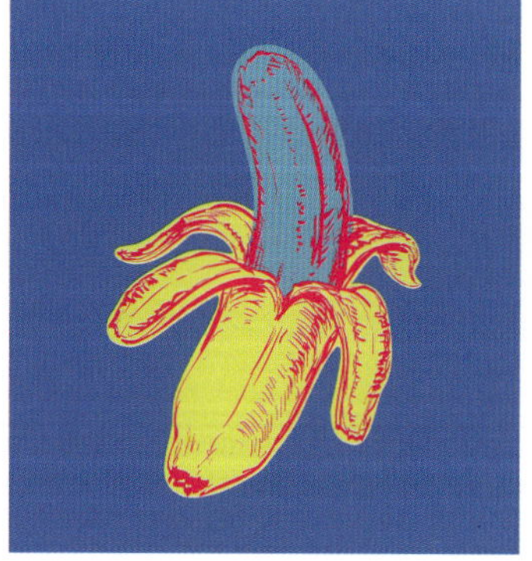 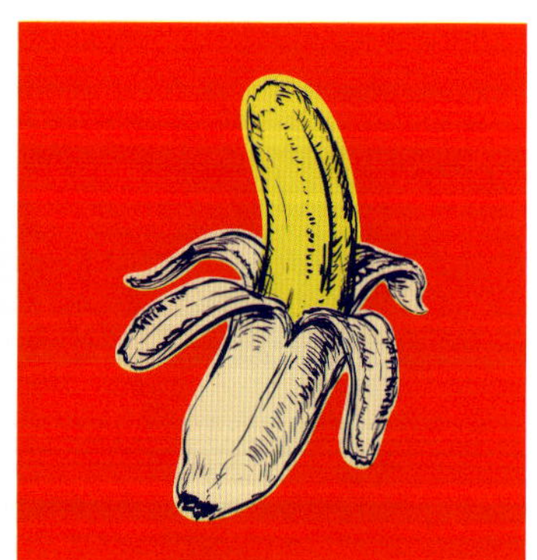

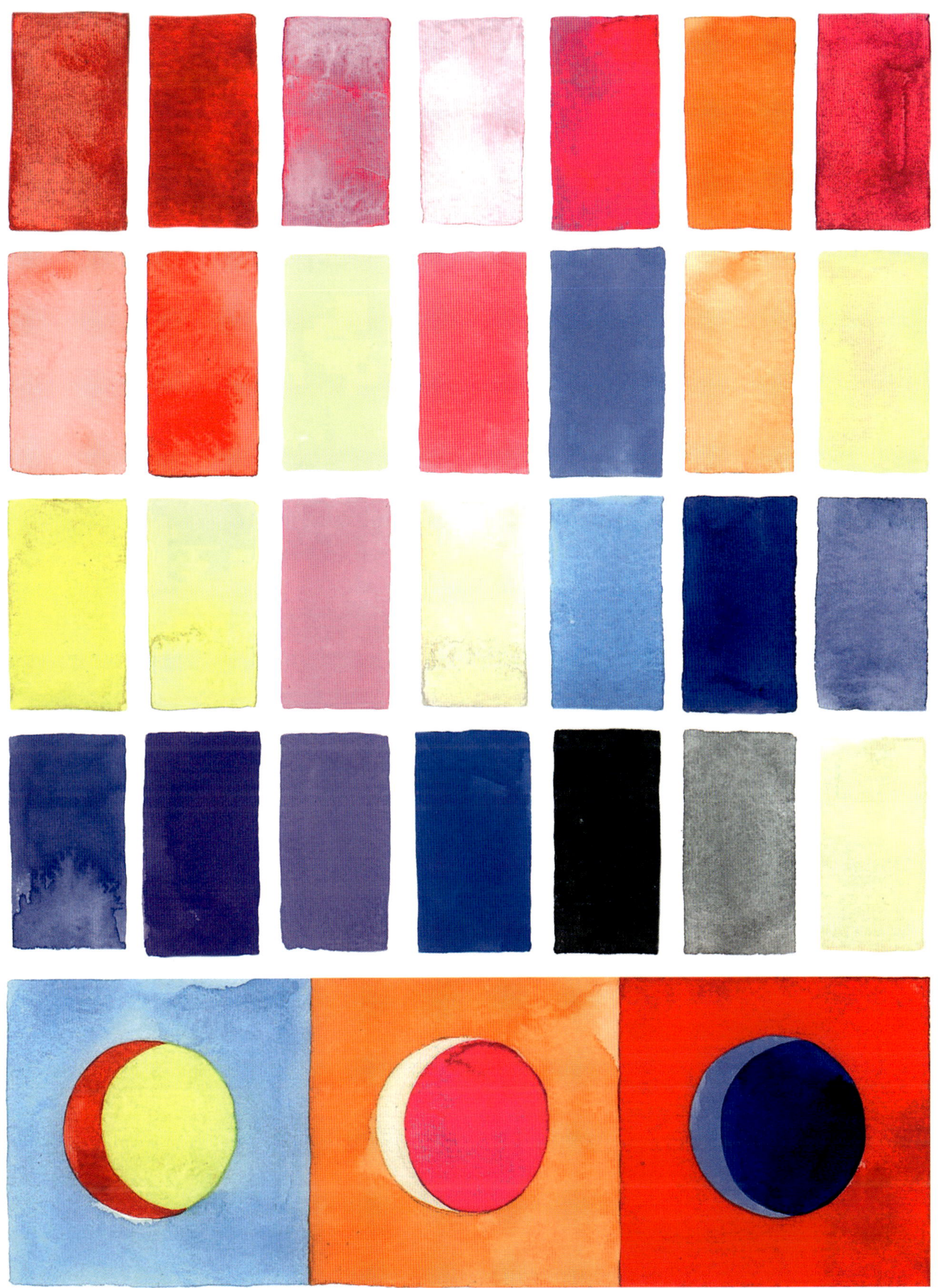

Ornamental Arts & Crafts

I credit the Arts and Crafts Movement for giving me the courage to become a full-time artist. The type of art I enjoyed making in my early twenties was decorative and ornamental, not really statement pieces, or art I thought could be hung in a gallery. When I began admiring this movement, which dates to Britain in the late eighteen-hundreds, I realized that art also represents an important role in decorating objects, specifically in a romantic, folk-inspired style.

William Morris was the main influence of this movement, and our reference picture is part of a collection at his company. The palette in this movement is harmonious because the colors mostly represent craftsmanship and natural tones. There's no blending in this style of art, just sections or layers of lighter and darker shades (for example, the two pinks in the tulip or the green dots that cover the background).

I could spend hours staring at Arts and Crafts designs. The shapes and compositions are truly a gift to humanity. I hope you find this movement equally inspiring!

COLOR NOTES My palette is heavy in natural greens in a variety of tones that are bold but slightly muted. For deep blues I like to use indigo as a base, with a touch of white gouache for a creamy effect.

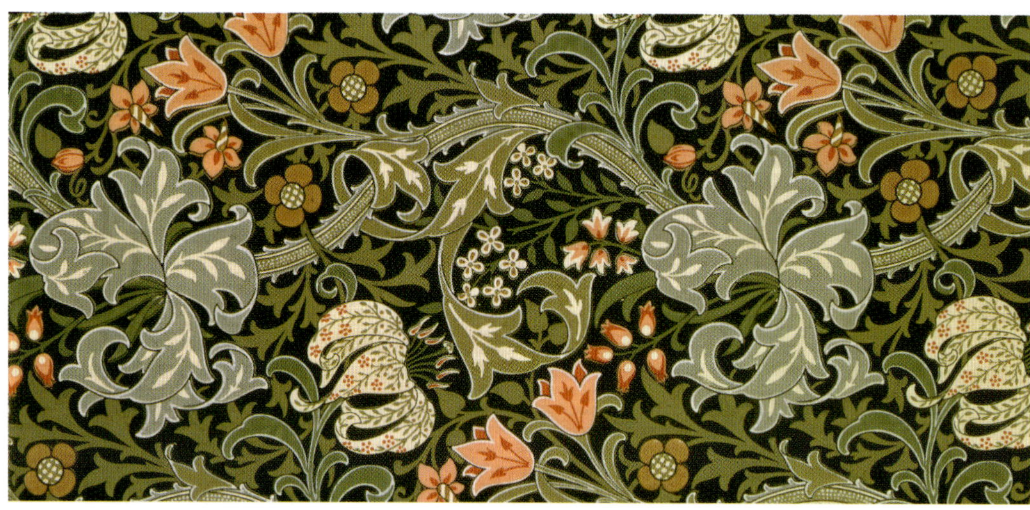

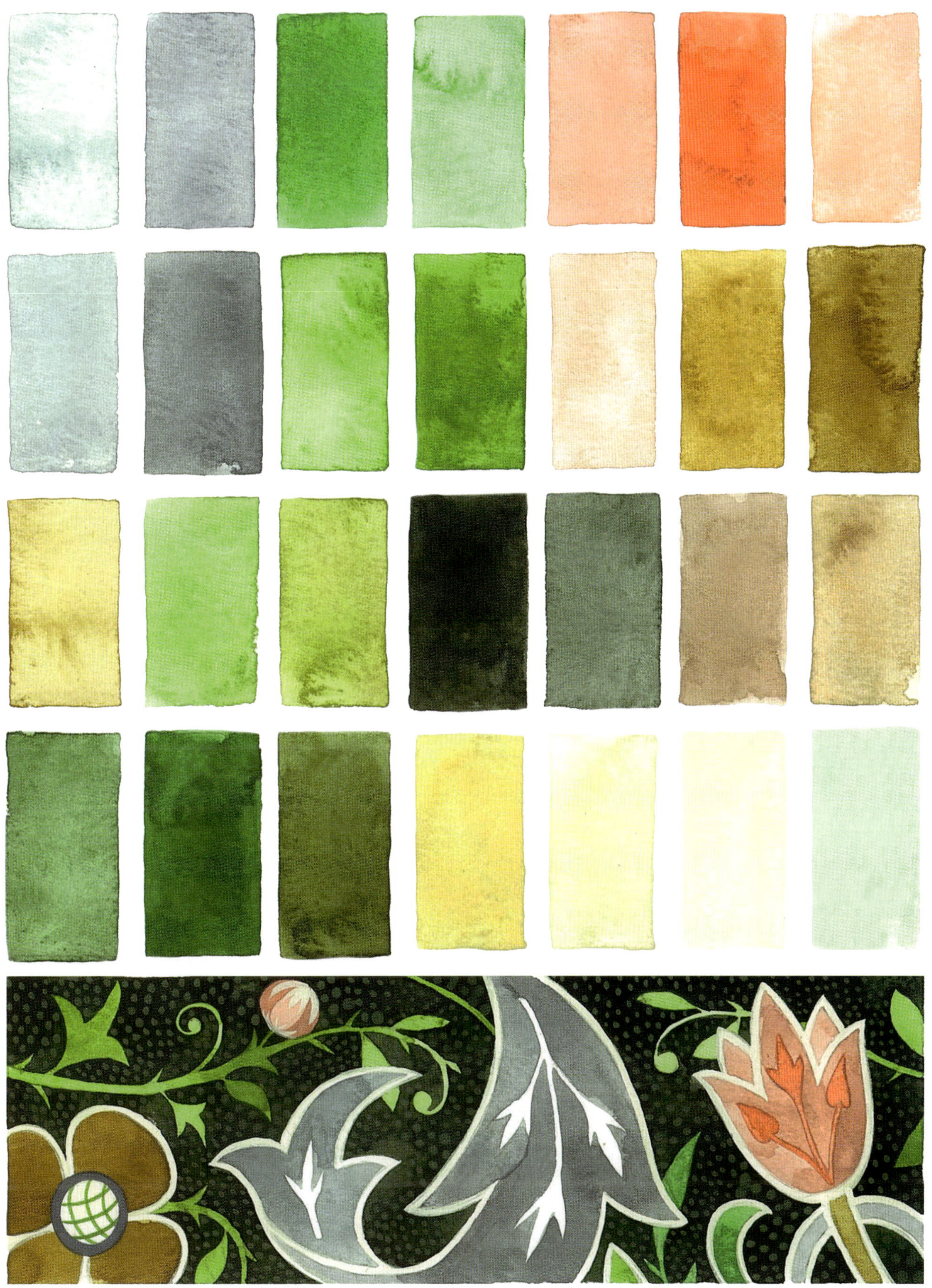

Cosmic Magic

There's a very special place in my heart for galaxy paintings. They're one of the first textures that defined my artistic style back in 2011, when my art career was beginning to take off. I fell in love with what watercolors can do when you learn how to mix wet on wet and add white spatter once the layers dry.

Some of my favorite colors for galaxy paintings are magenta and ultramarine. Space images like this are usually dark and cool with specks of pinks and violets. A mix of indigo and black watercolor works really nice for the deep space areas. You can use white ink, gouache, or acrylic with a flat brush for the spatter effect.

COLOR NOTES Most pan sets come in a variety of natural pigments, so I turn to Dr. Ph. Martin's Radiant Concentrated watercolors for a little extra fluorescence. These watercolors are dye-based instead of pigment-based, so their colors differ immensely from traditional pan sets or even tubes. In fact, they're so intense that I use them mindfully—instead of using directly from the bottle, add just a bit to a pan-set mix to make the colors more vibrant.

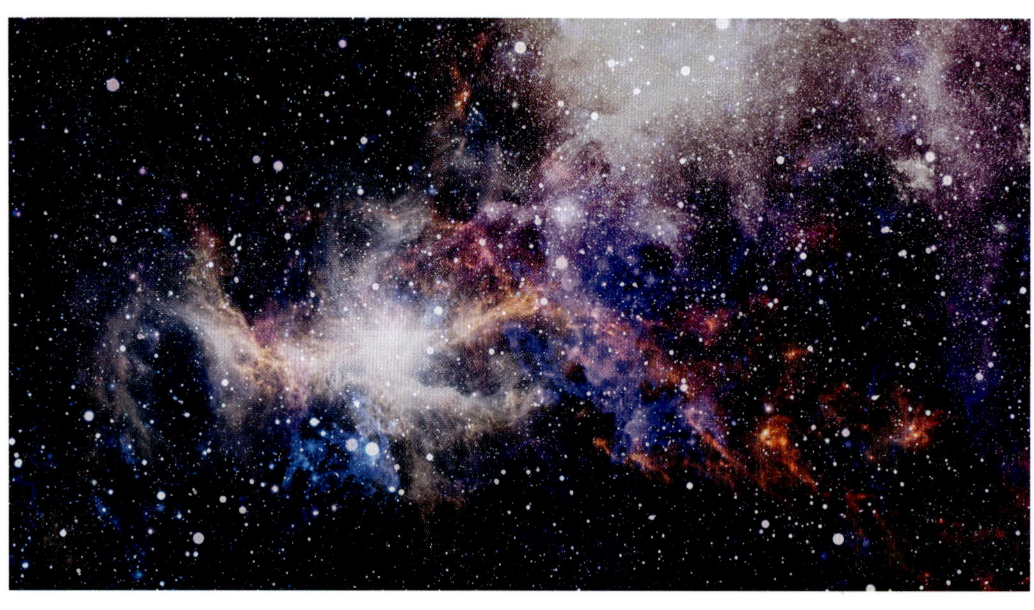

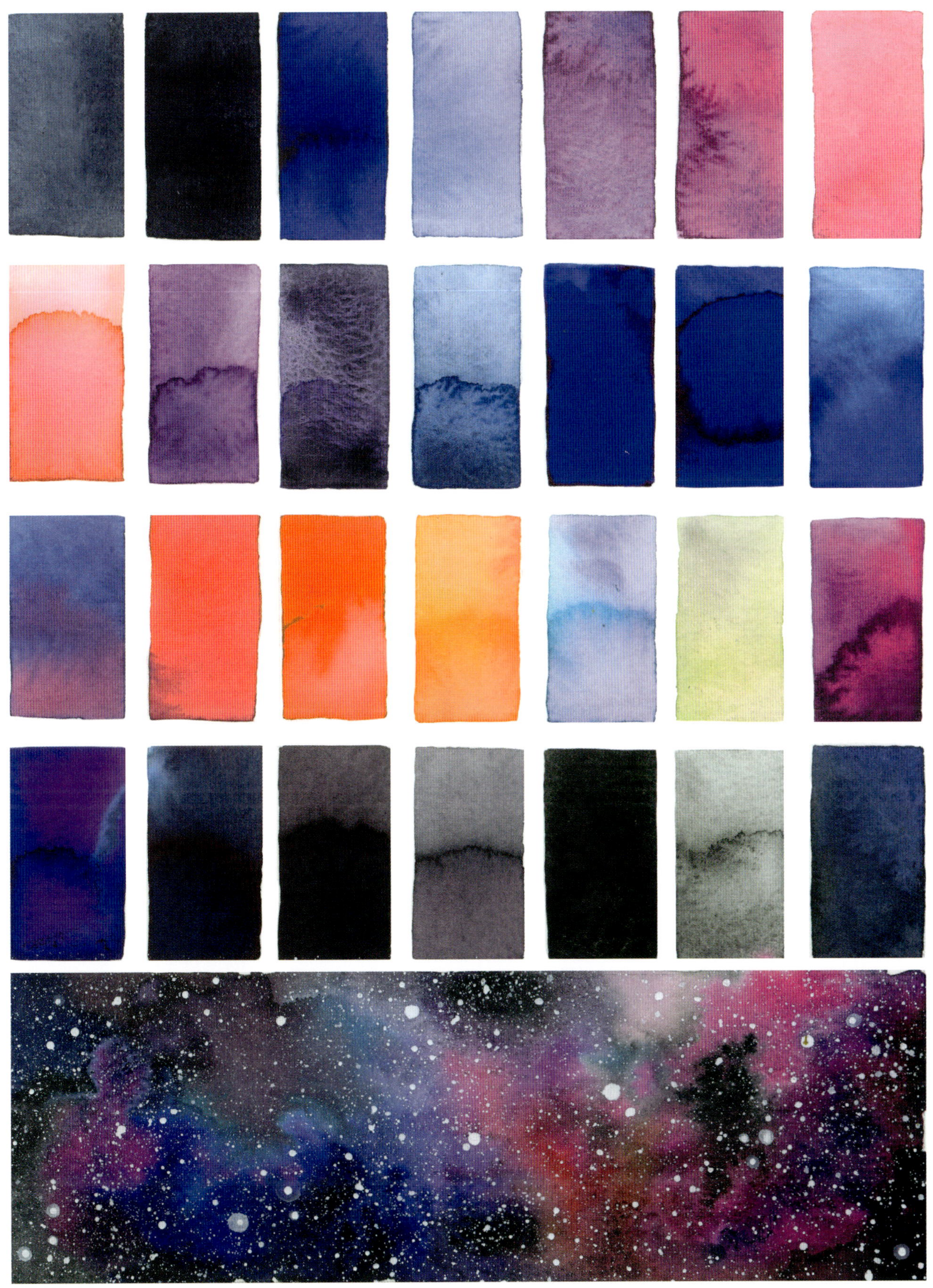

39

Glowing Sunset

The glowing Maldives sunset below is a complete dream of a palette; It's harmonious, mostly analogous, and extremely pleasing to the eye.

For me, this palette evokes the setting sun's powerful rays that dance in tiny sparkles on the ocean's waves.

COLOR NOTES This predominantly warm palette includes bright magentas, deeper mauve for shadows, and a wide range of yellows, oranges, reds, and pinks. Even the small touches of blue (for the sky) and green (for the water) work with the warm theme.

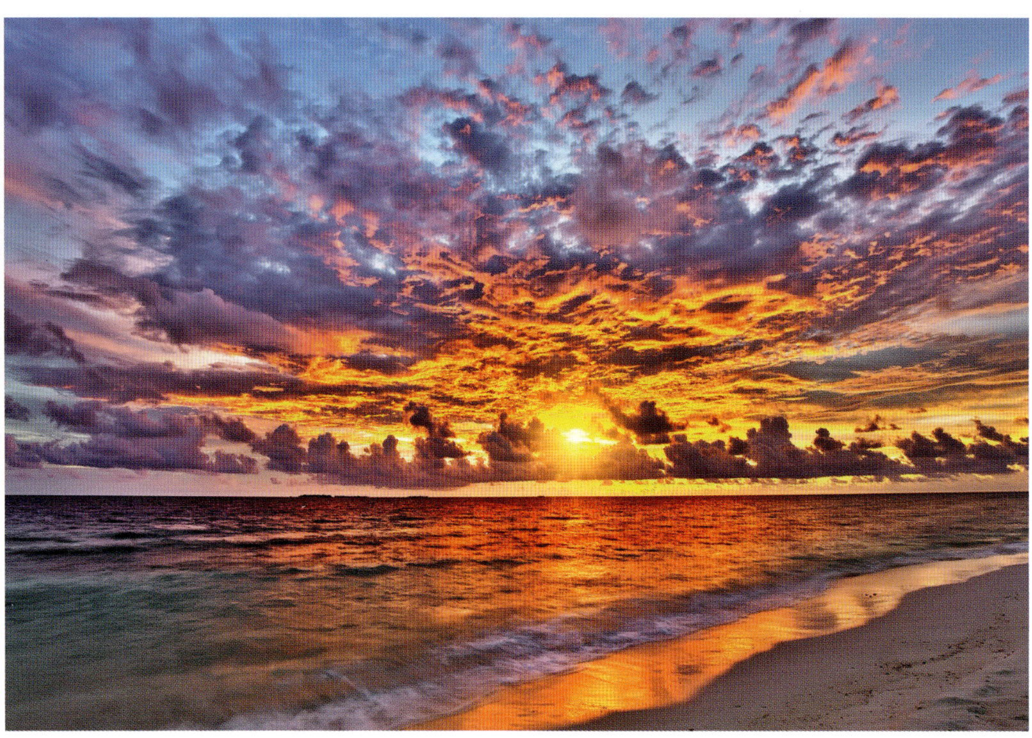

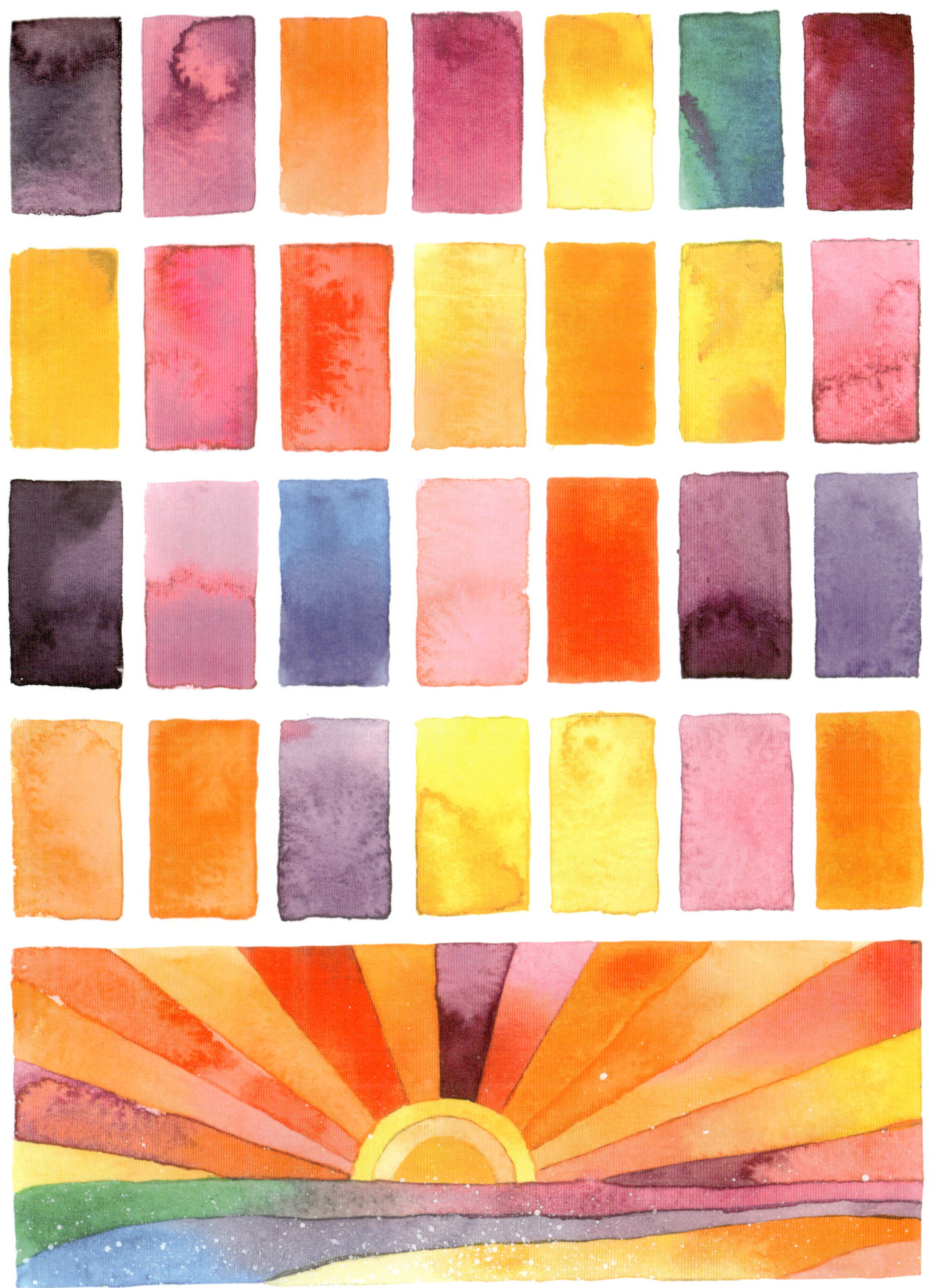

41

Northern Lights

It's my dream to travel to Iceland and see the stunning light display called aurora borealis, or northern lights. Can you even believe this happens on Earth? This magnificent, mostly wintertime occurrence lights up the sky with bright greens, and occasionally electric blue, ultraviolet, iridescent yellow, and pinks (as below).

The inspiration board is a wet-on-wet wash with white specks added once it's dried completely, so the stars don't blend into the sky.

COLOR NOTES I mainly used Dr. Ph. Martin's in this palette because of their radiant quality. My preferred tones are Magenta, Moss Rose, Ultramarine, Juniper Green, April Green, and Black. I also used indigo from my pan set and Opera Pink from Holbein.

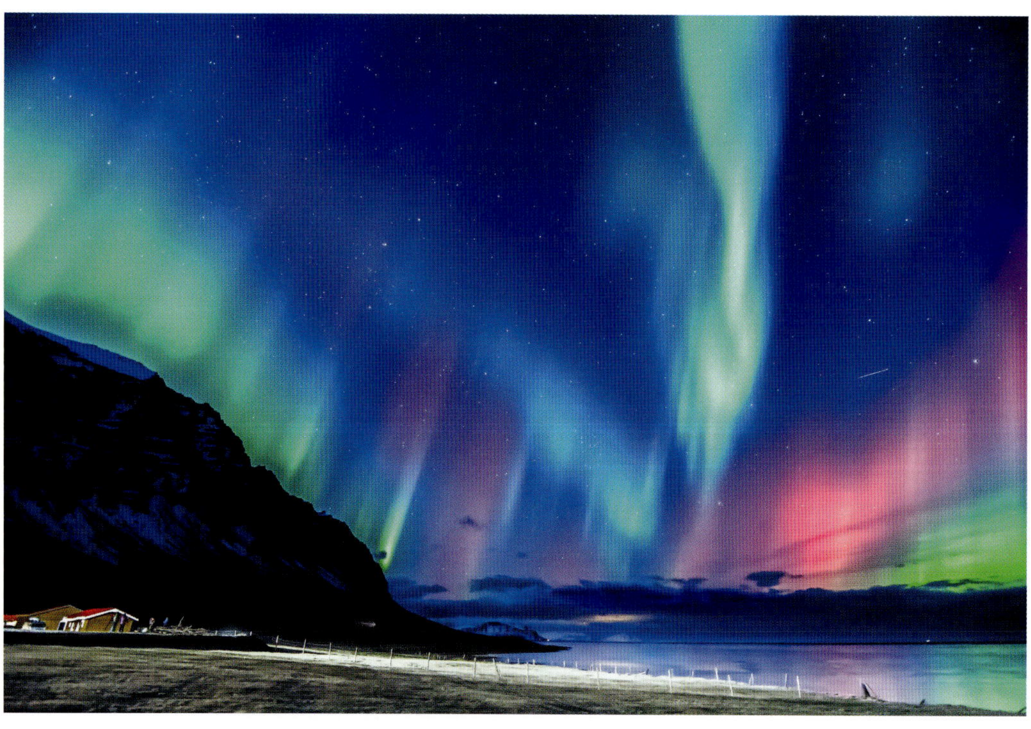

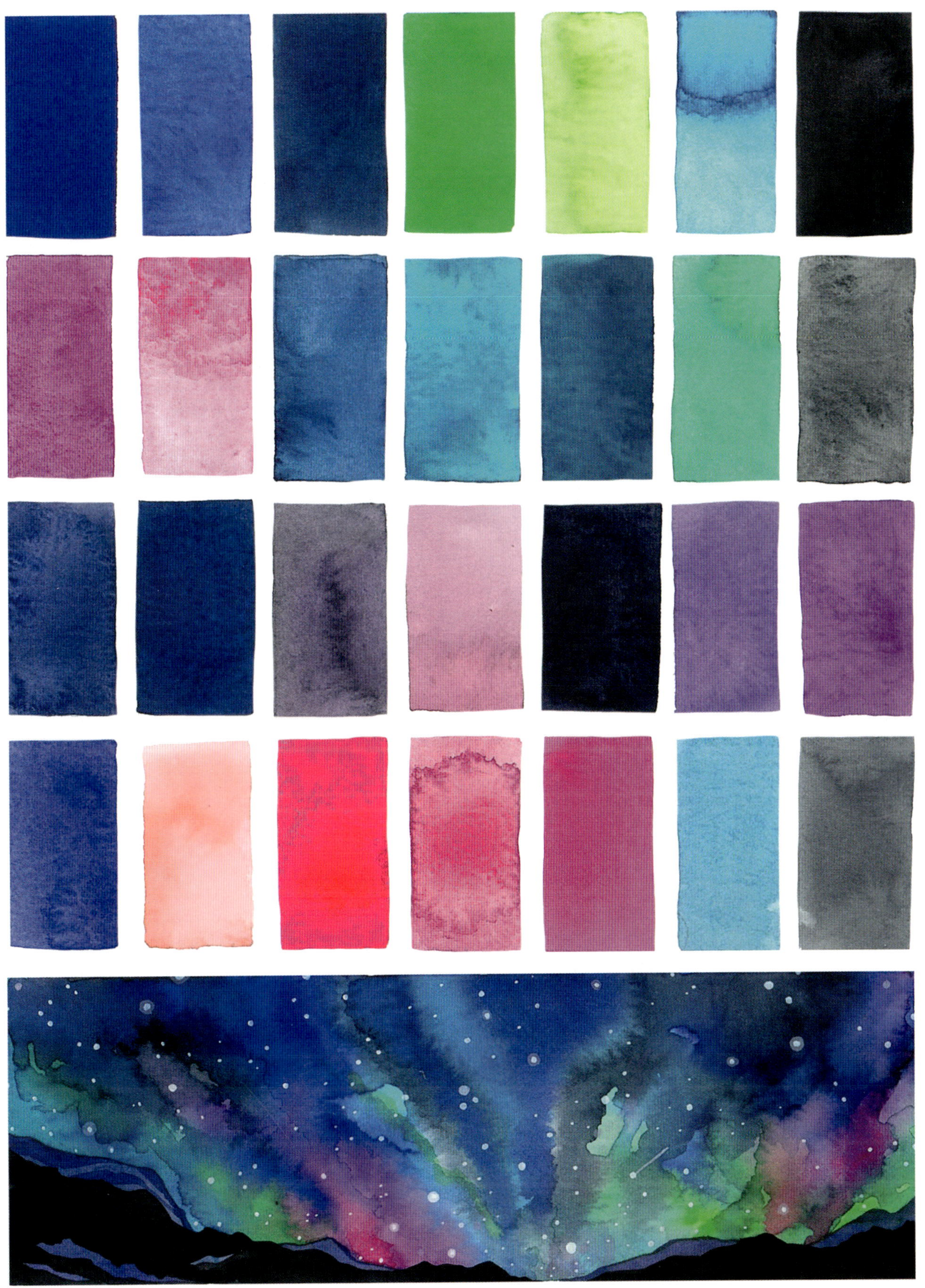

43

Pastel Sunrise

This image reminds me of my hometown of Cancun, where we'd get glorious cotton candy sunrises over the Caribbean Sea. Mother Nature's spectacle! I'm reminded of words like relaxing, soothing, dreamy, and innocent. It's no wonder pastel colors inspire such sweet sentiments.

COLOR NOTES I prefer watered-down neons such as Holbein's Opera or Dr. Ph. Martin's Moss Rose. I also really enjoy creamy watercolors like Holbein's Lavender and Shell Pink, which are a bit more opaque.

Add a bit of white gouache to bright colors for perfect pastels. Since watercolor's nature is translucent, light colors are traditionally created by making a watered-down mix of color. Also consider adding a bit of this opaque pigment to your watercolors to make colors that are chalky and creamier.

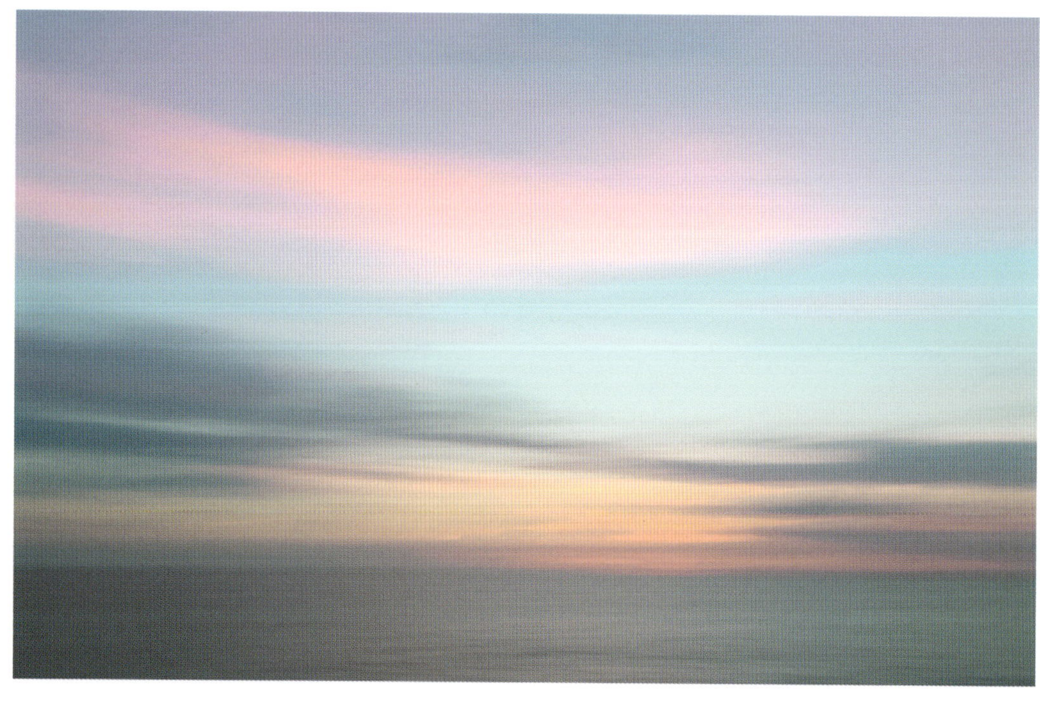

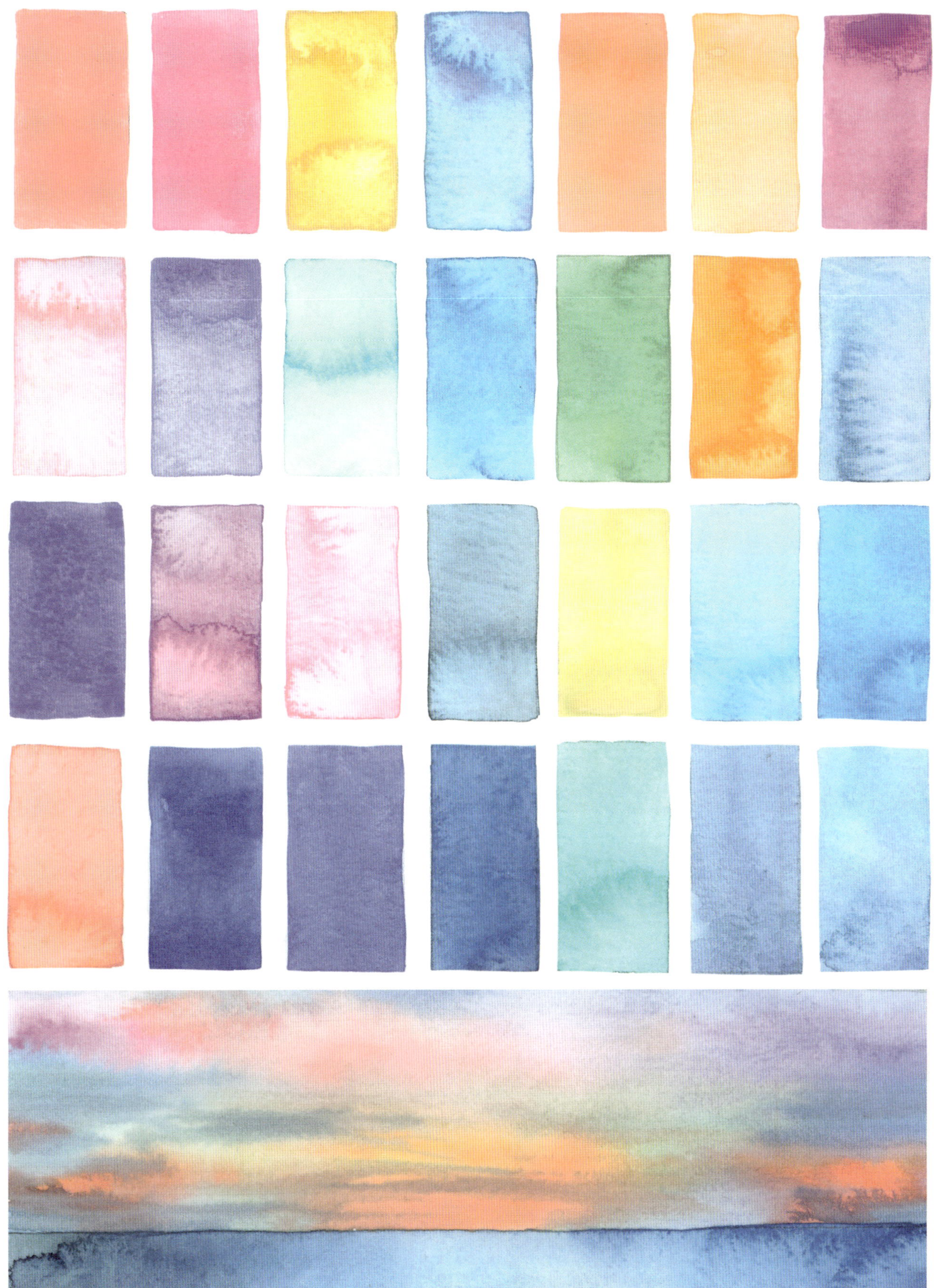

EXPRESSIVE SKIES

Lightning Storm

I am completely fascinated with this picture! There's so much force and energy to a lightning storm. It's also completely terrifying. But in the end, it's a part of nature and as beautiful as a calm sunset.

I tried painting some realistic lightning bolts in my inspiration board, and now I can't wait to integrate this element into a full painting.

TECHNIQUE NOTES You might think this photo is just blue and black, but if you look closely you can train your eye to observe variations in hues, tones, and lightness. In fact, the mixing possibilities are endless even with just four colors (indigo, Payne's gray, turquoise, and black). Between the color combinations and different values (depending on the amount of water), this is a harmonious, cool palette.

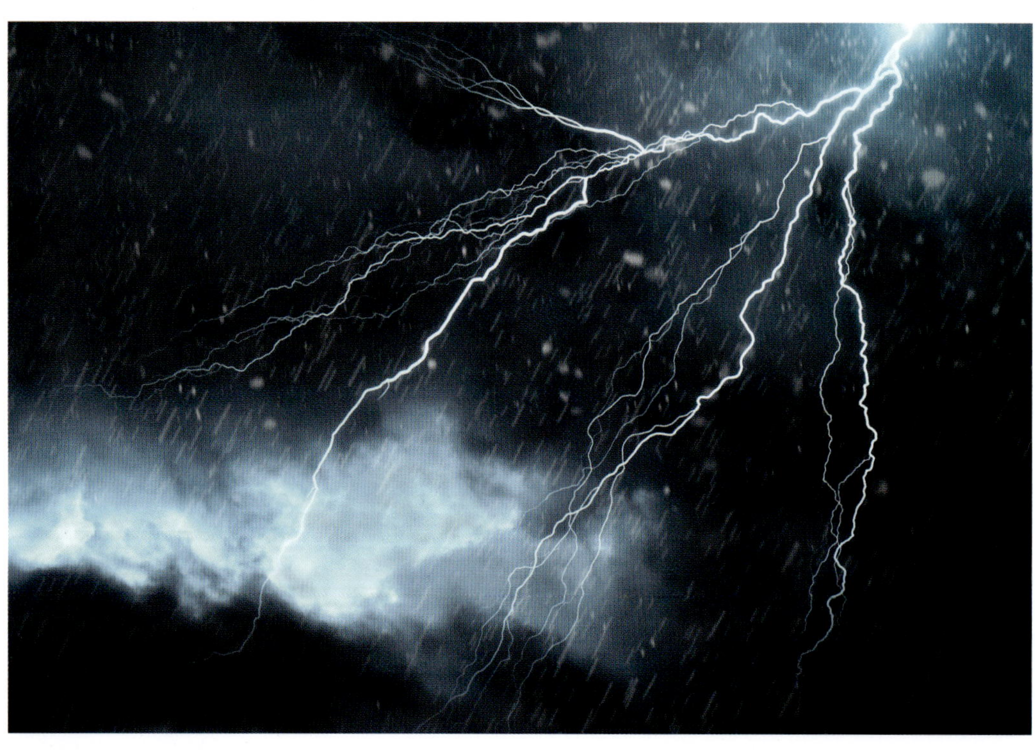

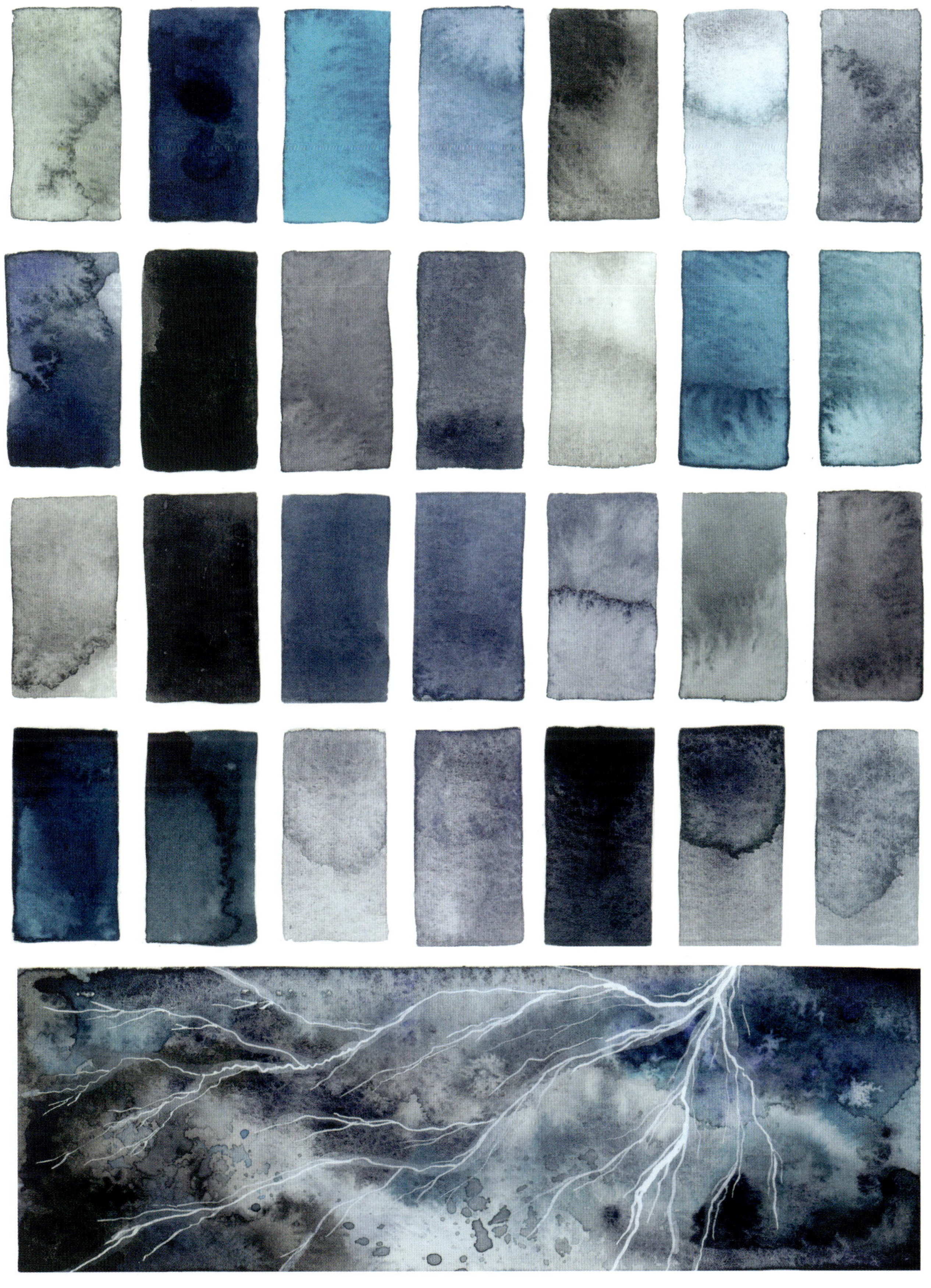

Matryoshka Dolls

I remember seeing a Matryoshka doll at my grandmother's house. She was born in Belarus but came to America when she was just a little girl. The ornamental paintings on the nesting wooden dolls were aesthetically pleasing, and they opened one after the other to reveal a tinier version of the doll hidden inside the larger one, and so on.

It's said that the Russian dolls, also known as stacking dolls, originally represented fertility and motherhood. The largest doll is the family matriarch, an important symbol in Russian families, and the dolls inside represent sons and daughters in generations to come.

Russian folk art usually consists of a darker and deeper color palette, closer to colder seasons like winter and fall rather than spring or summer. The reds are bright but deep. Yellows tend toward warmer hues, giving the impression of gold.

Traditional Russian folk art is a great place to find ornamental references. The shapes and motifs are similar, but each doll is uniquely hand painted and so inspiring!

COLOR NOTES Complementary tones are an amazing tool to desaturate or darken specific shades. In this case, I use Holbein's Pyrrole Red when I need a red with orange undertones. Mix different reds by experimenting with this base tone and then add slight touches of greens to the mix to go deeper, similar to a brick tone. The same process works in reverse. To achieve dark forest greens, just add a small touch of your red mix and it will naturally get darker. If you mix the same amount of the red mix with the green mix, you'll get a beautiful brown. By mixing in touches of ochre, your browns will be deeper or have golden shades.

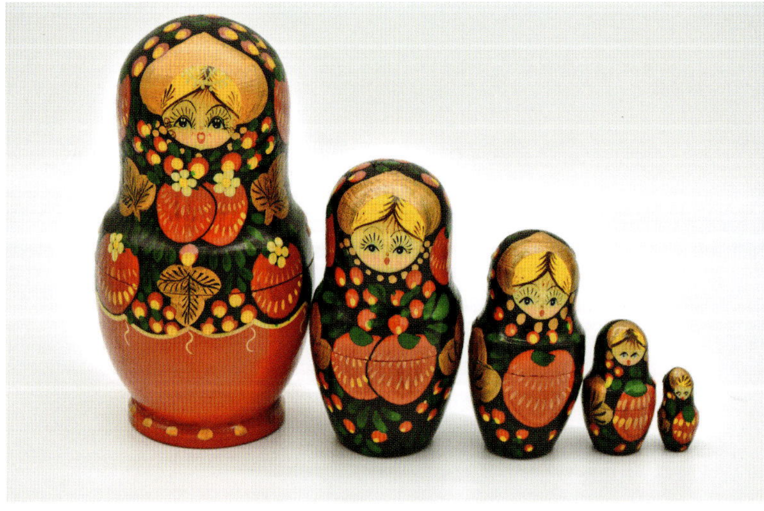

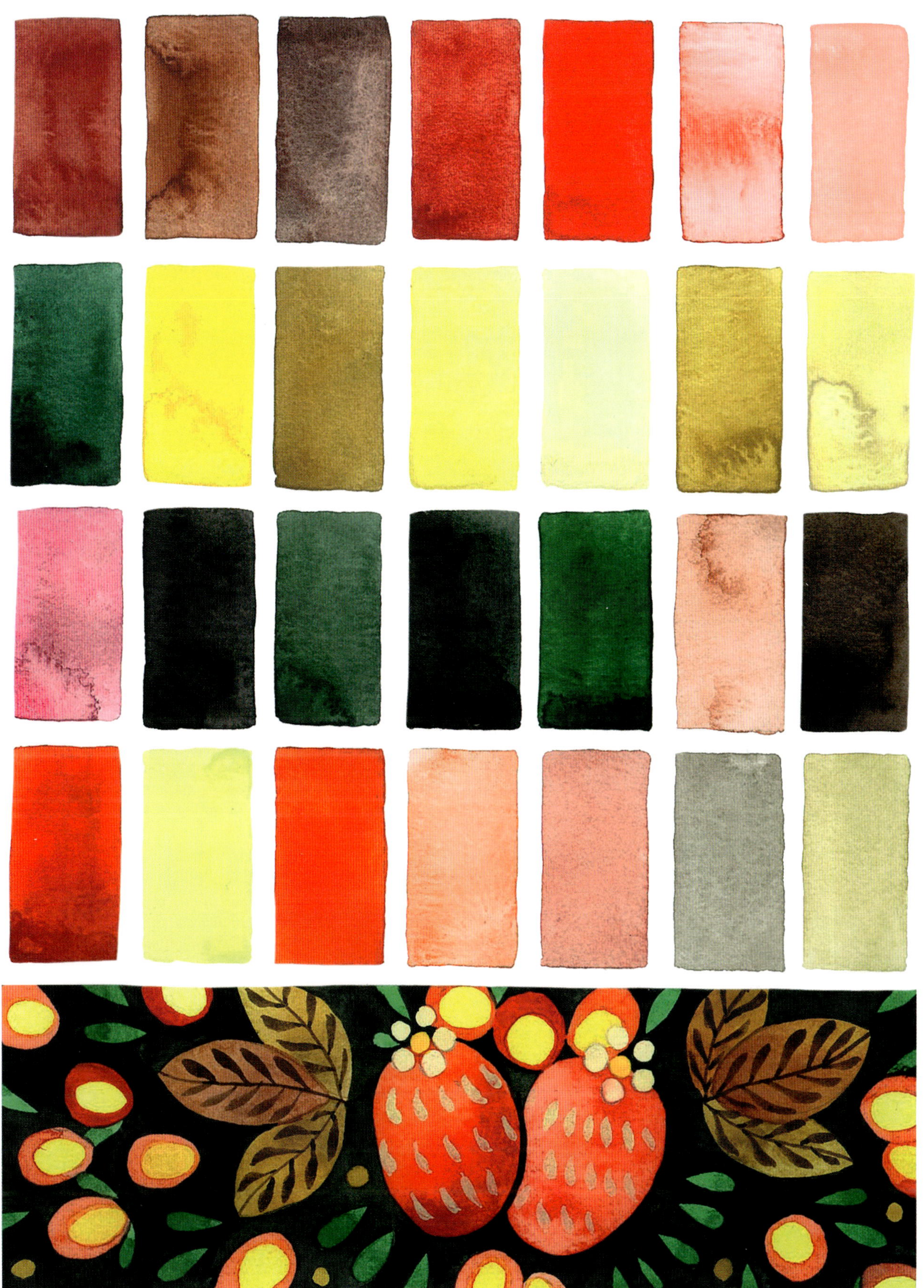

49

African Geometric Textiles

I've always admired African culture and the deep, bold, and bright textiles. The inspiration for this color and texture swatch comes from a picture of West African fabric at an outdoor market in Accra, the capital of Ghana. When I think of Africa, I imagine the sun shining brightly on colors like the ones shown in the fabrics below.

The palette in this image has a lot of contrast with its bold use of primary colors, black, and hints of pastels. At a quick glance, the predominant colors are red and yellow. I chose a scarlet red as a base; to my eye it's not too warm or too cool, just the perfect classic red. I also worked with variations of yellow, ranging from lemon yellow (cooler) to marigold yellow (warmer). Beautiful orange tones emerge from an area where the yellow and red threads intertwine.

Observing these rugs closely, I imitated a couple of the geometric patterns. What patterns can you find in these textiles? Try it out!

TECHNIQUE NOTES I used the white gouache trick to make that perfect pastel pink in some of the block sections. Simply add white gouache to your red mix to make creamy light pinks that are chalky, not transparent.

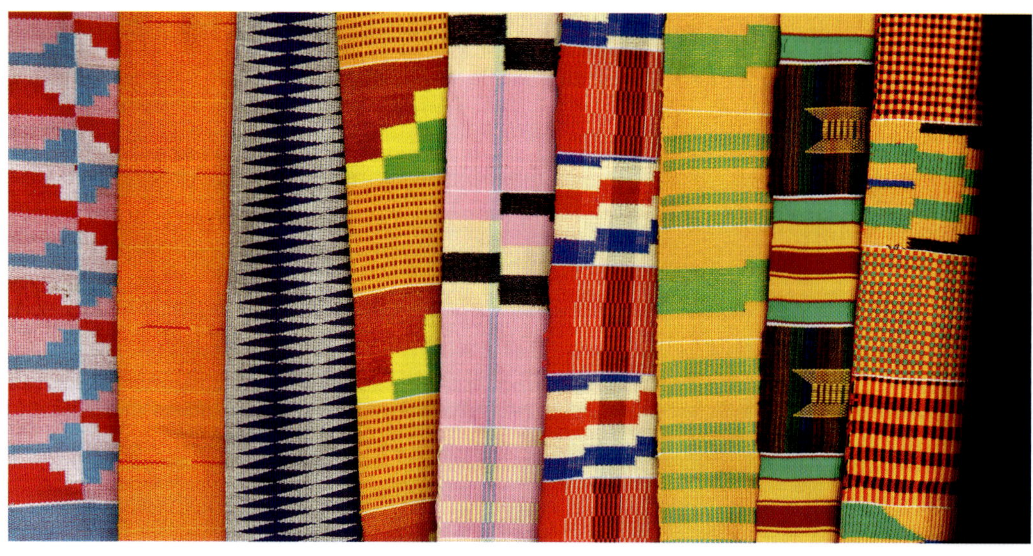

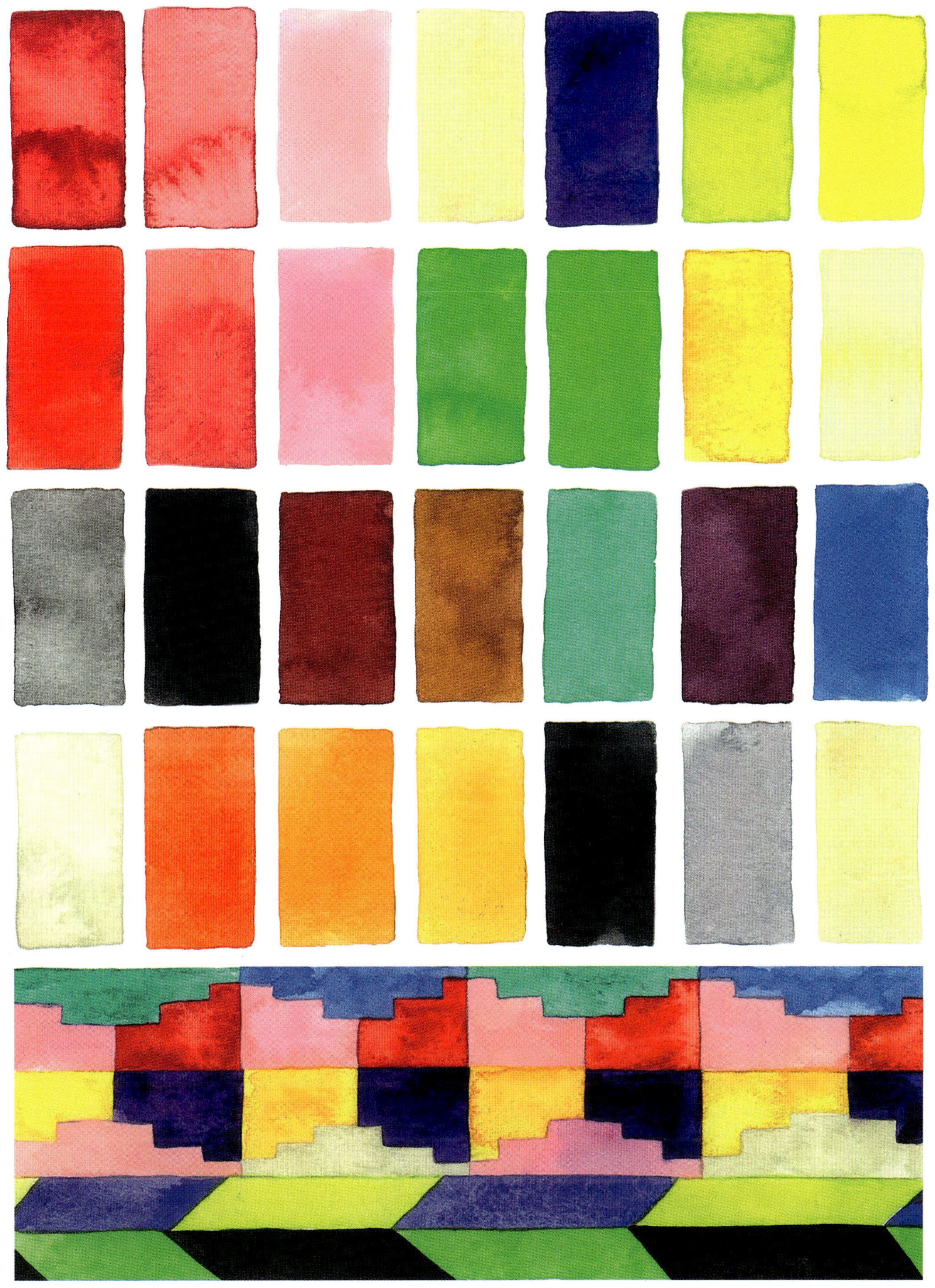

Hungarian Embroidery

I didn't know much about this style of embroidery, but was pleased to see these beautiful shapes consisting of bright, cheerful florals, spiral ornaments, and foliage. The folkloric motifs are embroidered on all kinds of crafts: women's clothing, table runners, pillowcases, and doilies, to name a few.

After reading more about this traditional folk art, I learned that the craft took shape during the beginning of the eighteenth century and originally incorporated Renaissance and Baroque elements. I swooned over all the beautiful examples of embroideries online and was inspired to swatch a design inspired by these swirly florals.

The palette is bright and cheery but also quite bold. There's really no blending or gradients in this style. Instead, a variety of colorful threads make up these beautiful designs. I enjoyed using bright pinks as a base and mixing this pigment with touches of blue to make deep magentas, or a little speck of white gouache for the pastel pinks.

Overall, this folk art is a beautiful source of inspiration and so happy to look at!

TECHNIQUE NOTES Great examples of bright pinks are Dr. Ph. Martin's Moss Rose and Holbein's Opera Pink, both highlighted in my favorite paints on pages 24 to 25. You can add equals part of yellow to make a bright orange. I also enjoyed working with brights such as Cadmium Yellow, Sennelier's beautiful Dioxazine Purple, and an extremely watered-down version of Dr. Ph. Martin's Juniper Green, which in my mind looks more like a turquoise blue. I also played around freely with a variety of greens in my pan sets to find the right shades in the inspiration image.

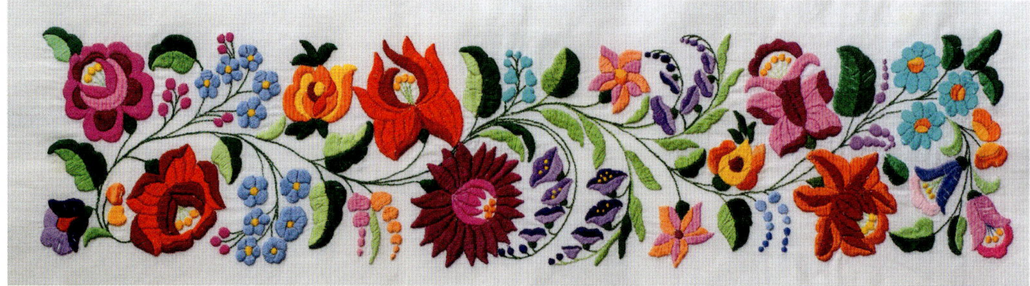

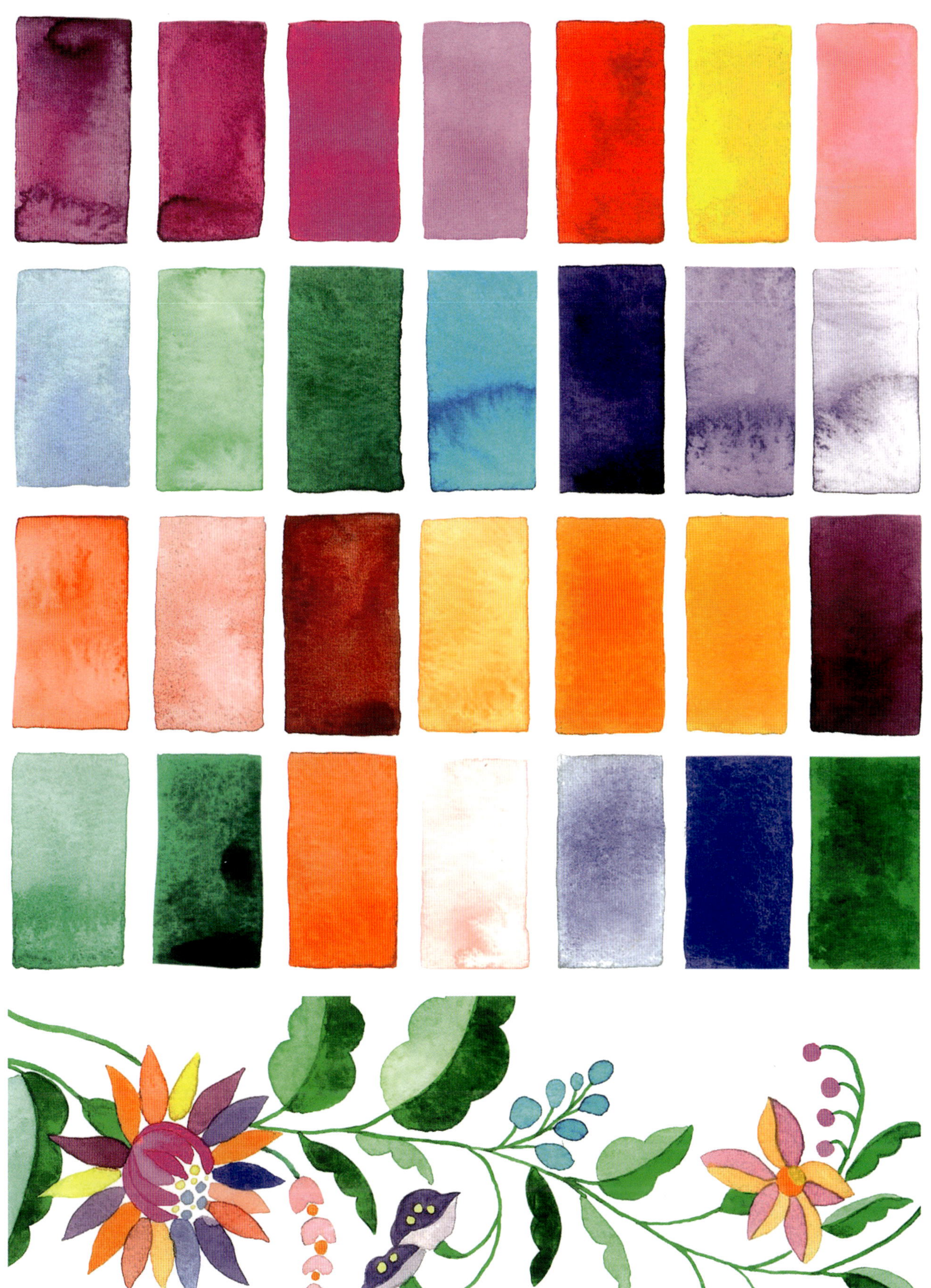

Mexican Talavera

Growing up in Mexico, this type of dinnerware always felt cozy and meant that I was about to eat a delicious homemade, artisanal meal. It's not uncommon for families to have bits of this type of folk art around the house, but it's more typical for old Haciendas or classic Mexican restaurants to serve meals on Talavera.

Talavera is specific to the Puebla state in Mexico, where you find specific types of clay, including blue, yellow, black, green, pale violet, and orange. I went to college there and I remember this beautiful artwork on plates, ceramics, and tiles.

I'm naturally inclined to florals, so this inspiration board was such fun! I painted a bright, bold orange flower with concentrated paint around the edges and a bit more water as I approached the center of each petal. I repeated that technique with the blue flowers on each corner.

COLOR NOTES Our example centers heavily on yellow with hints of other colors. The bright primary and secondary color palette is festive and joyful. I had a great time playing around with my pan set, testing all kinds of colors, and simply observing which ones best matched the colors in the photo. Experiment with the paints you have; the palette has easy-to-match, basic colors.

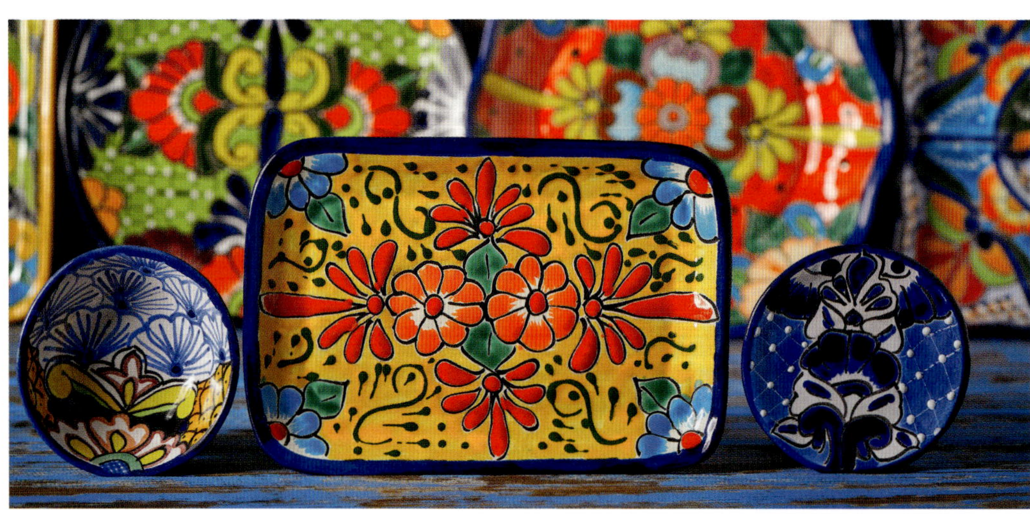

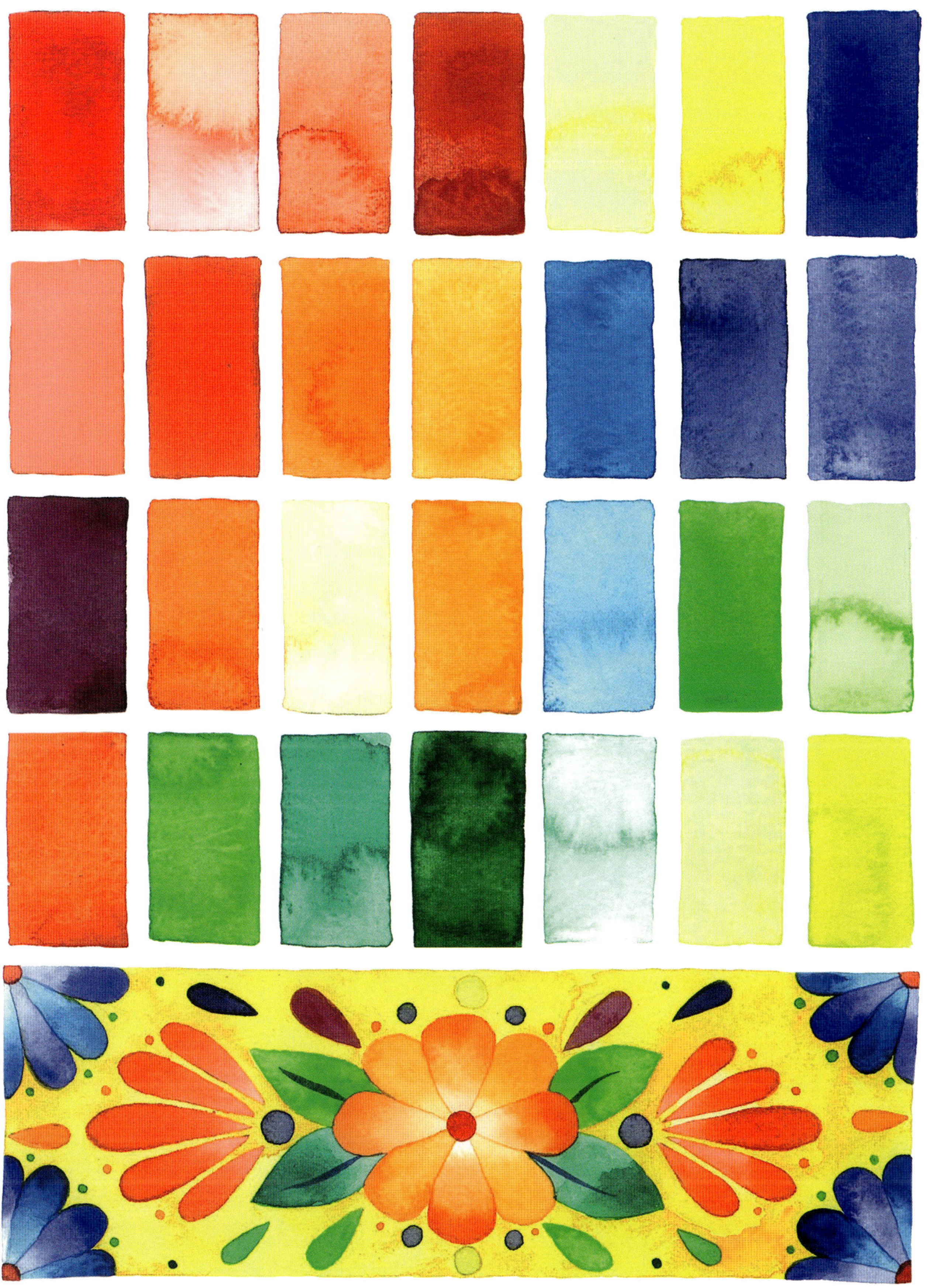

Aboriginal Dot Art

I've never been to Australia, but the indigenous culture has always fascinated me. This beautiful dot art, which can be seen in various media, has been found on stones that archeologists have dated to 60,000 years ago. There is no written language in the Aboriginal culture, so these drawings and symbols are incredibly important. Some dot art has been thought to contain hidden symbols in, or under, the designs.

The palette is warm and neutral, reflecting the natural materials used to create this style of artwork. Locally sourced materials originally included ochre or iron clay pigments to produce yellow, red, and white. Black pigments came from charcoal.

TECHNIQUE NOTES I used a variety of yellows, oranges, and reds to create this swatch. Since I'm looking for a toned-down yellow that complements the earth, not a super bright yellow, I need complementaries to help desaturate. To do this, add touches of violet to your yellow mix, a touch of green to your red mixes, and a touch of blue to the oranges. You can also create interesting and earthy browns using this method.

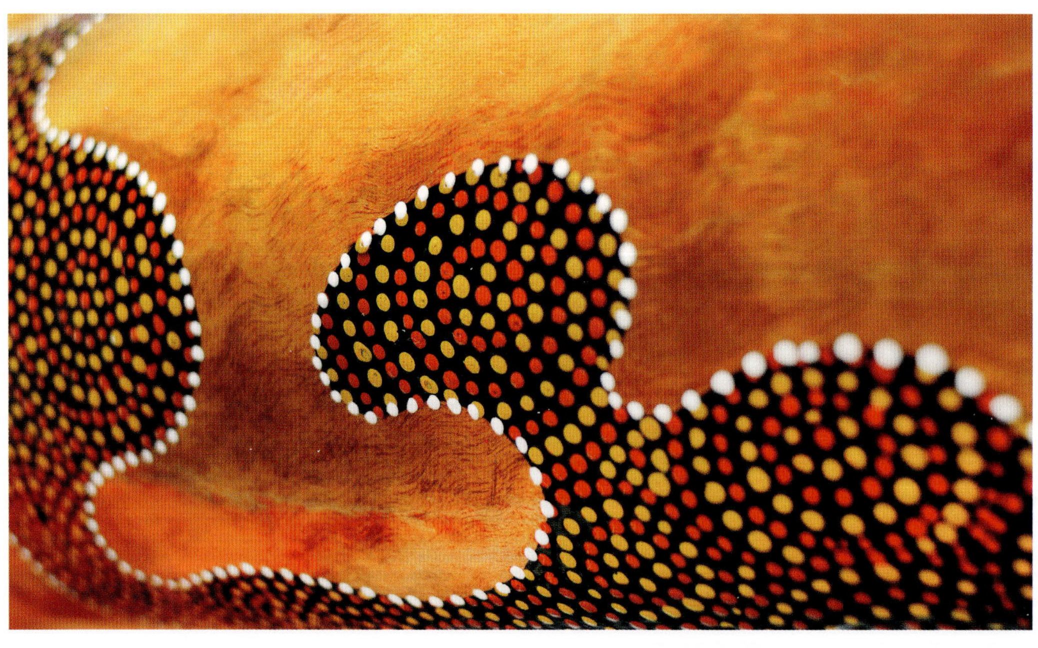

COLOR HARMONY FOR ARTISTS

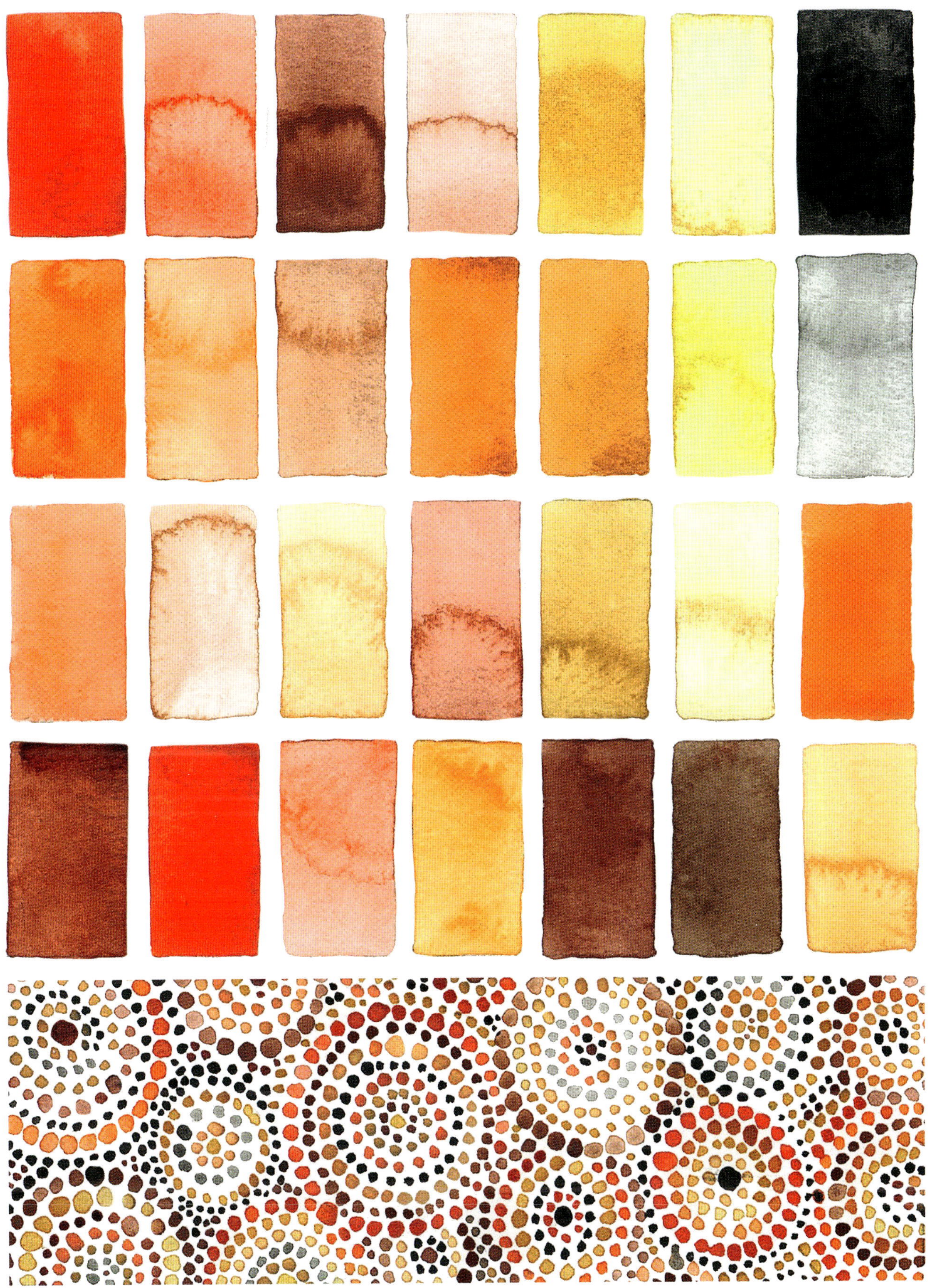

Portuguese Azulejos

A few things might come to mind when you think of Portugal: Porto wine, seafood, and beautiful Azulejo tiles that cover entire buildings. These pieces of public artwork date to the Moors' invasion of Spain and Portugal in the thirteenth century. The word "Azulejo" comes from the Arabic word for small polished stones.

These simple stones became more ornamental over the years, and now Azulejos famously decorate everything from cathedrals to train stations, palaces, restaurants, bars, and even regular homes.

See how gorgeous tiles give a country character and public beauty! Look to tile designs for your inspiration—there is so much to discover!

COLOR NOTES The sample here consists of a harmonious mix of earthy, muted tones and bright, bold jewel tones. Colors like emerald green, olive green, and bright sapphire contrast beautifully with deep mahogany and ochre hues. Daniel Smith has an amazing pigment called Sap Green that works great for olive or swampy greens. For bright emerald greens I enjoy using Holbein Viridian Hue as a base. Schmincke's Naples Yellow works beautifully for the hints of cream. You can also use my white gouache trick and add a delicate touch of peach and yellow to your mix.

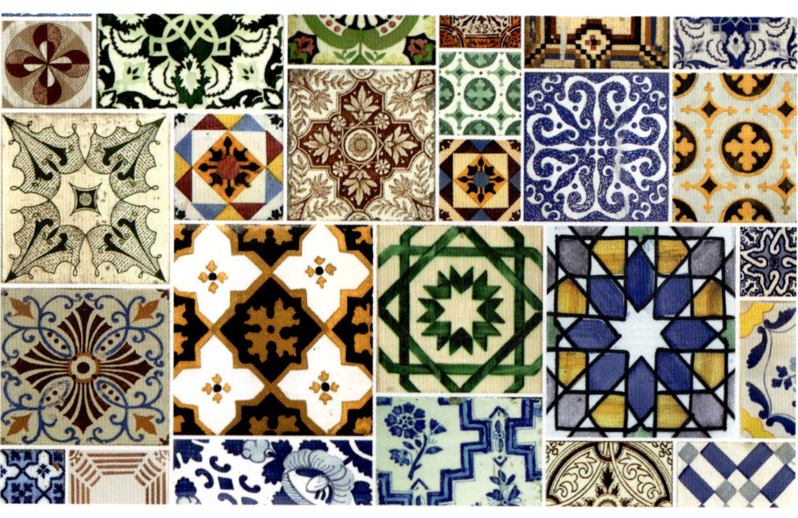

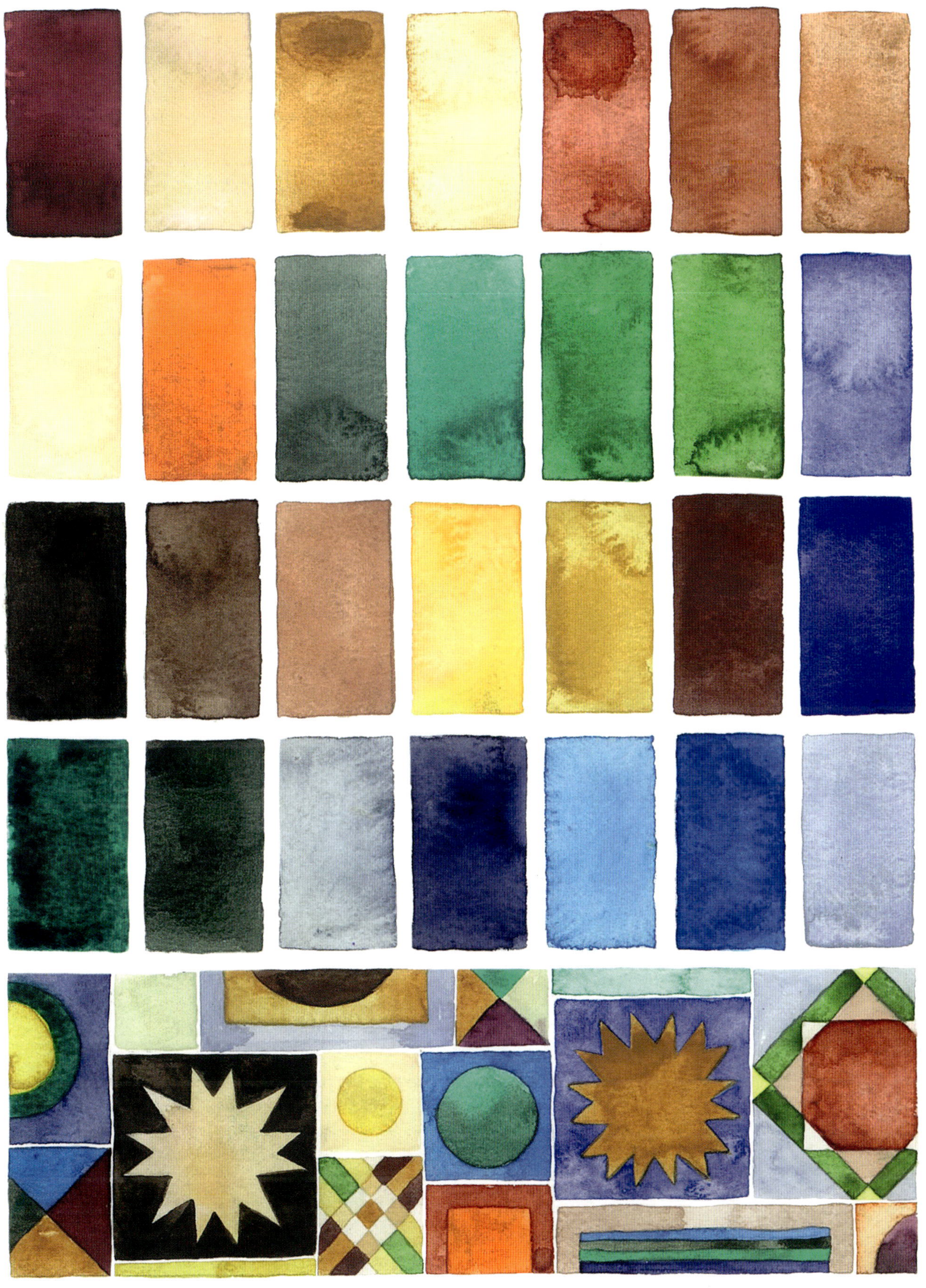

Lai Thai

Lai Thai is a beautiful ornamental, two-dimensional style of traditional Thai art. Its character is said to be influenced by Buddhism and its symbols reflect kindness, gracefulness, and an overall love of beauty.

I was most inspired by this painting's engaging use of detail and fine lines in the moving water. The tetradic palette creates harmony, with blue as a main color and combinations of green (on the cool side) and touches of red and orange for warmth.

> **TECHNIQUE NOTES** Experiment with the different blue pigments of your pan set to see how they look on paper. Since blue pigments tend to appear darker if they're in square cake form, it's important to test them first. I also recommend adding touches of green to make warmer blues, or violet to deepen and darken your different blues.

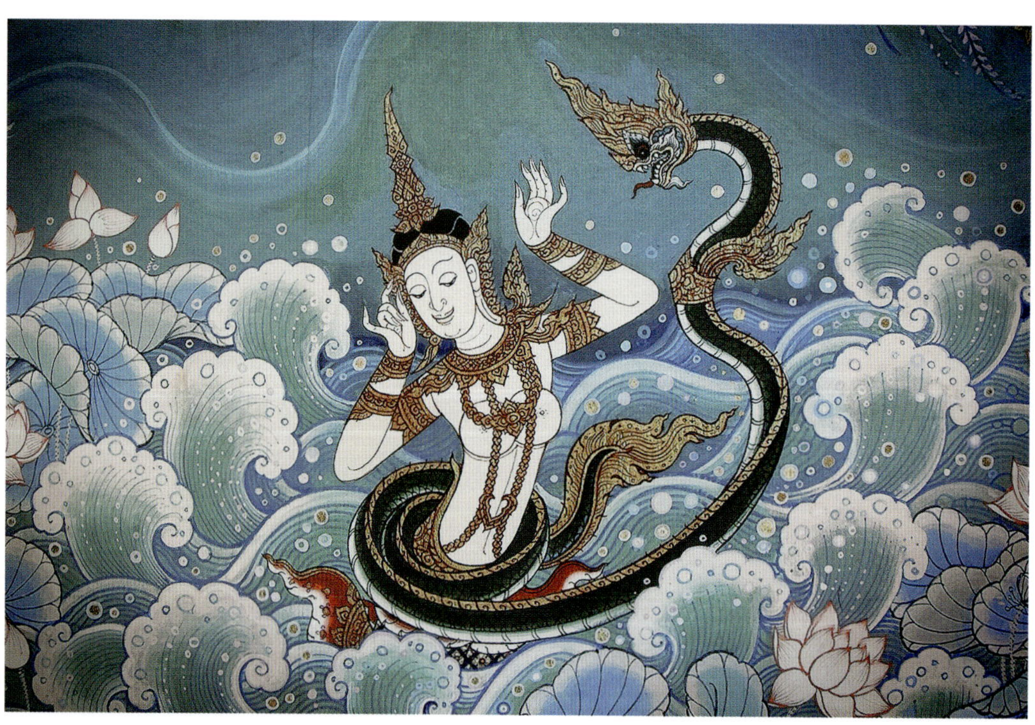

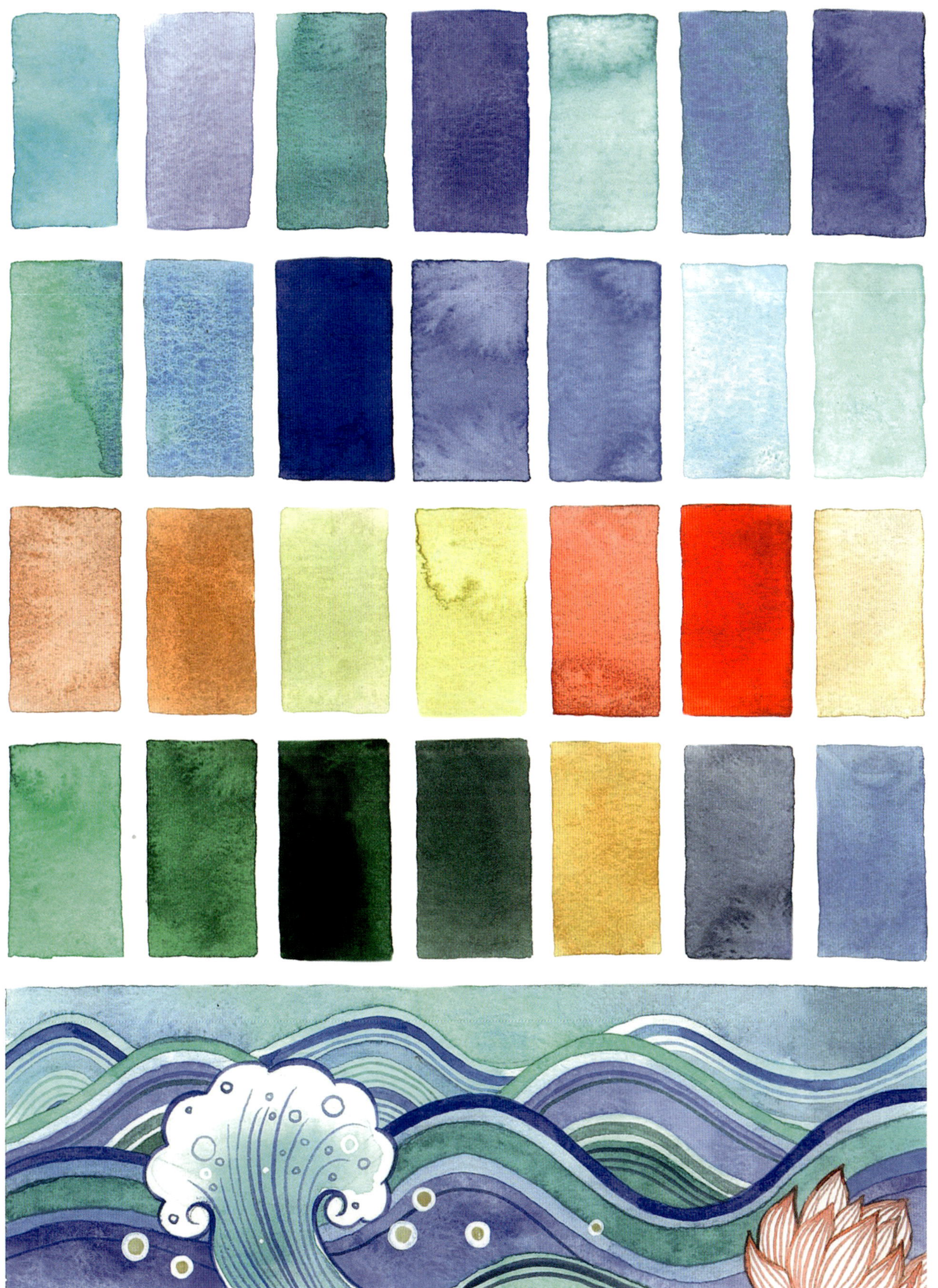

61

Scottish Kilt

Kilts are traditionally worn on special occasions by men and boys in Scotland. The knee-length skirts with pleats at the back are usually made out of plaid fabric. Plaid, also known as tartan pattern, is comprised of crisscrossed horizontal and vertical bands in different colors.

To me, this palette and pattern symbolize formal occasions and seriousness. Complementary colors (green and red) stand out, which demonstrate perfect contrast. There is no real blending or gradation, but because threads intertwine (a red that threads together with green) some appear darker, similar to a brick red.

COLOR NOTES Forest greens, navy blues, crimson reds, and lemon yellows stand out in this palette. I did a little texture swatch by layering different watercolor bars over dry layers.

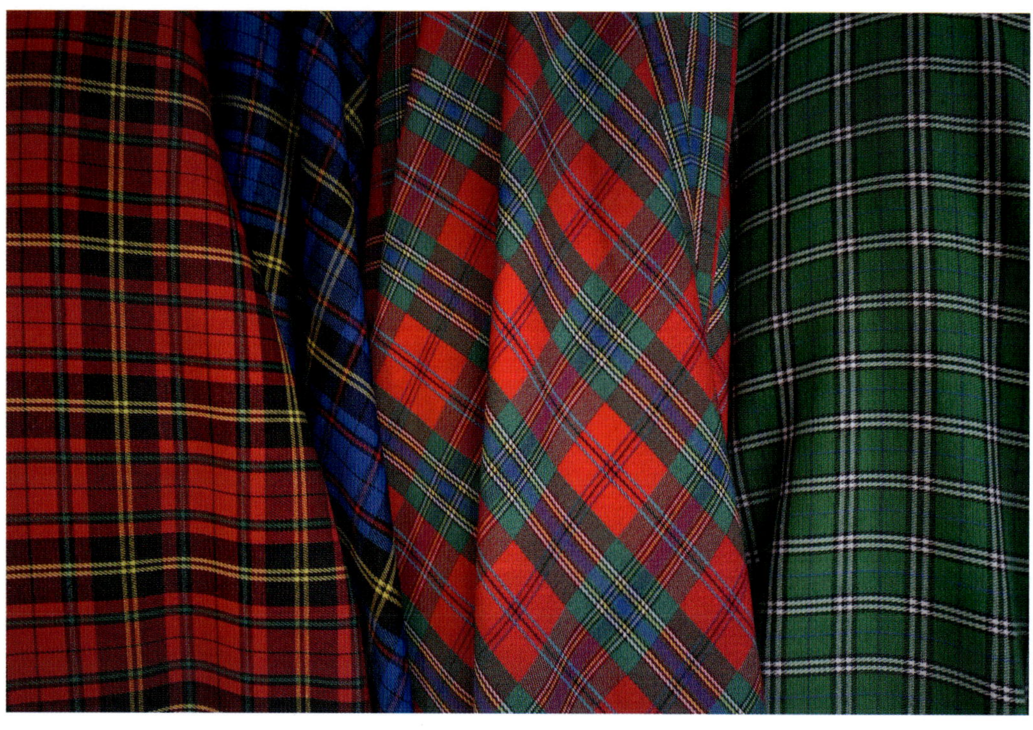

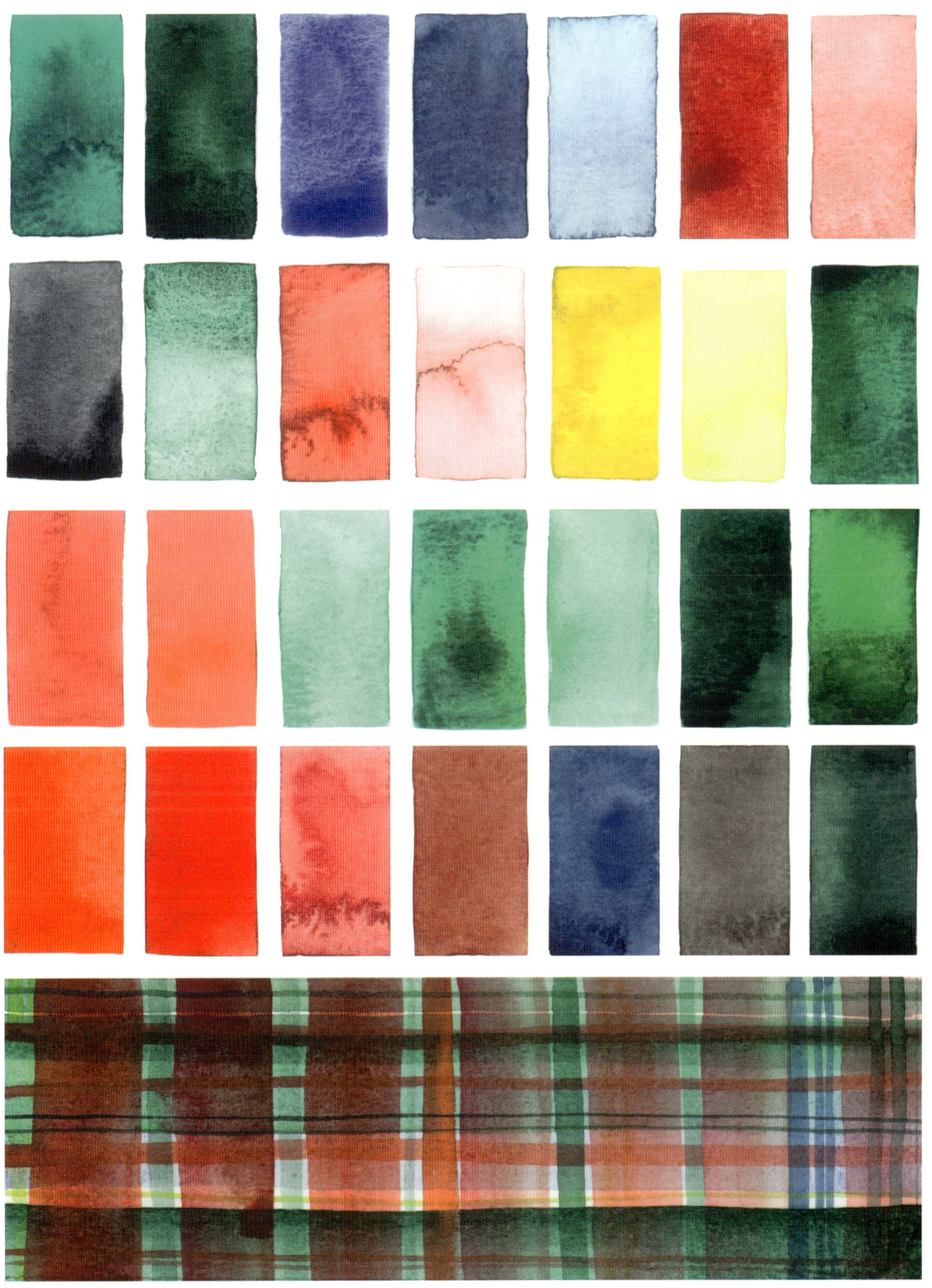

Peruvian Textiles

Friends who have traveled to Peru have shared stories about walking for hours around markets with of all kinds of beautiful textiles, ponchos, rugs, bags, clothing, and hats. The patterns, in natural alpaca wool and other fibers naturally tinted with local flowers and plants, highlight unique indigenous designs, geometric shapes, and even little alpacas.

I love the way the deep black wool contrasts with the bright colors and the natural fibers.

COLOR NOTES I was excited to use Opera Pink as a base for the wonderful pink pigments in these designs. Sometimes they're concentrated and appear bright pink; other times they're watered down and mixed with Moss Pink for tonal variation. I also used Dr. Ph. Martin's Mahogany for deep purples and to mix with the pinks for mid-violet magenta hues.

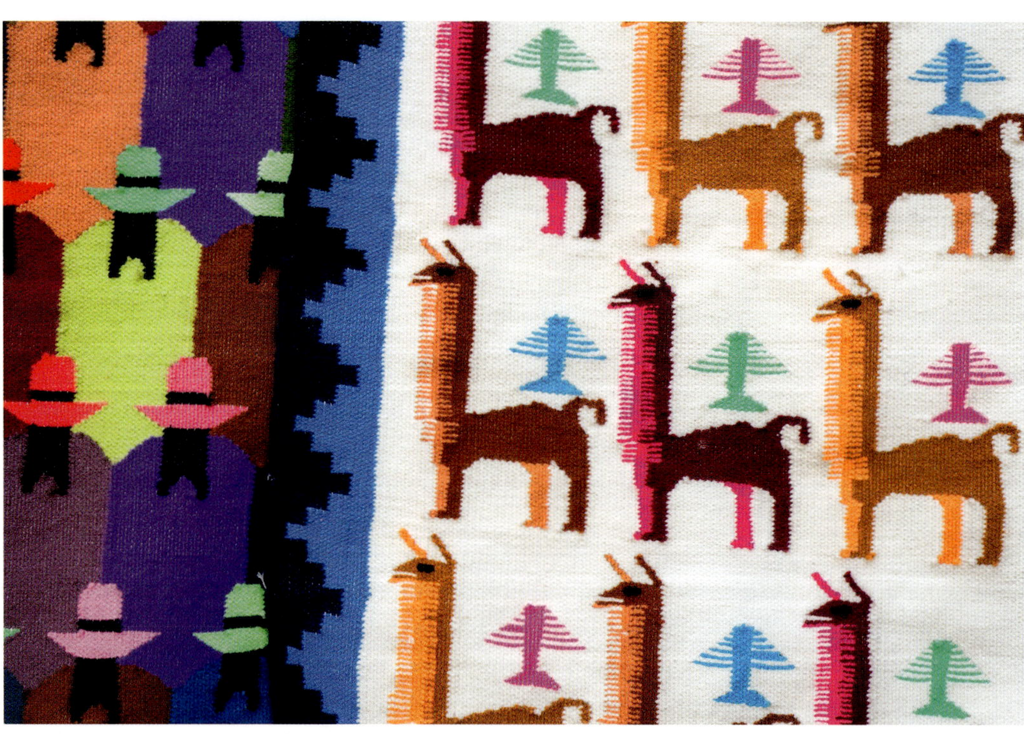

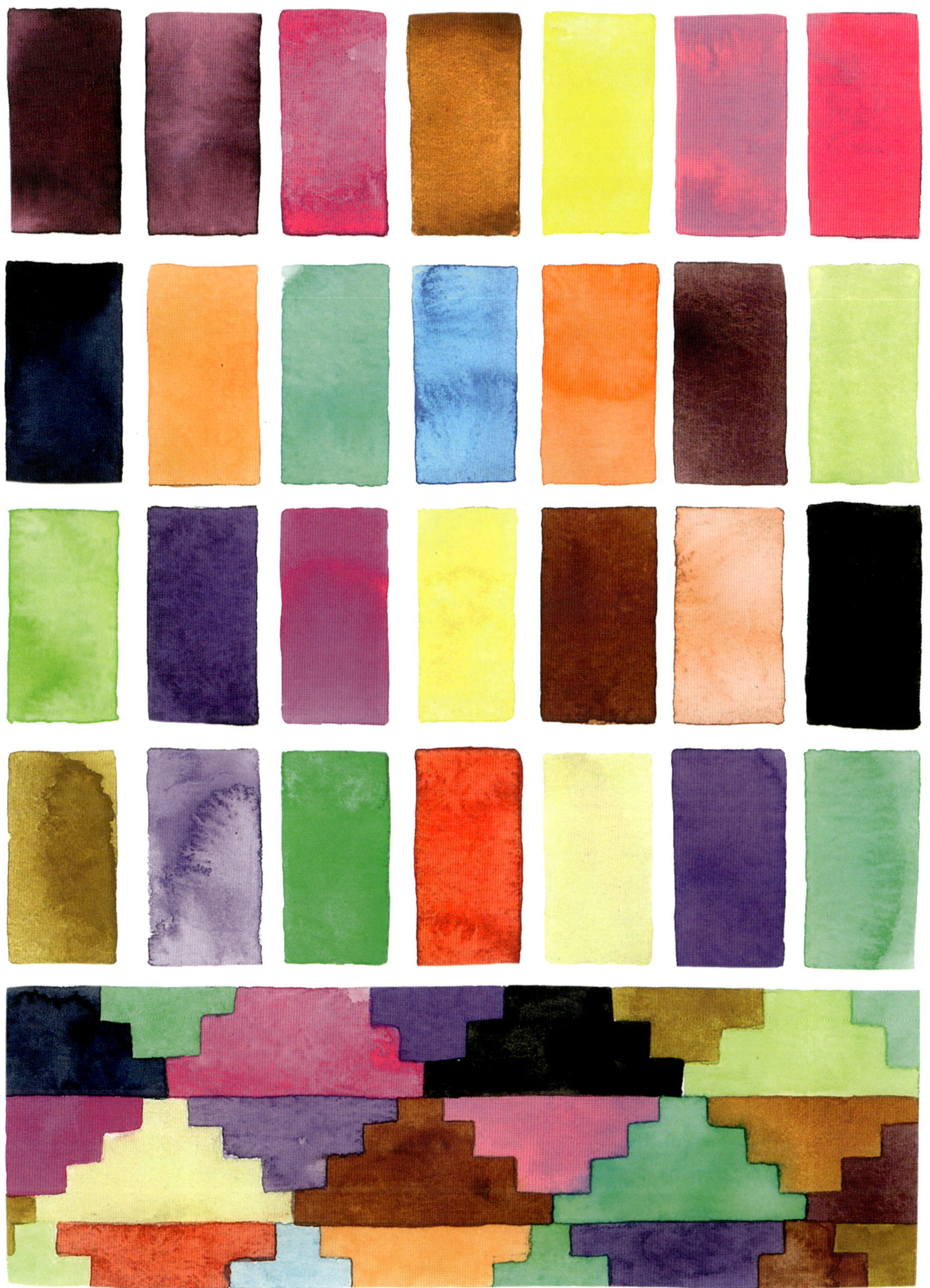

Serene Flamingos

This palette is so serene and dreamy. It influenced me to paint delicate gradients in my creative inspiration board that imitate the peaceful waters where flamingos take a long rest.

The palette is soft overall, with two main colors (pink and blue) and a wide range of variation. The third color is just a touch of watered-down black for the flamingos' beaks.

When working with a variety of pinks, I suggest a base of Opera Pink instead of a red. We all learned early on that red and white do in fact make pink, and this will work if you have a limited selection of base colors. But I find that pigments or dyes like Opera (I enjoy Holbein), Moss Rose, and Persimmon (Dr. Ph. Martin's) have a certain neon hue that's hard to find in conventional pan sets.

I also enjoyed testing a variety of blues in my pan sets and comparing them to the colors in the water, which are mostly diluted and soft.

> **TECHNIQUE NOTES** When painting with bright pastels, have a tube of white gouache handy. Watercolor painting usually requires watering down the paint and using the white of your paper to achieve light tones. Gouache (sometimes referred to as opaque watercolor) is also water based, so they actually mix well. The white gouache also helps when you want to make your watercolors creamier and chalky, like the variety of pinks in the flamingos' feathers.

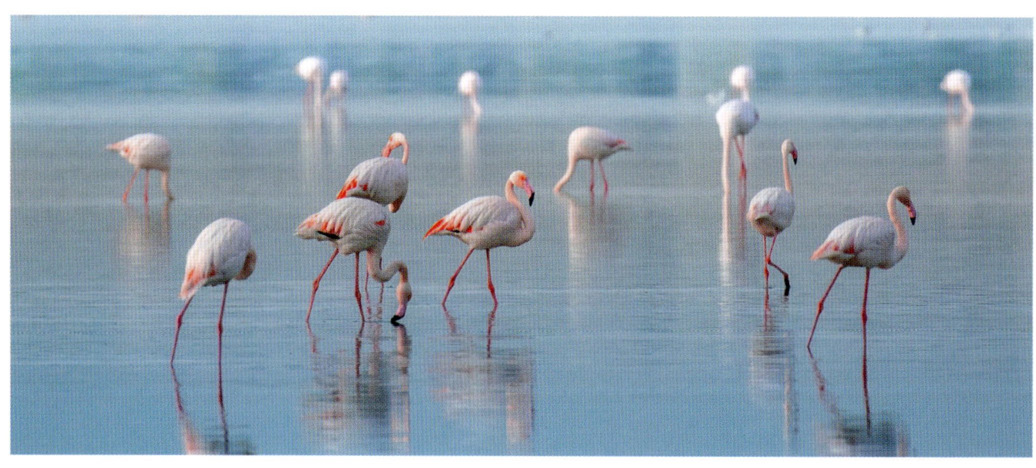

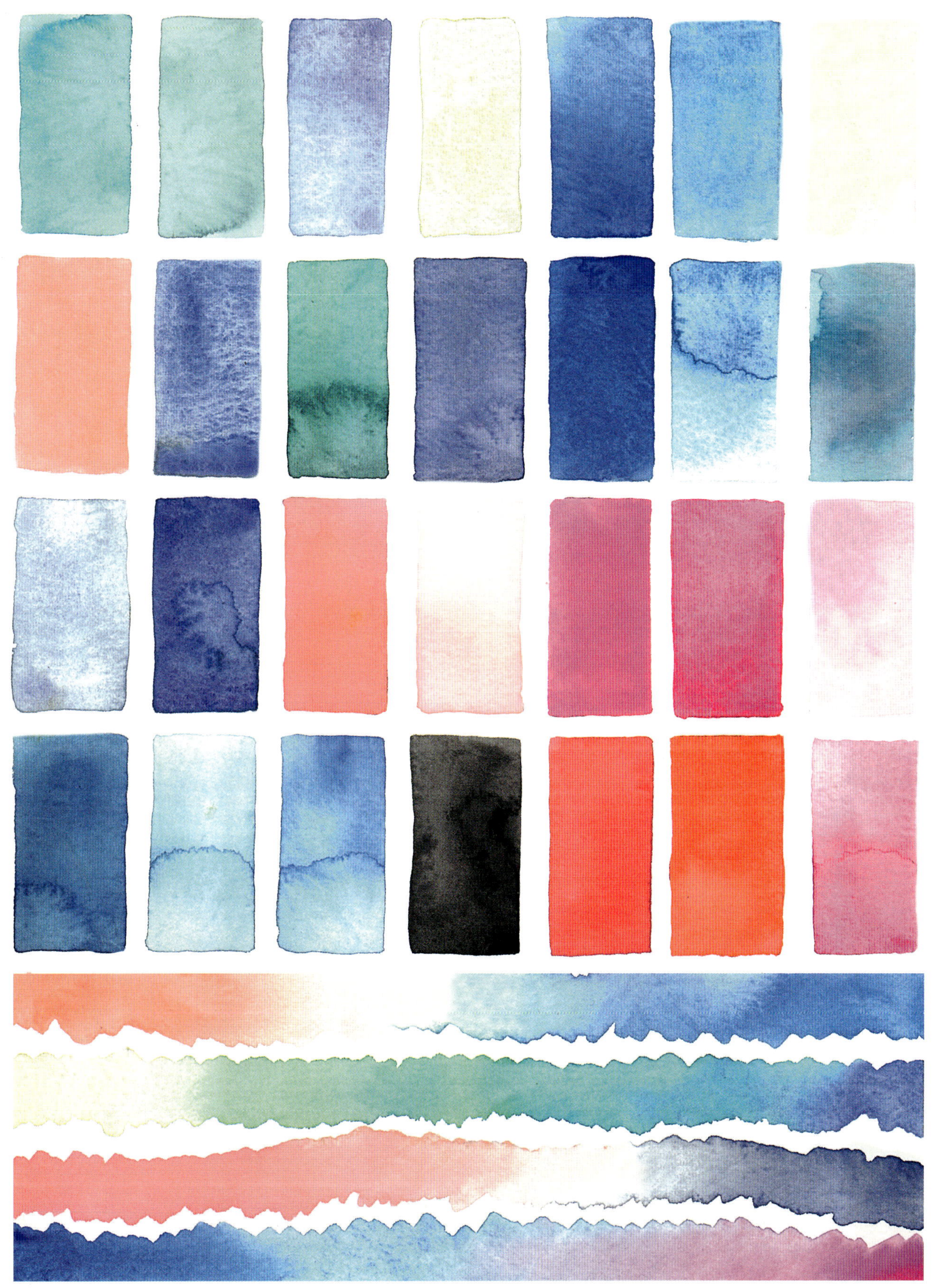

67

Angelfish

Snorkeling was a big part of weekend activities growing up in Cancun, Mexico. I remember the first time I saw an angelfish: It was so beautiful because its shape and colors were so different from the other fish I'd seen.

This palette is another example of nature using complementaries to achieve color harmony. The overall yellow-orange tones contrast perfectly with the violet blues.

Sea life can be quite exciting, and the electric color palette never disappoints. When I find a bright inspiration image like this, I like to use Radiant Concentrated watercolors by Dr. Ph. Martin's to complement my pan set. I usually mix these vibrant paints into my pans or tubes, because they are kind of over the top and highly pigmented. Adding just a touch of these dyes into my other paints works beautifully to make a large variety of tones in the same palette. I also used liquid watercolors in Prussian Blue and Daffodil Yellow.

Have you ever explored a coral reef? It feels like you're in outer space. Inspiration is everywhere!

TECHNIQUE NOTES Although the image represents a complementary palette, notice that there is no real blending. Remember, if you mix complementaries equally, you'll end up with a shade of brown. So while the colors interact, they switch from one to another within the scales. And these scales are exactly what inspired my texture board!

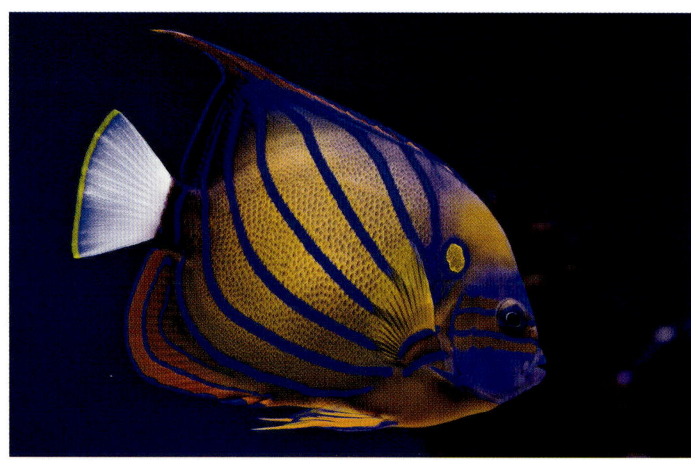

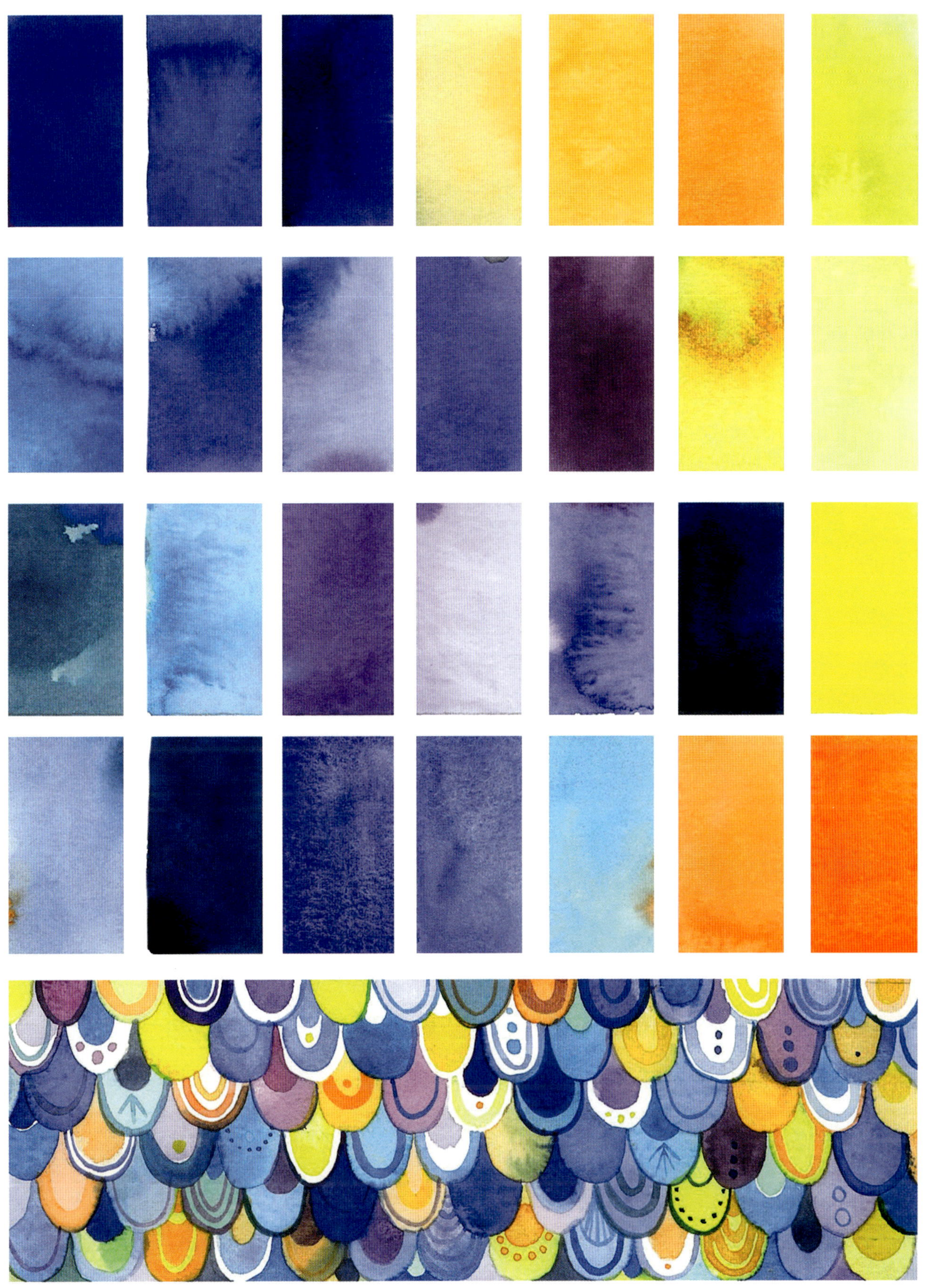

Fluffy Bunnies

This image is downright cute! Although rabbits aren't the cuddliest of animals, they do inspire tenderness. Their color palette is sweet and their fur is soft and fluffy.

The palette's furlike colors range from light peaches to pastel ochres and soft browns. Begin by creating a variety of neutral mixes of paint (browns, ochres, blacks) and carefully add touches of white gouache to each mix. Mix them together for a wider range of tones.

Mixing white gouache paint with watercolors will also turn your watercolors opaque for a chalky appearance. For example, if you add a touch of white gouache to black watercolor, you'll get a nice charcoal tone or light creamy gray, depending of the amount of black you use.

The fluffy nature of the bunnies' fur made me think of puffy clouds!

TECHNIQUE NOTE   Use white gouache to help you achieve creamy tones instead of just transparent watercolors, and for light tones like the ones here.

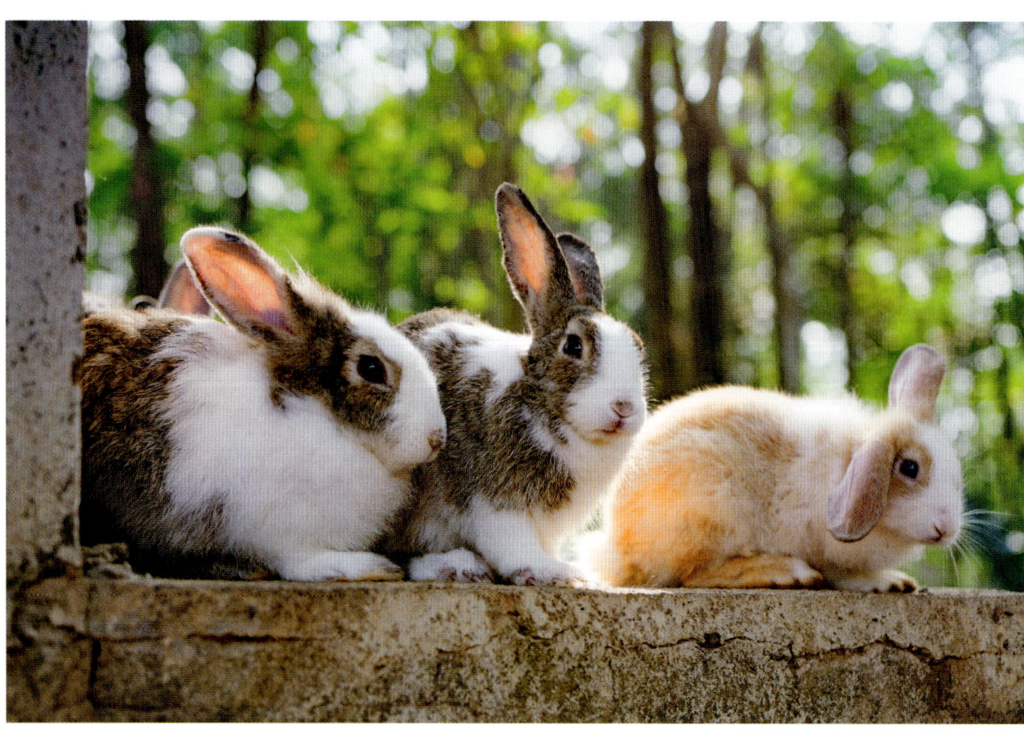

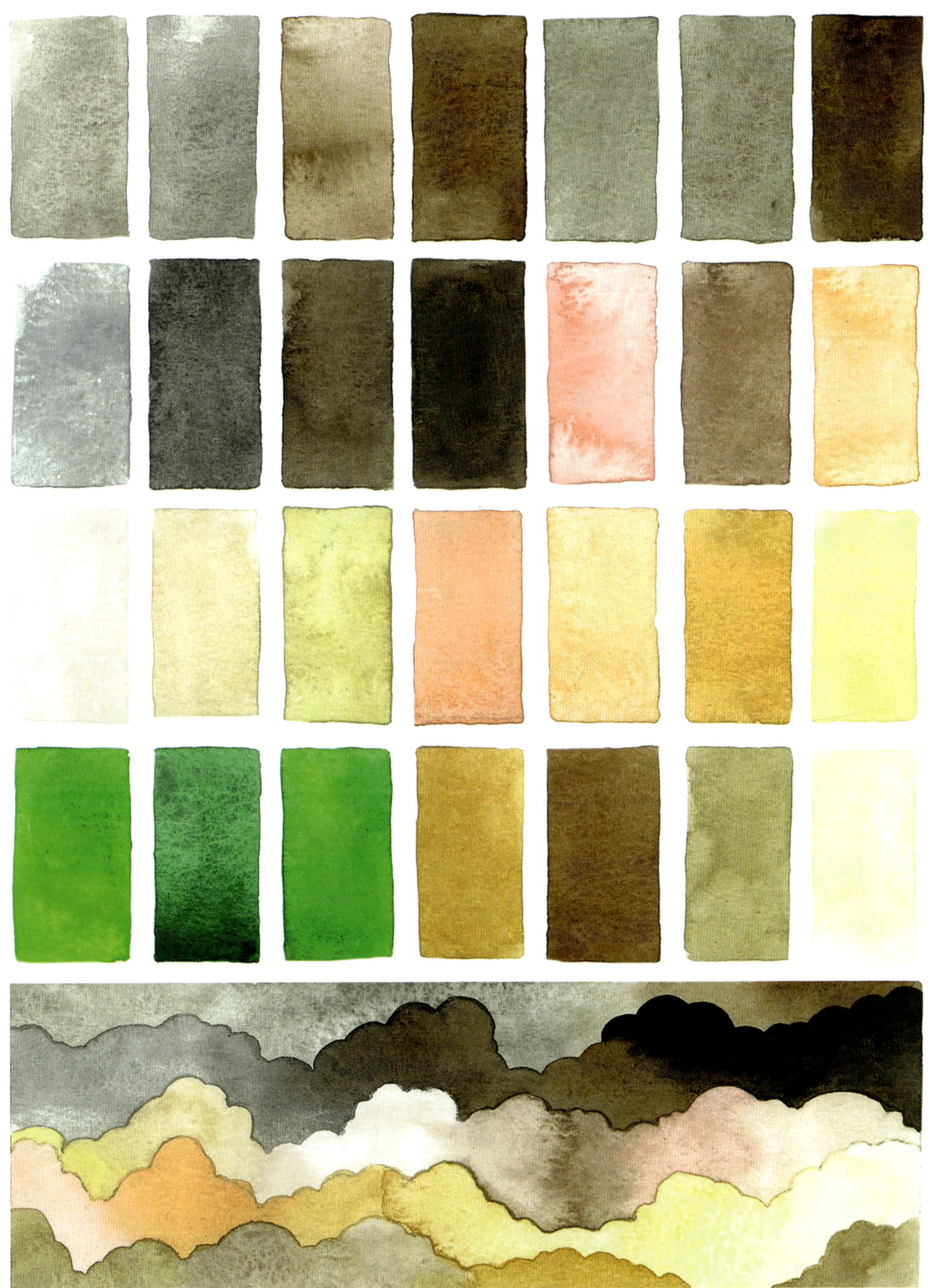

Neon Butterflies

Butterflies always make me think of flying flowers! I love the variety in color and design within each wing, along with the fine details in black and white that contrast the bright colors.

For swatching I used standout colors such as Moss Rose, Magenta, Daffodil Yellow, Juniper Green, Persimmon, Ice Blue, Ultramarine, Black, and Mahogany.

I felt like this inspiration painting called for something free and loose, with touches of spatter. Once the main layer is dry, go in with white gouache and black watercolor to add little details to the wings.

TECHNIQUE NOTES   This is one of the few palettes where I used just Dr. Ph. Martin's liquid Radiant Concentrated watercolors and didn't mix with my pan set. Regular or natural pigments don't really come in the types of bright and fluorescent colors shown in the inspiration photo. Liquid watercolors are so radiant because they are dye based, not pigment based. But liquids aren't lightfast and your painting will fade over time if it's near a sunny window. For design work like this, though, they work like a charm.

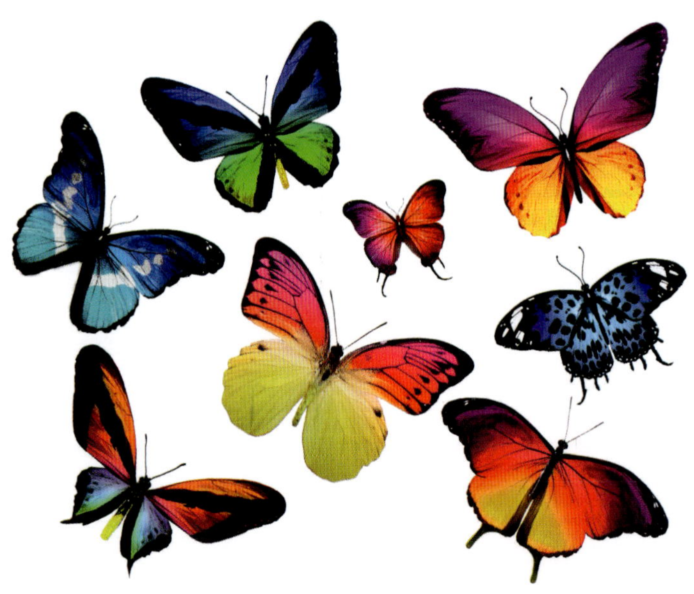

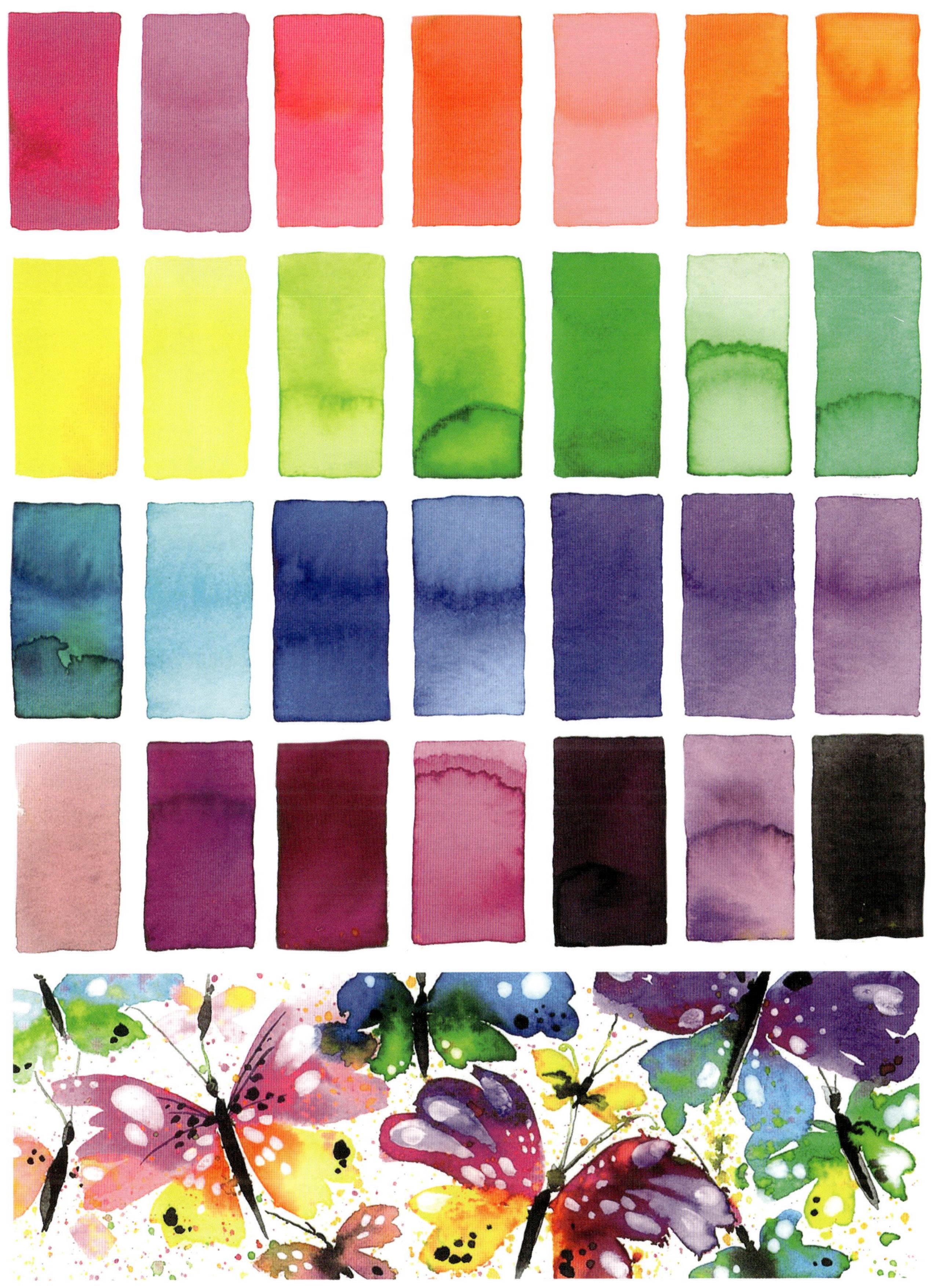

Leopard Print

I'm a huge fan of all kinds of felines! They're beautiful and mysterious, and this gorgeous leopard is no exception. This cat was resting on a tree in his natural habitat of Sri Lanka. The coat is a rusty yellow covered in dark rosettes. The entire image is swatched in the palette, but the leopard's coat inspired the inspiration box.

Begin by creating a variety of oranges and yellows and carefully adding their complementaries to desaturate the brightness for more natural hues.

To paint a texture like the leopard print with watercolor, create a light base layer using the watered-down ochre yellows and wait for the first layer to dry completely. Once this initial layer has dried, you can continue to paint irregular circles in medium-value oranges and then wait for that to dry, too. Your final layer will consist of using the darker browns from the palette to create elongated, rounded shapes around your irregular circles.

COLOR NOTES This palette is another example where complementaries create deeper colors, specifically with yellows and oranges in the base coat. Yellow's complementary is violet, and orange's complementary is blue. The large variety of yellows and oranges exist in the animal's fur tone, and also because of the light and shadow captured in the photo. It's always important to observe closely so you can create swatches that cover the entire range of color.

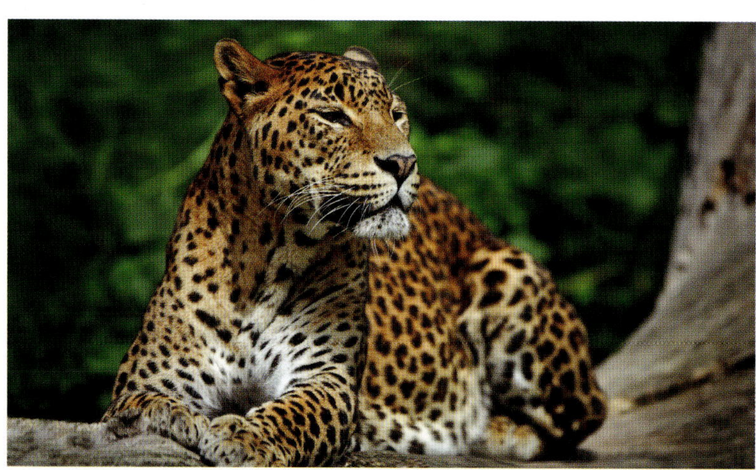

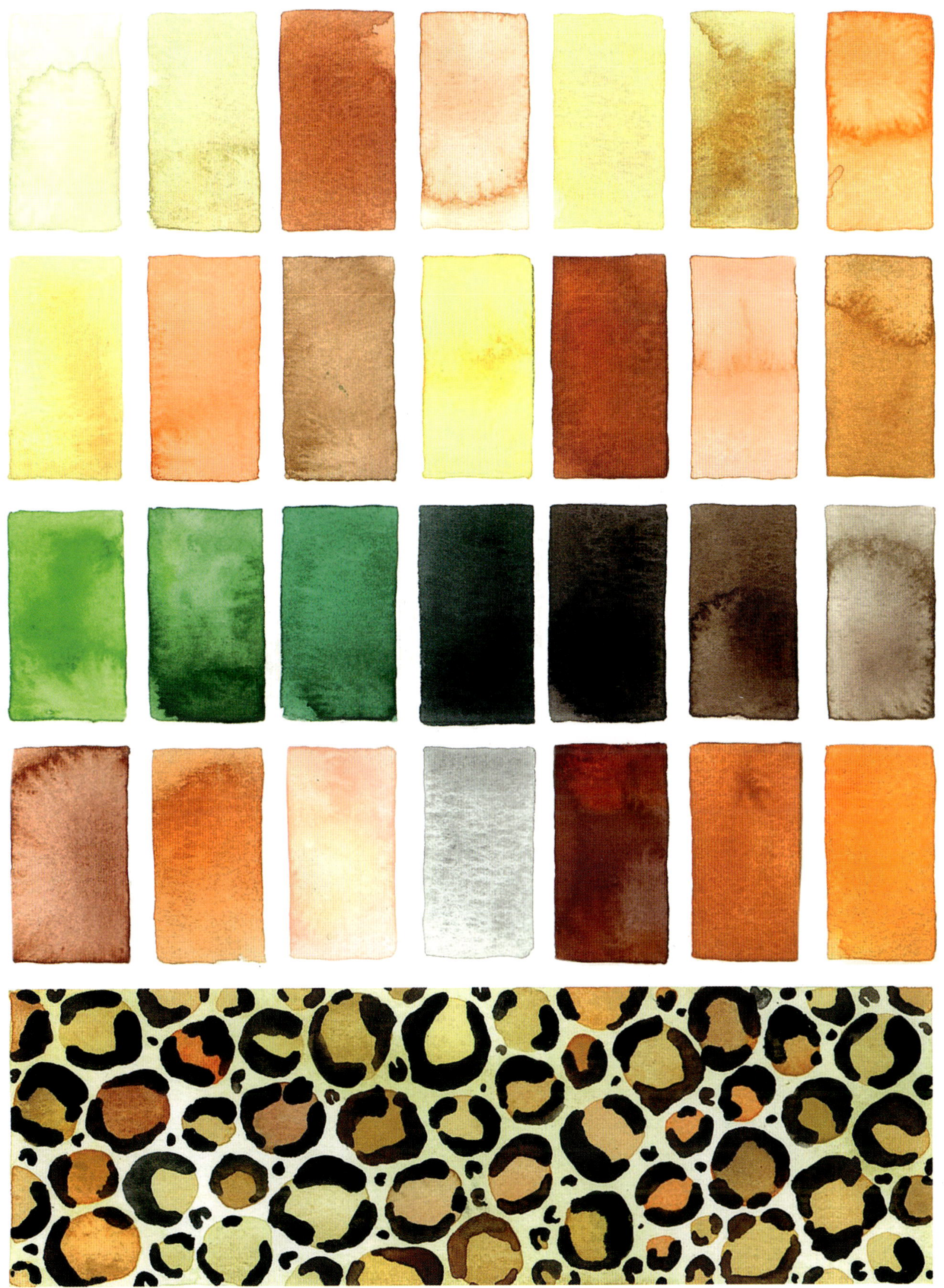

Exotic Macaw

The scarlet macaw, a large parrot from Central and South America, is a perfect example of what you can do when you mix primary colors. I'm fascinated by the gradients in each feather; all three primary colors blend gently into a hint of the secondary color (green).

I illustrated a more precise texture inspired by these feathers. Naturally!

TECHNIQUE NOTES Even though the main colors look like just the three primaries, there's actually a large range in color because of the shading and the way light hits each feather. For basic primaries I like scarlet red, lemon yellow, and cerulean blue. Mixing these three in different combinations can produce all the colors of the rainbow.

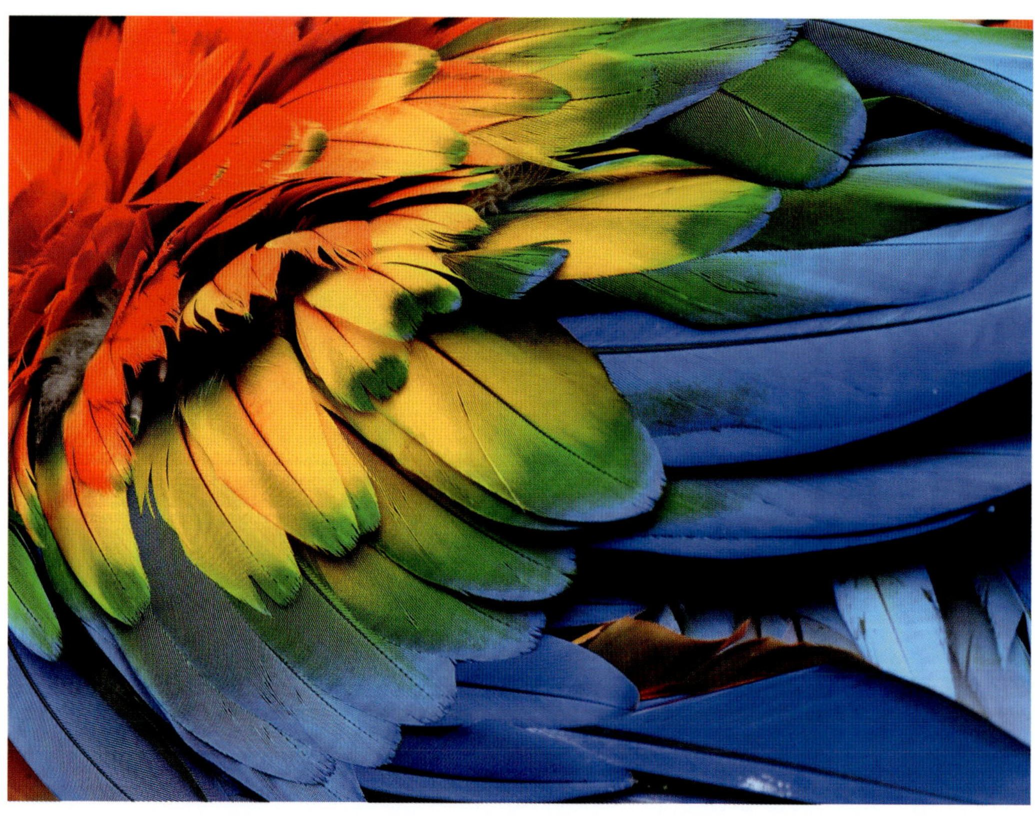

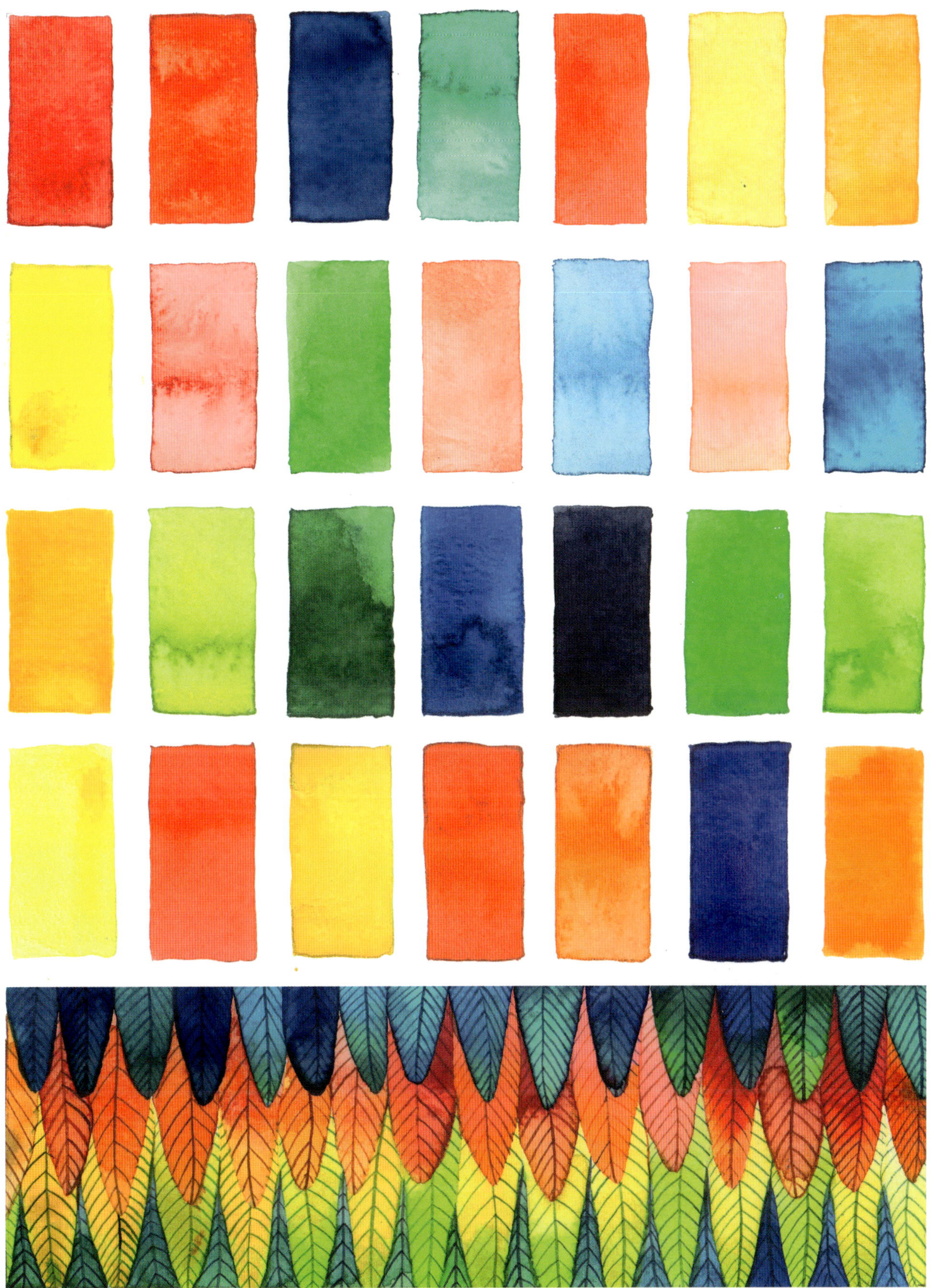

Changing Chameleon

These creatures are beyond magic! How cool is it to be able to change colors? Not only do chameleons change colors depending on their surroundings, they come in a large variety of colors. This specific lizard's palette is heavily green with blue-green accents.

I was inspired to create a texture this time, too. Sometimes something as simple as adding different-sized dots can turn out quite fun. It's also very relaxing to paint.

COLOR NOTES This image is generally an analogous harmony scheme. It ranges from blue to turquoise, green, lime, and all the way to lemon yellow, with the exception of red details, which are the complementary of green. In other words, green's opposite is red, so that makes perfect contrast.

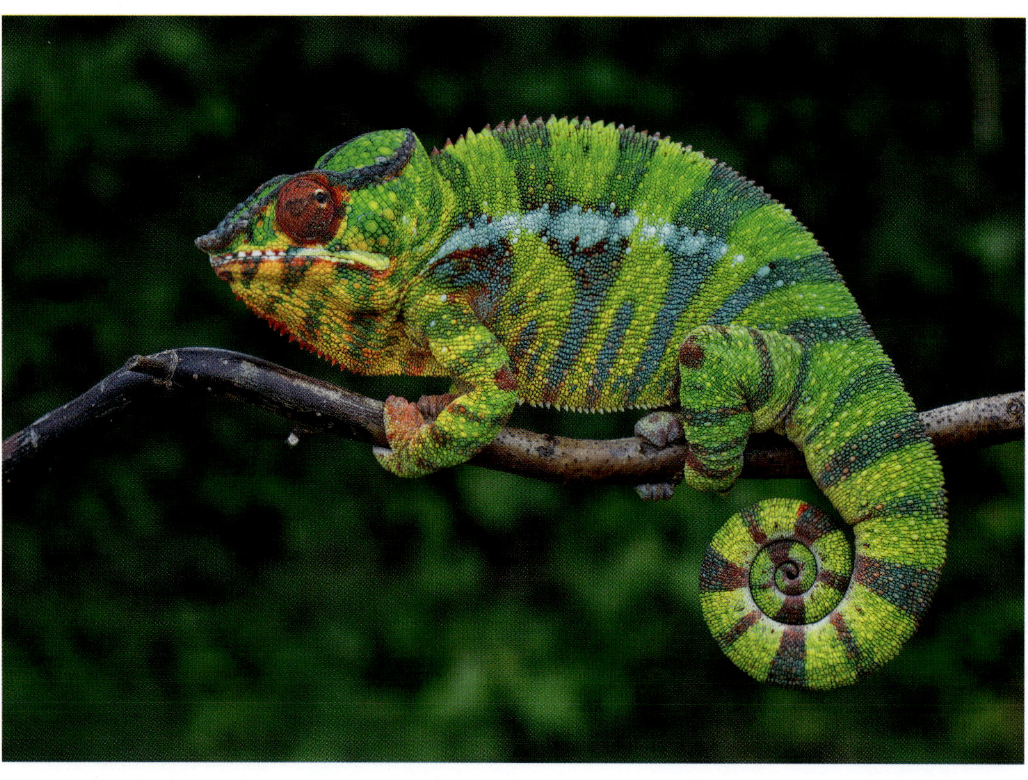

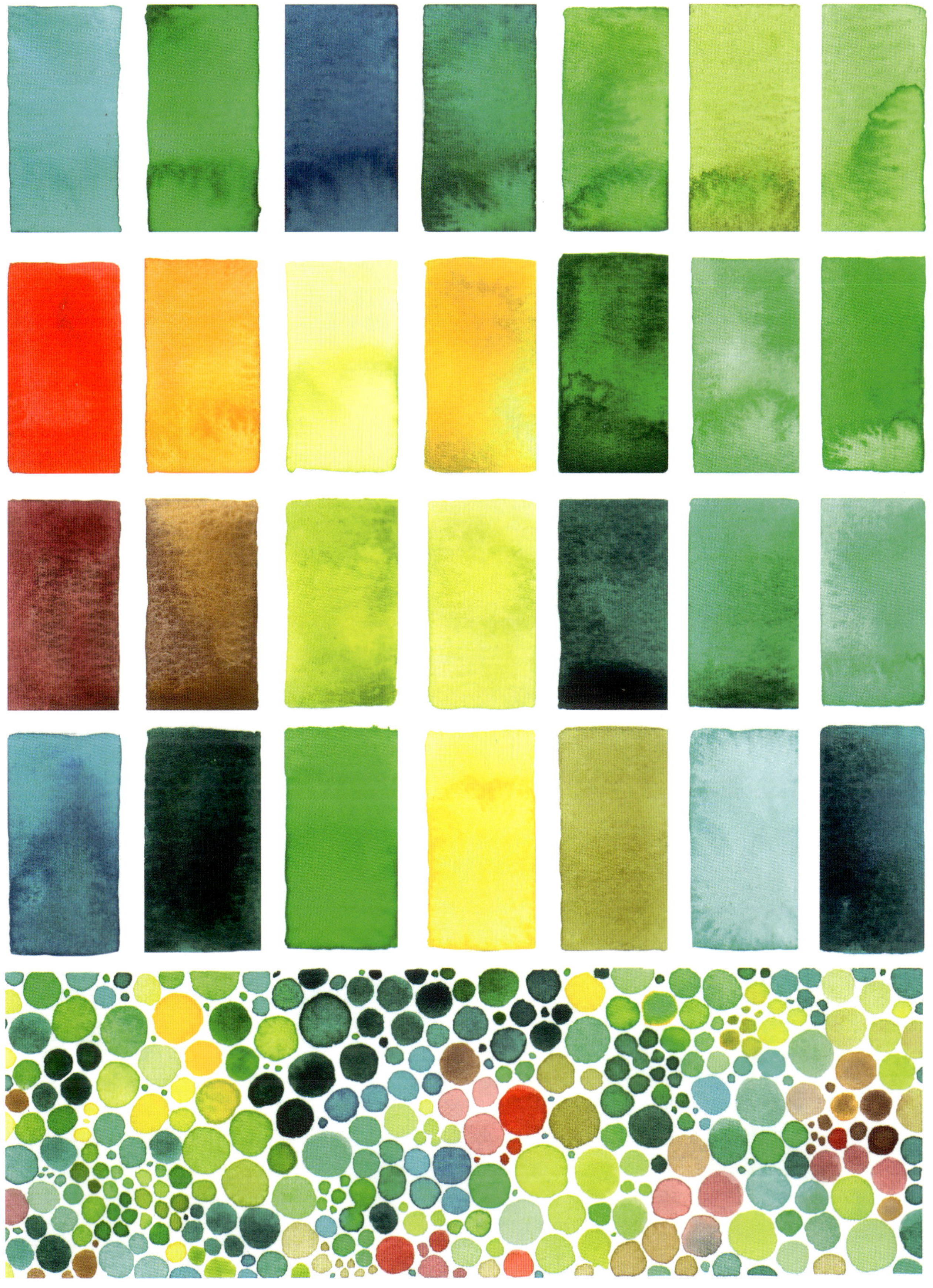

La Parroquia

San Miguel de Allende is a colonial town in the Bajío area of Mexico, famous for its cobblestone streets, artisanal shopping, and the *Parroquia de San Miguel Arcángel*, which is one of the most photographed churches in Mexico.

Like many Mexican towns, San Miguel de Allende is vibrant and colorful. What's really appealing about this image is the contrast between the clear blue sky and the orange architecture. The complementary colors—opposites, in other words—create contrast and harmony simultaneously.

The pointy shape of the church inspired me to create a texture of long triangles using the wide range of oranges to represent the buildings and hints of blue and green for the plants.

COLOR NOTES This is also an example of a split-complementary scheme on the color wheel, with orange as the predominant color and green and blue on the other side of the wheel.

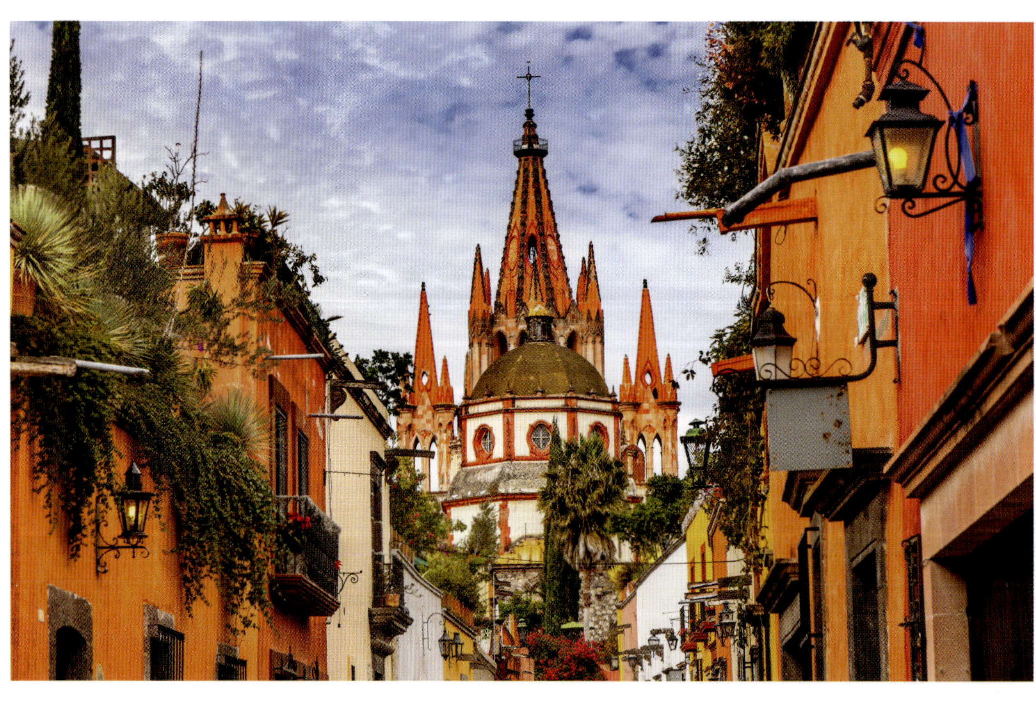

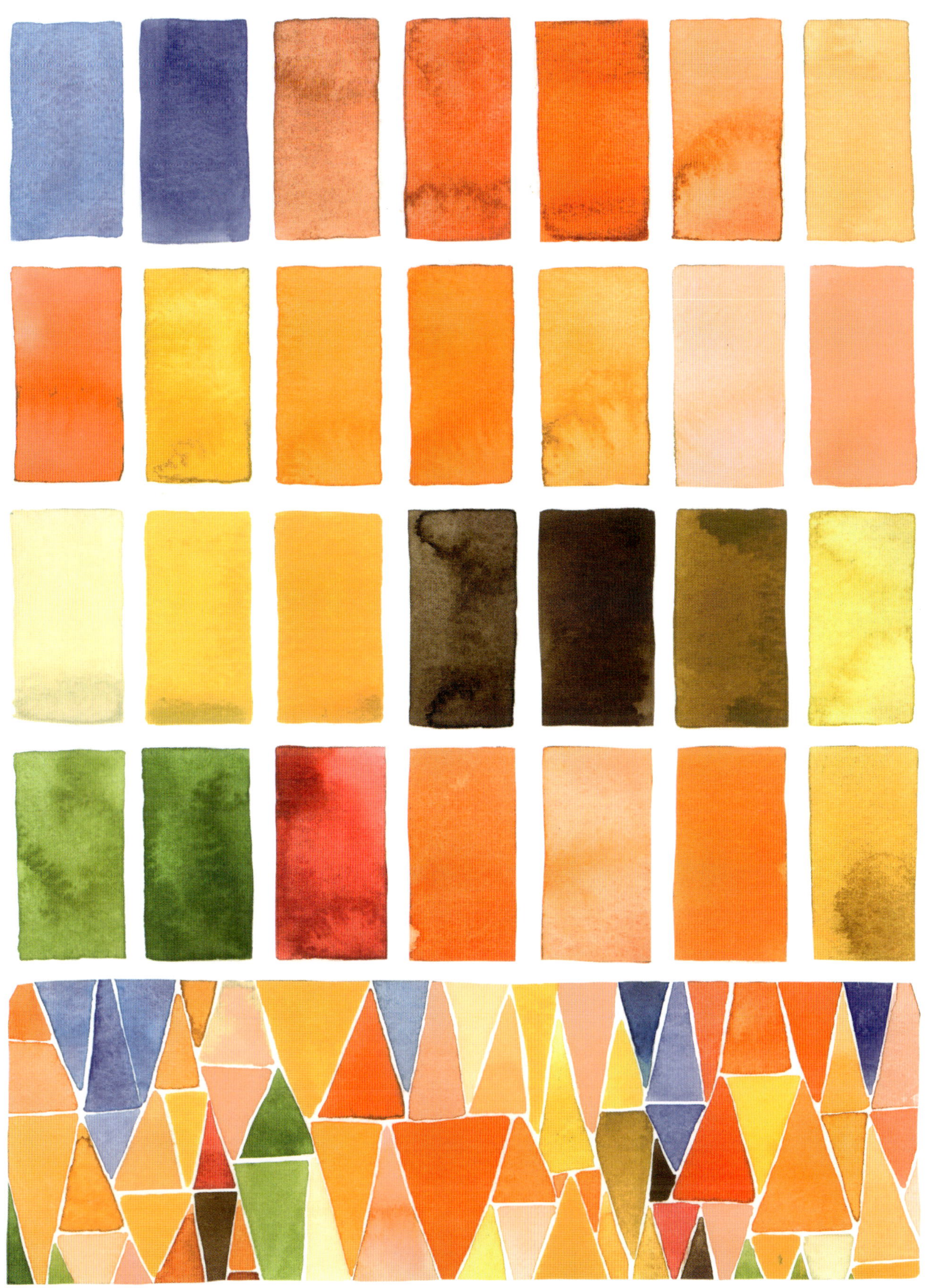

Oia Village

When booking my family trip to Greece last year, I knew there were a few things we just couldn't miss: the Parthenon, eating a million Greek salads, and hitting the impressive museums. But most of all, I was eager to visit the beautiful islands of Mykonos and Santorini because I had seen hundreds of photos. I was in awe of the unique style of these islands—rounded edges in architecture, cobblestones, and mainly the distinctive white and blue paint on outdoor structures.

I highly recommend visiting Greece, for the lovely people, impressive history, and inspiring locations!

TECHNIQUE NOTES Blue is the most important color in cool palettes. In this image we see various blues in combination with neutral colors, like shades of white, light browns, and soft ochres. I used all kinds of blues here, mixing some Dr. Ph. Martin's droppers, such as Ultramarine and Juniper Green, into my larger variety of pan set watercolors. I played around not only with color mixing but amounts of water to achieve lighter tones and deeper shades.

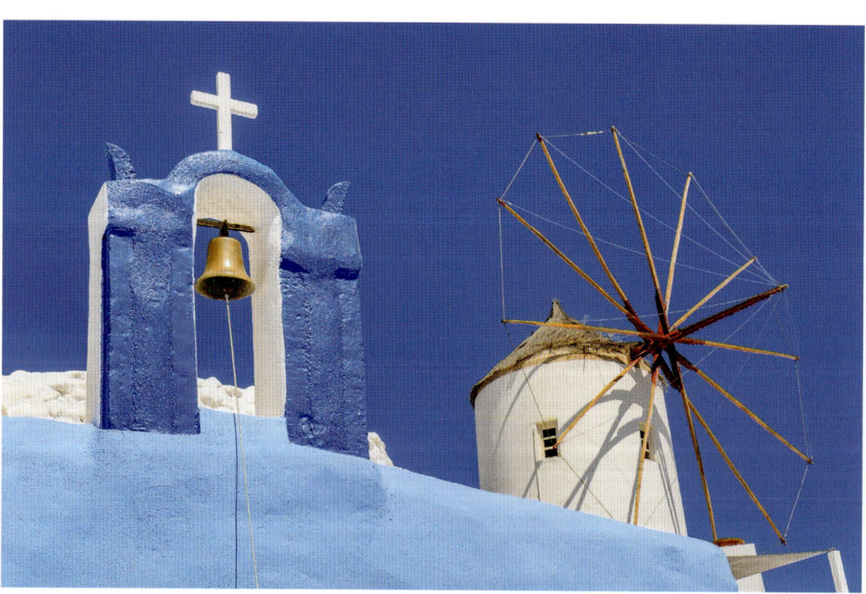

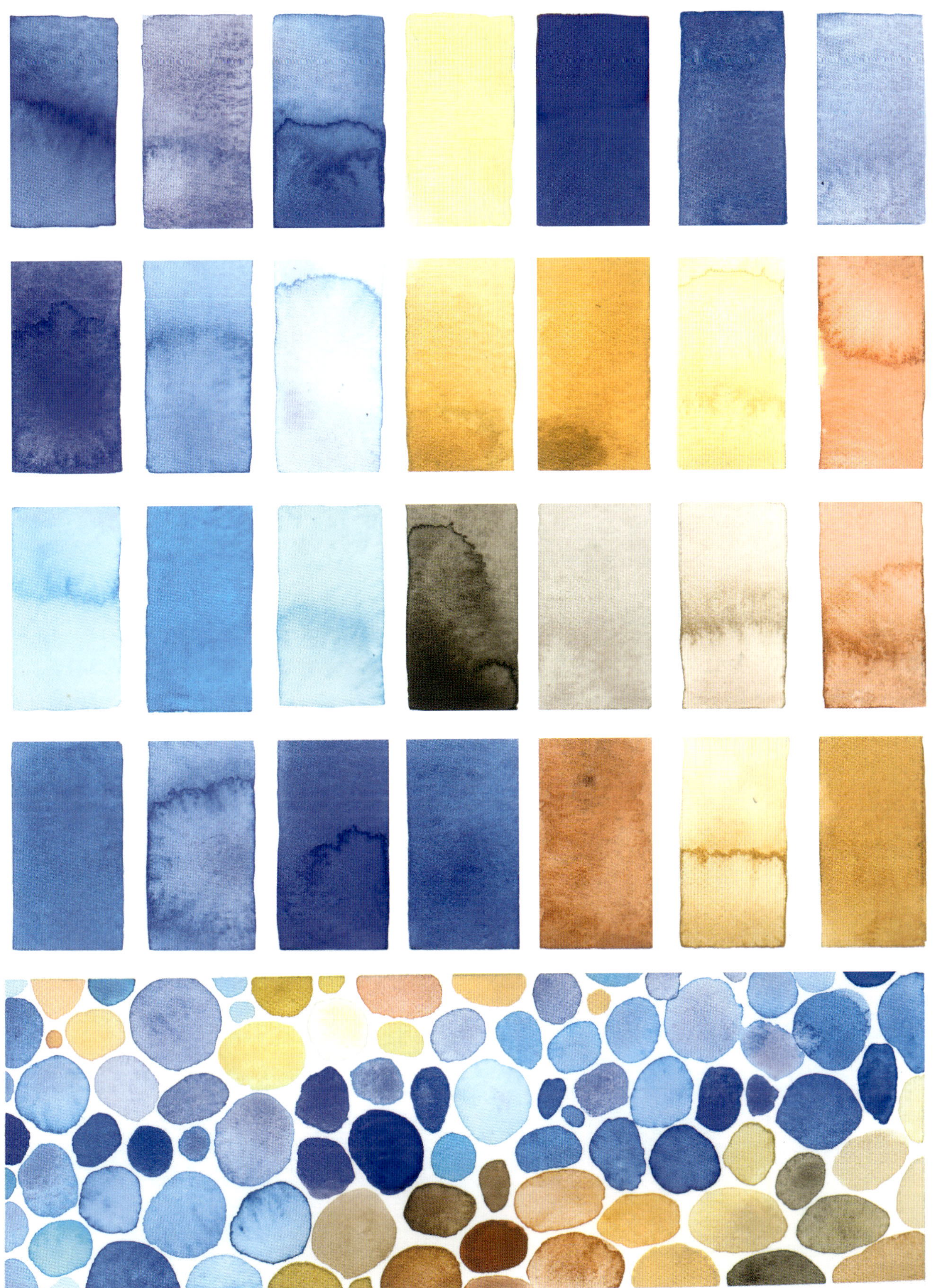

Spring in Kyoto

Kyoto was the imperial capital of Japan and has long-established cultural aspects. It's famous for traditional townhouses, historic monuments, Buddhist temples, and my favorite: the cherry blossom trees in this photograph.

Cherry blossoms, or *sakuras*, are known for their precious light pink flowers, which harmonize perfectly with the muted natural tones and textures of traditional Kyoto. This swatch has numerous low-contrast neutrals that depict the natural elements of the environment (stone, wood, and brick), so the palette is muted and clean with a combination of light browns, ochres, and grays.

Seeing the sakura blooms peak at the beginning of April is on my bucket list!

COLOR NOTES Cherry blossoms are a beautiful example of complementary harmonies in nature; pink is a light version of red, which is the opposite of green. The greens aren't obvious, hiding in the leaves of the tree when they begin to blossom.

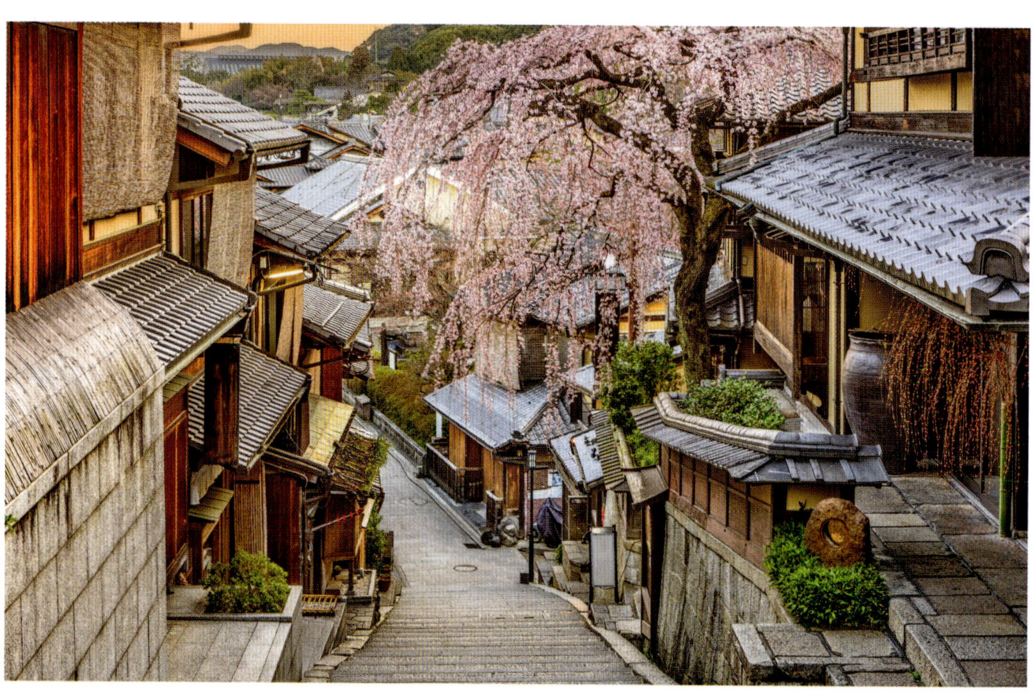

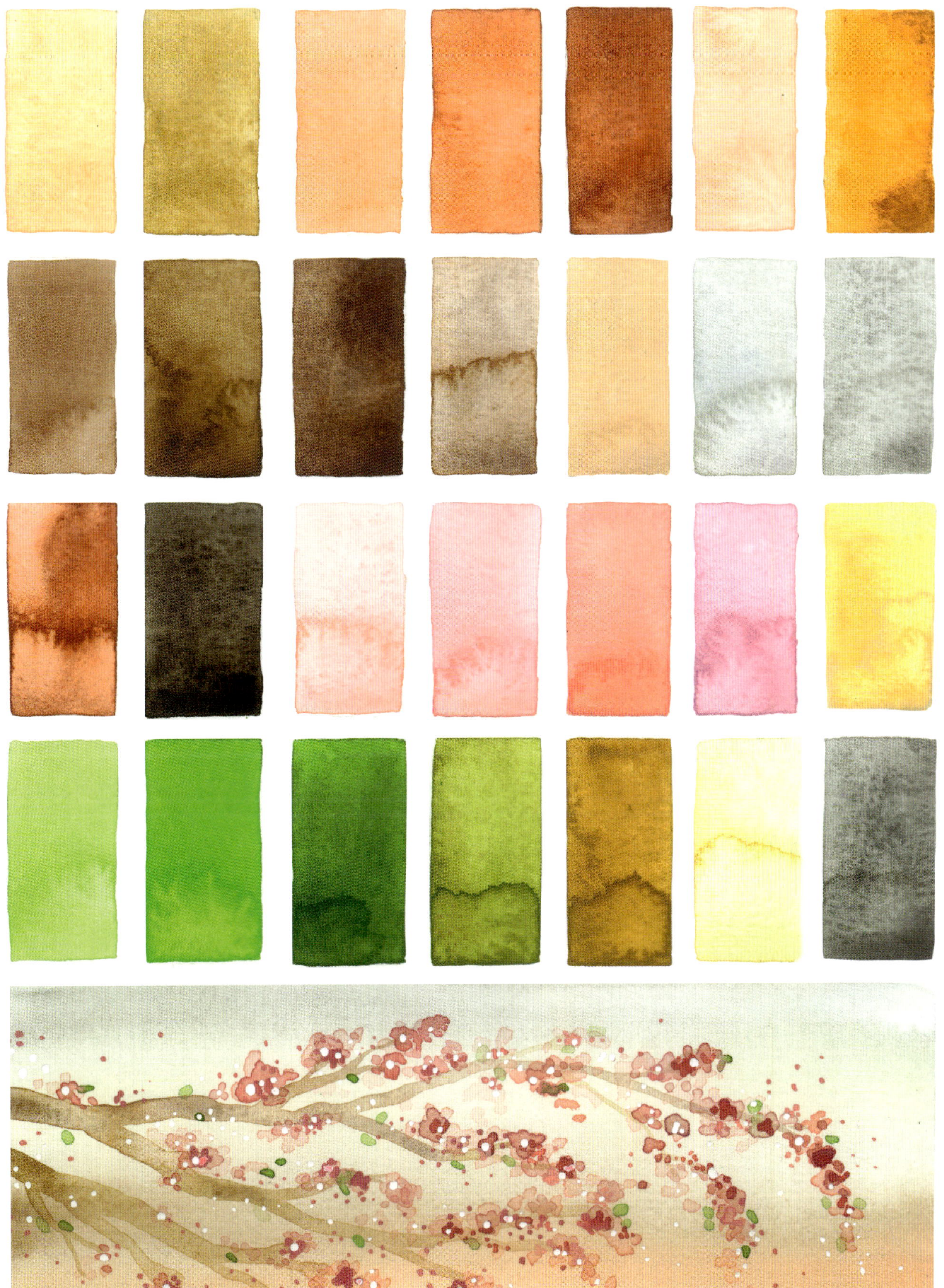

Sunny Seville

Seville is the capital of Andalusia, the southern region of Spain. It's famous for flamenco dancing, oranges, and tapas . . . and my paternal grandmother! As you'd expect, I have a very special place in my heart for Seville and its warm, sunny skies.

One summer, when I was eighteen, I traveled to Spain with my entire family. We focused on Seville for a large part of our trip because our extended family is based there. Everything was beautiful and felt like a dream, especially for a teenager beginning her art and design studies! Ever since then, the *Plaza de España* (Spain Square) and its gorgeous tiles and warm palette have stayed with me. The plaza, built in 1928, is a perfect example of regional architecture influenced by the Renaissance and Moorish Revival, a beautiful mix of European architecture and Asian character.

This detail of the tiles on the landmark's exterior reveals a palette that's a perfect example of analogous harmony (three colors that are next to each other on the color wheel); in this case, blue, green, and the dominant yellow.

Tiles are always an amazing source of inspiration, and these designs are no exception.

COLOR NOTES The specific tone of yellow that I enjoy for warm, sunny hues is 2H Gamboge, from the Hydrus line of Dr. Ph. Martin's. You can deepen the gold tone with touches of ochre, or make it lighter and cooler by adding lemon yellow. I've found with yellows in general that it pays to have individual tubes or droppers. Yellows can get the dirtiest in pan sets, so it really helps to isolate them. I used Ultra Blue from the Radiant line by Dr. Ph. Martin's. I like to mix this type of paint with the blue from my pan set to get a nice variety.

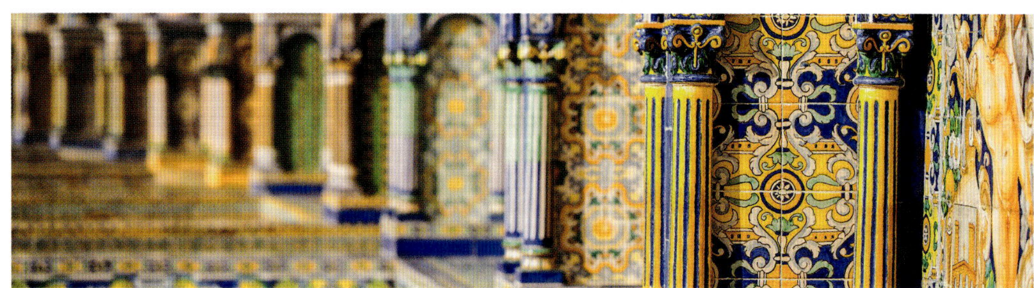

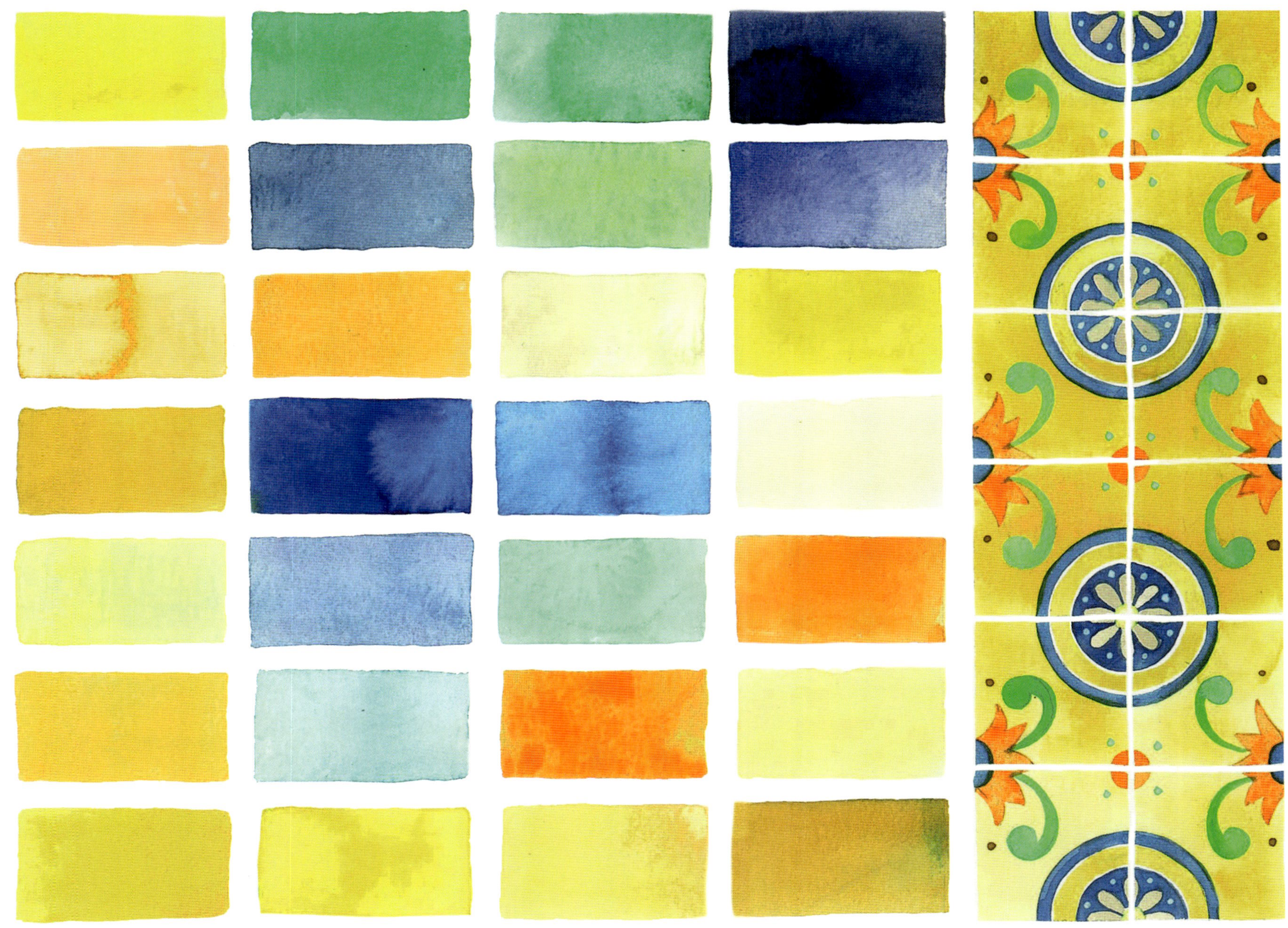

Jewel Box

The tomb of I'timād-ud-Daulah is sometimes referred to as the "baby Taj" because it's regarded as a precursor of the World Heritage Site, the Taj Mahal. Also in the city of Agra, India, the mausoleum includes several buildings and gardens. This image is a detail of a wall decoration. The beautiful arabesque and geometrical designs that cover the entire exterior are one of the most important aspects of this tomb.

This palette is extremely pleasing and calming, with a variety of neutral tones like light browns, gray, and light peach hues.

TECHNIQUE NOTES I remembered that the granular texture of a Lunar Black paint by Daniel Smith on my pan set palette reminded me of marbled properties, so I decided to add hints of the black to some browns. This kind of paint has magnetic shavings in the formula, which makes specks of pigment repel each other for a beautiful stonelike texture. The palette in general is a harmonious neutral mix of black, brown, and ochre, either watered down or mixed with a touch of white gouache for a pastel look.

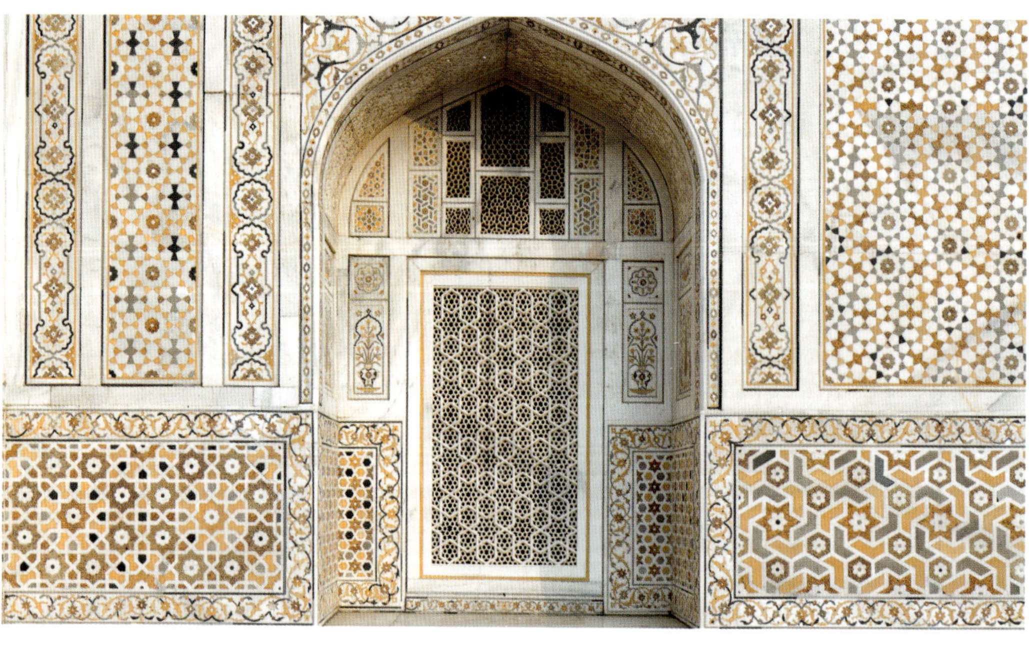

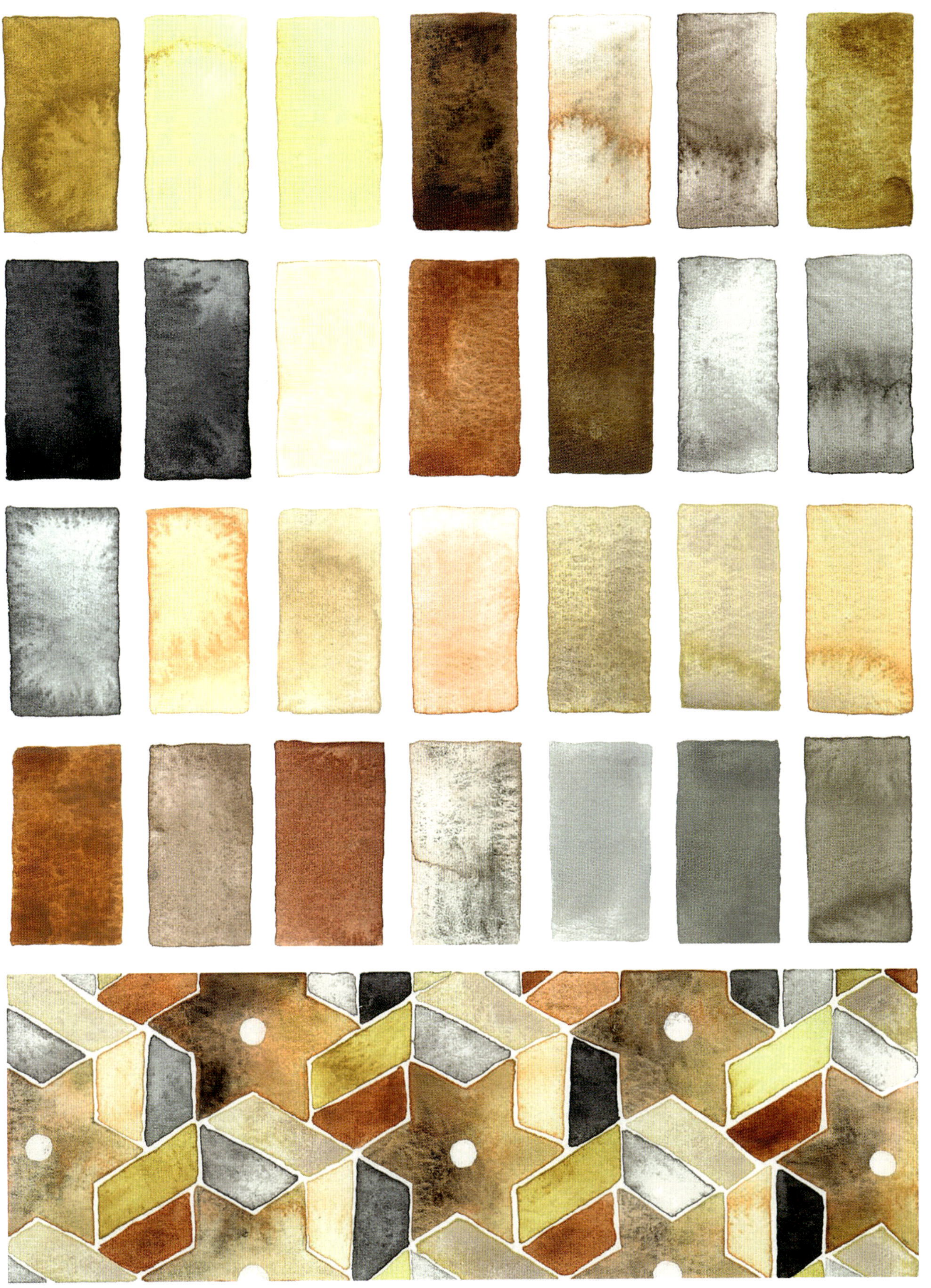

Forbidden City

The famous Forbidden City in Beijing, China, is a major complex of palaces that housed emperors, ceremonies, and government for about 500 years. Now a World Heritage Site, it welcomes millions of visitors a year.

I was really inspired by the colors of the sunset reflecting over this magnificent palace. I started swatching reds and creating variations of warm purples and mauves by adding touches of blue. I also created a variety of yellows and then mixed those with my original red mix. In fact, I created the majority of this palette by playing around with the three primary colors (red, blue, yellow). Another accent is a beautiful emerald green.

Every detail in the palace refers to religious principles and auspicious signs. I looked closely to find the inspiration for the texture I created with this palette.

TECHNIQUE NOTES Because of its vibrancy, my favorite royal blue base is Dr. Ph. Martin's Ultramarine, which I mix with the other blues on my palette. To create a bright red base, I like to mix a bit of Scarlet with Persimmon, also by Dr. Ph. Martin's. I mix with my pan set to create various hues—a touch of cherry red makes the red slightly cooler.

The best way to re-create the many shadows in this picture is to use complementaries. To achieve the red structure's defined shadows and darker bricklike reds, for example, just add a touch of green to your mix.

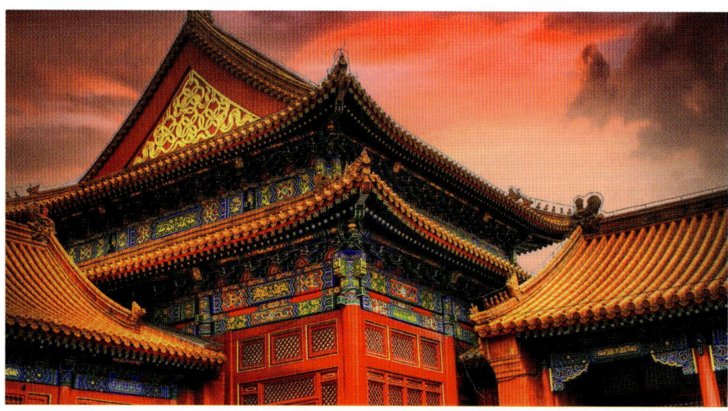

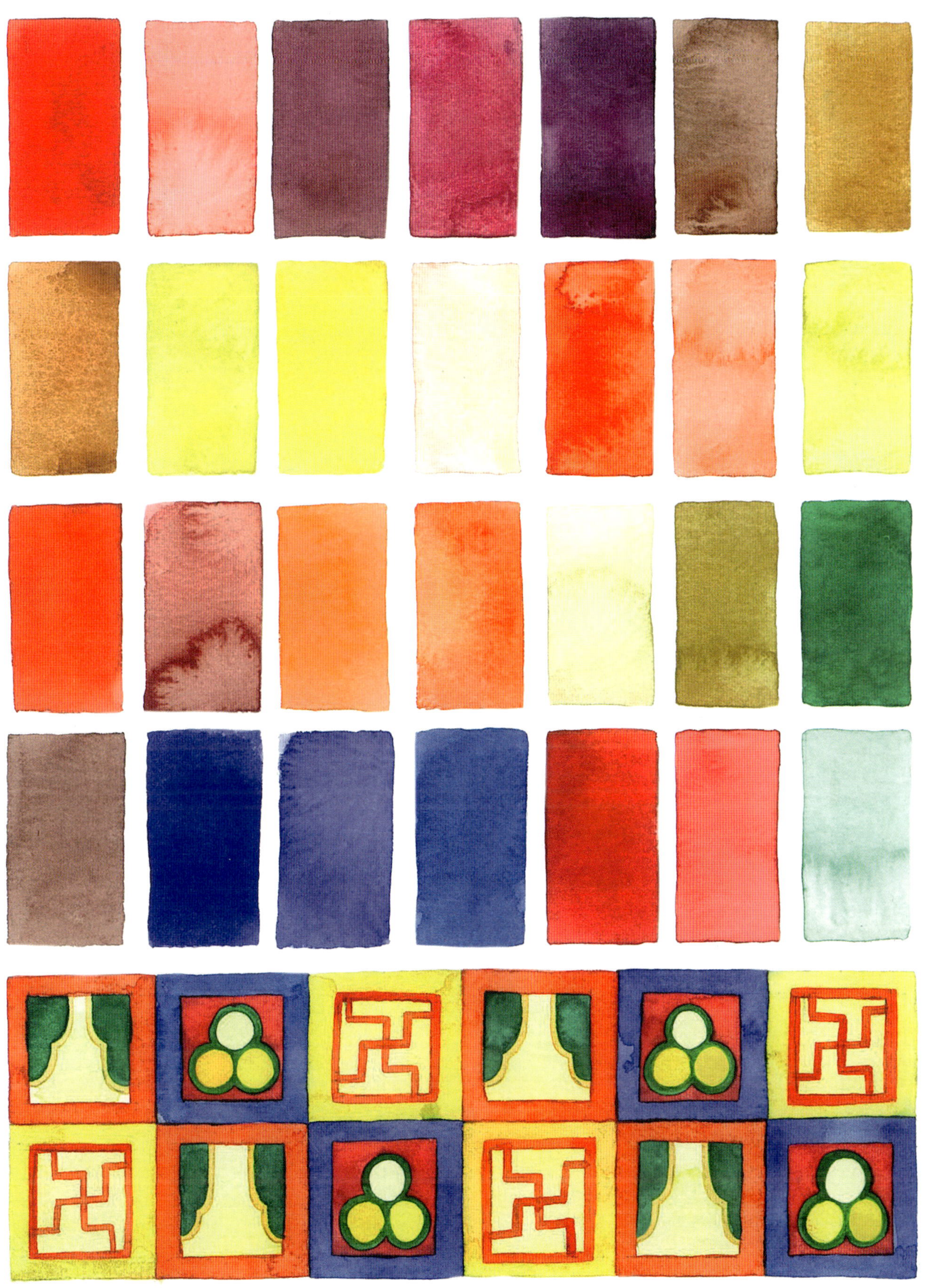

Terracotta Ksar

Every summer I organize a watercolor retreat with women from around the world who want to spend a week in a faraway land and be inspired by new cultures and surroundings. This year we chose Morocco, and it's not hard to see why. What a pink terracotta dream! This picture is of Aït Benhaddou, a Ksar or fortified village on the old caravan route along the Atlas Mountains, from Marrakesh to the Sahara. The magnificent sundown's pink hues reflect on the natural-colored structures made of straw and mud.

You can almost feel the warm air in this dreamy desert image. The palette is soft and muted, with accents of dusty rose in a variety of values and shadows.

TECHNIQUE NOTES To create a dusty rose, make a watered-down red mix and add a small touch of green (its complementary color). Play with adding touches of lavender and browns for options.

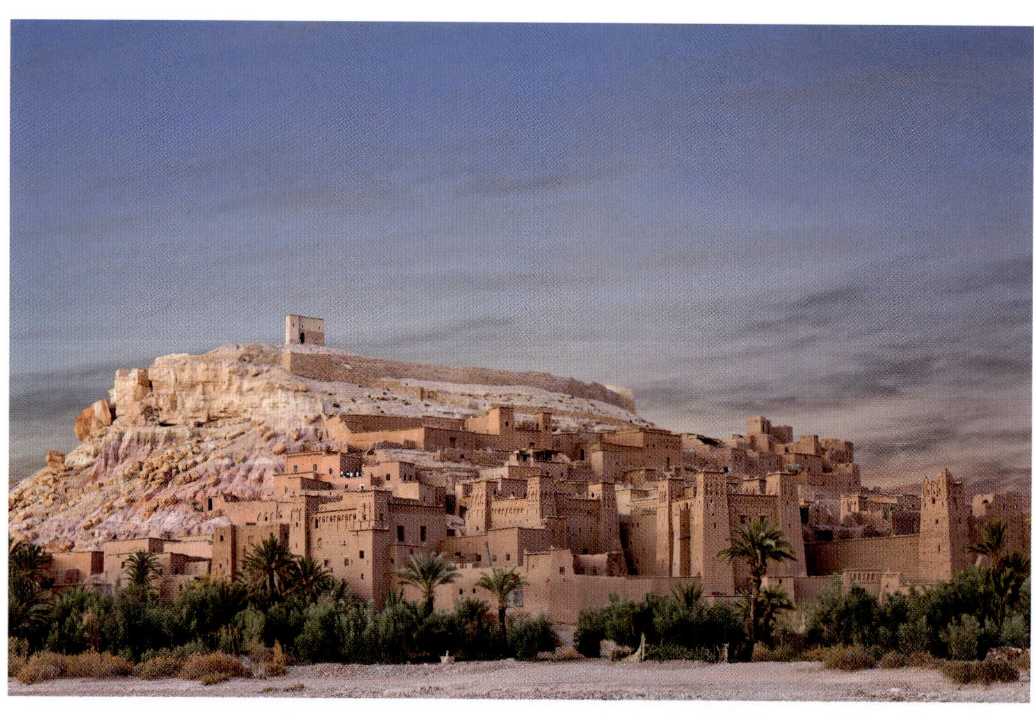

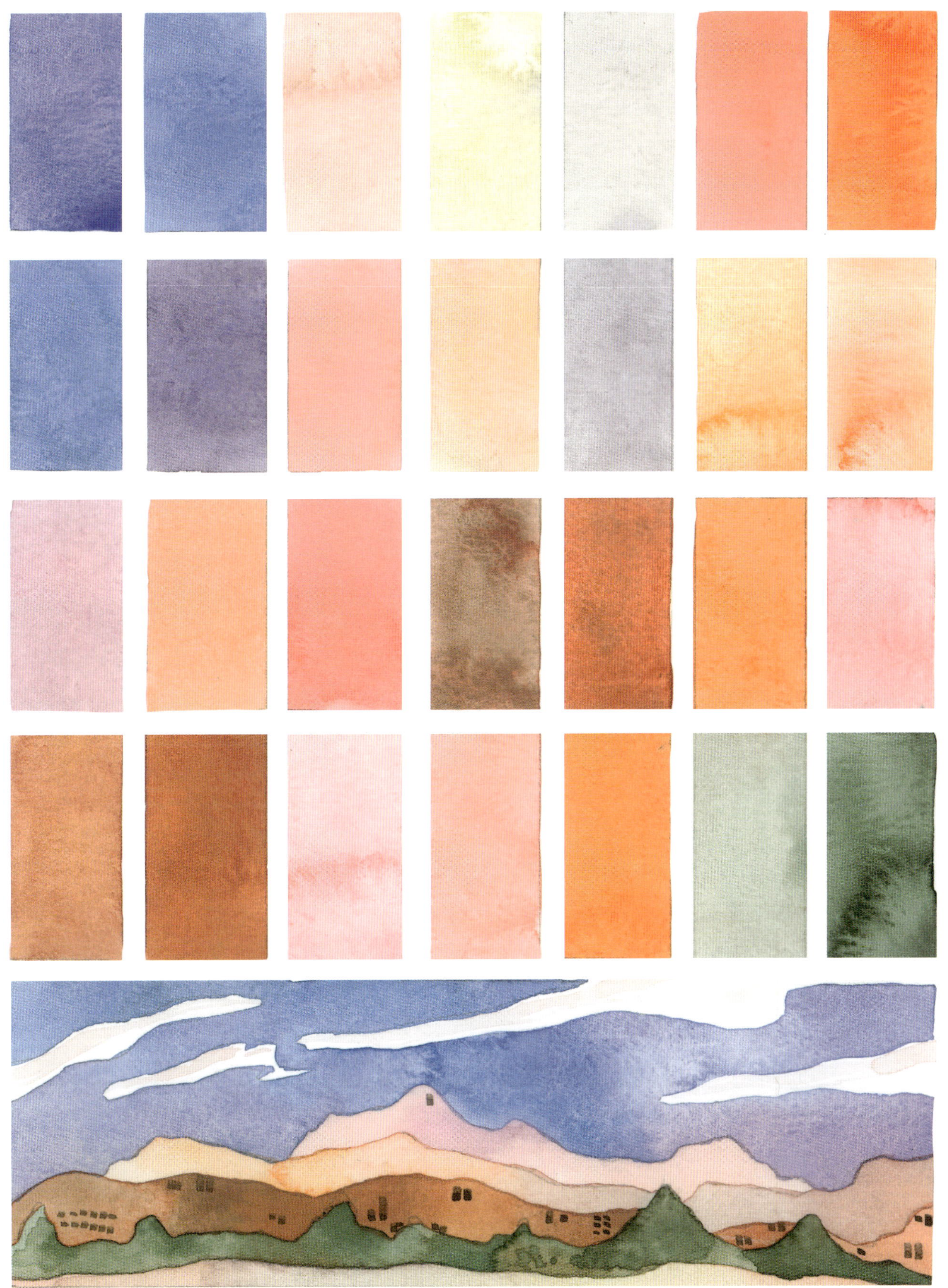

Caribbean Skyline

The story behind the Dutch capital of Curaçao's famous brilliant pastel buildings comes from legend. It's told that King Willem I named a governor to the Netherlands Antilles and stationed him in Curaçao. All the buildings in the capital (then Willemstad) were crisp white and reflected such harsh glare that the governor suffered terrible migraines. As a remedy he instructed the townspeople to paint the buildings in a variety of colors. Today, people travel to see the skyline of bright yet slightly soft pastels in this image.

I painted a geometric abstract texture inspired by the skyline and the water at the dock. These colorful buildings make me feel at ease and cheerful.

TECHNIQUE NOTES For my base colors I used Holbein's Shell Pink, a beautiful, rich, and creamy pastel pink tube watercolor. I used this as is, and mixed it with terracotta tones for the roofs.

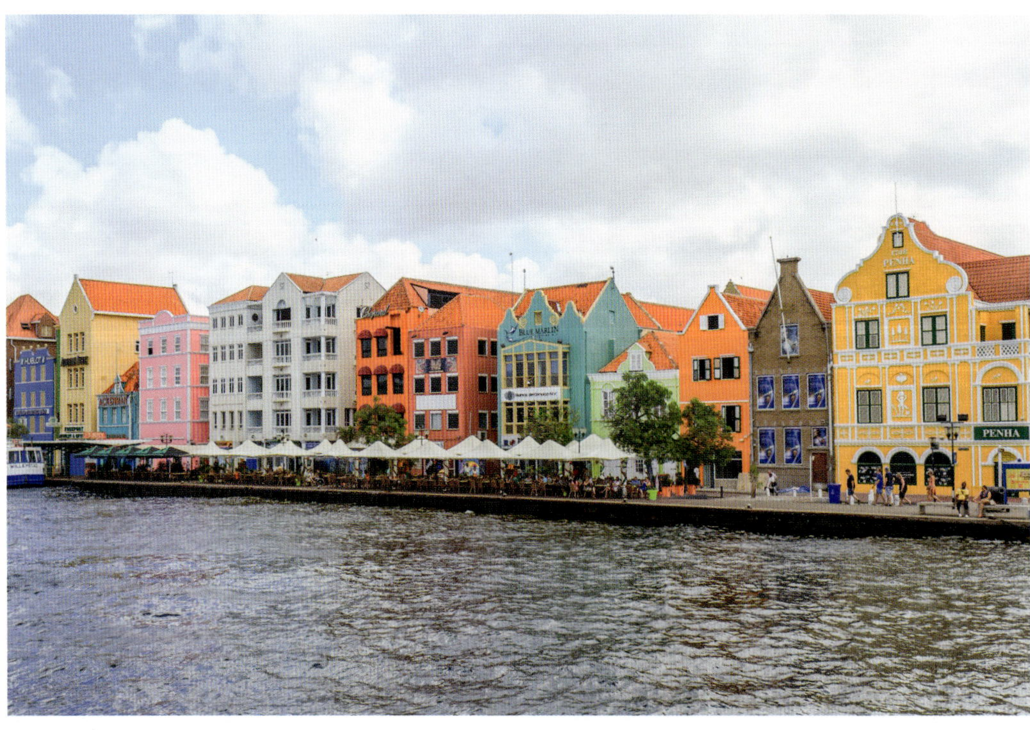

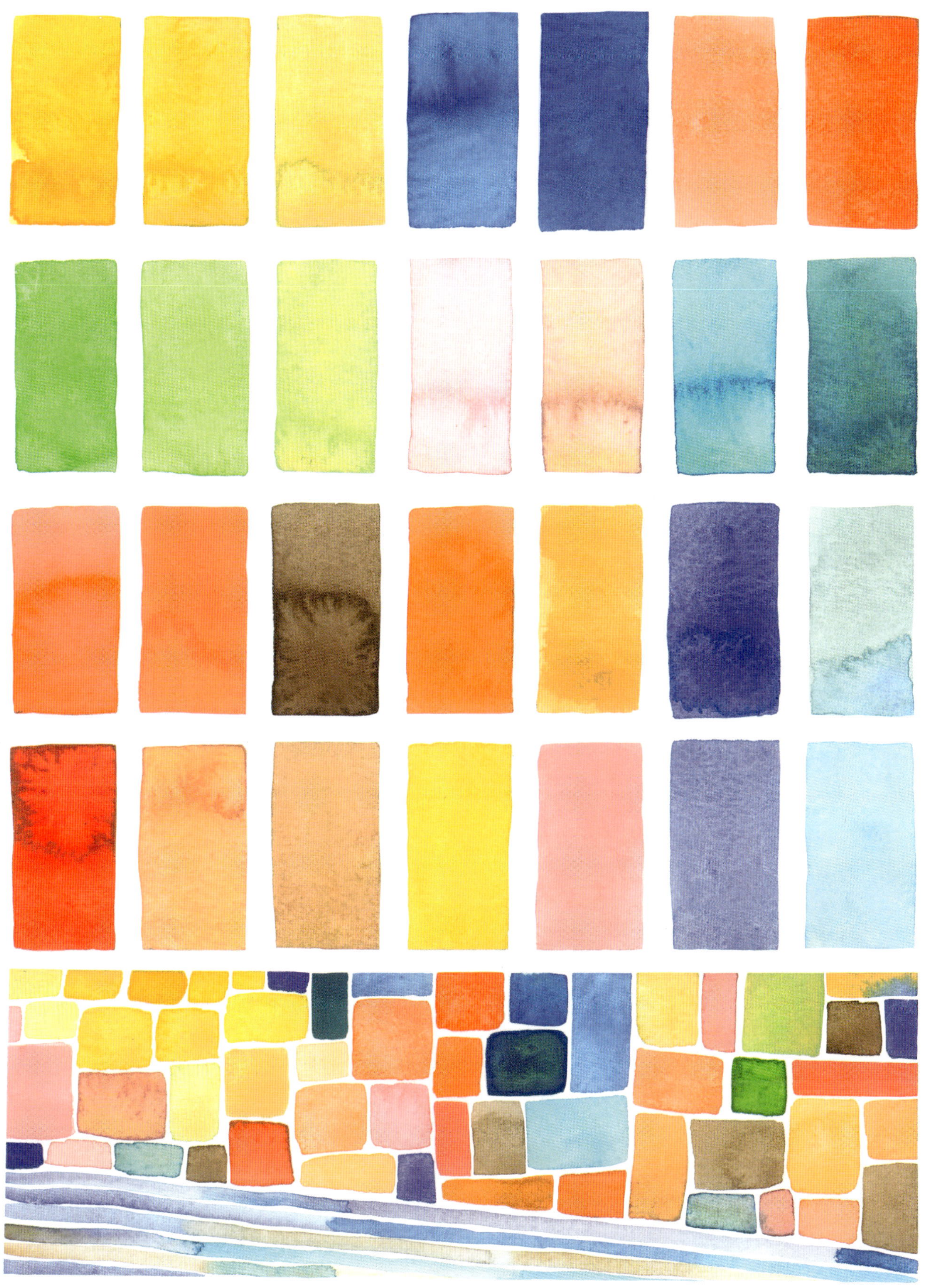

Park Güell

Antoni Gaudí is without a doubt the most famous Catalán architect of the *Modernisme* movement. Among the many Gaudí sites to visit in Barcelona, the most famous is *la Sagrada Família*. The style is characterized by its curves, organic shapes, asymmetry, rich ornamentation, and spectacular decoration. In this close-up of a bench at Gaudí's Park Güell, you can see a specific style of mosaic with tiles in all sorts of shapes, colors and sizes.

The direction of the lines and the irregular mosaic work on the bench inspired my texture board.

COLOR NOTES   Overall, this colorful image has a lot of variety, but it's overpowered by the brightness of yellows in all different shades. Ranging from gold yellow to lemon yellow and ochre, this predominantly warm tone is at the center of ceramic tile design. The image leans toward a warm palette in general.

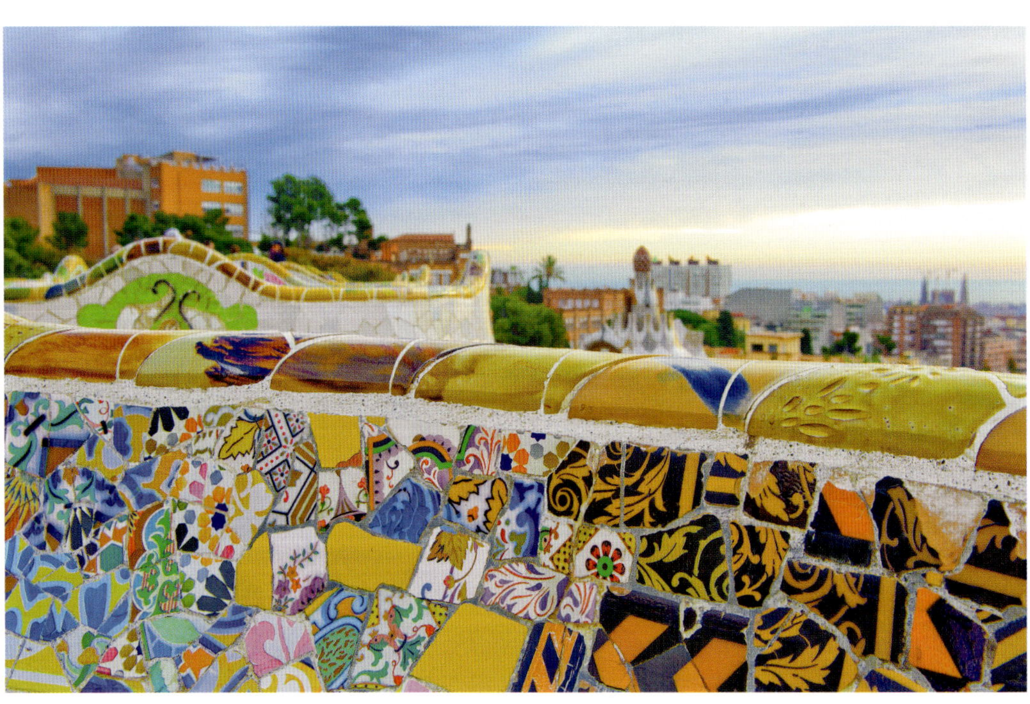

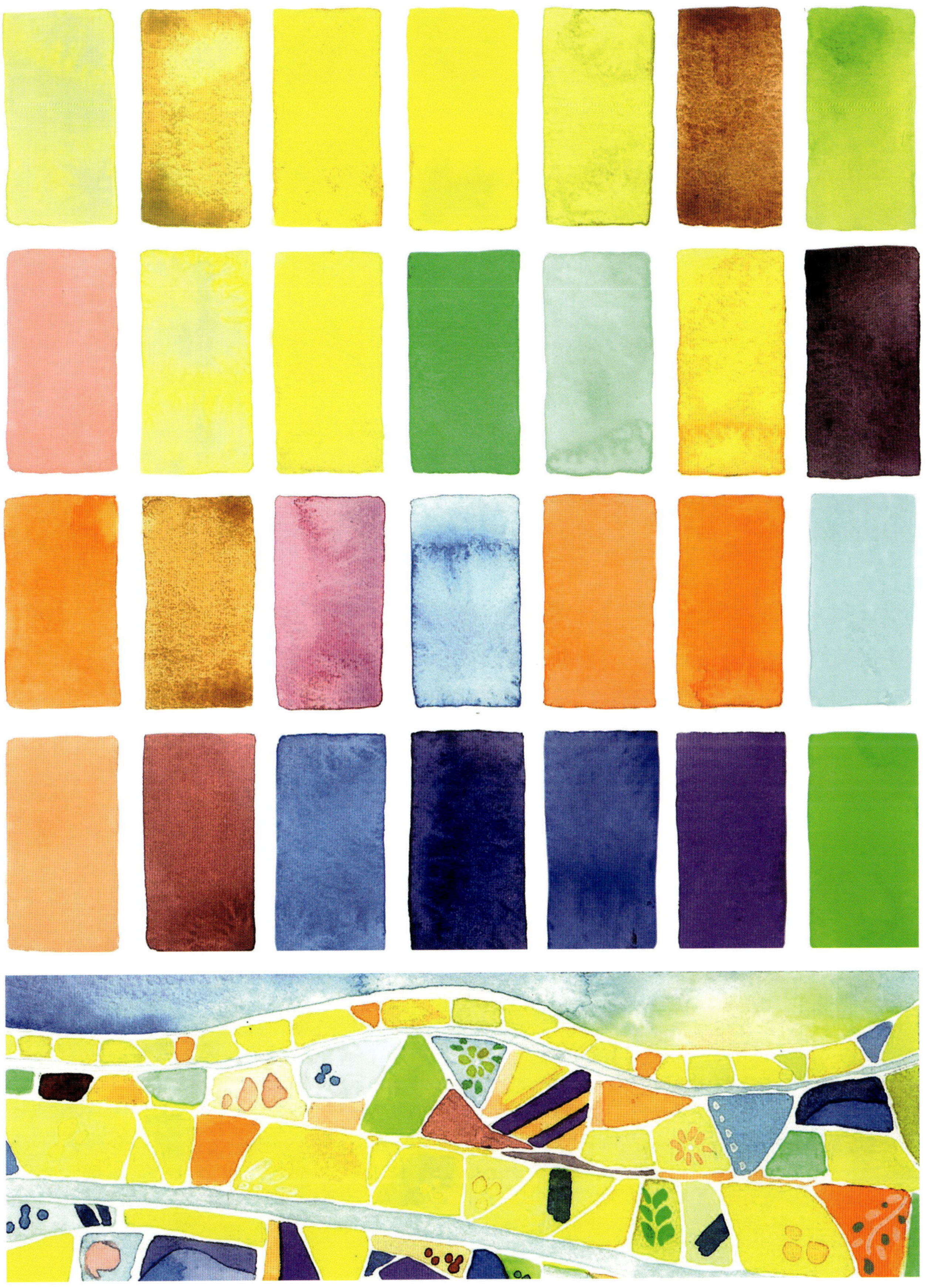

97

Swinging Sixties

As a child of the 1980s, I always felt like I missed out on the best decade of the century. The culture, music, and fashion of the 1960s fascinate me!

Choosing an image to represent this decade was difficult, but in the end I liked this sample of vintage fabric because the colors are bright yet muted. The palette also reminds me of all the amazing pictures in magazine articles from this era; The ambiance was colorful but the photographs always seemed slightly faded.

COLOR NOTES I used a palette of creamy bright pinks, olive greens, light violet, a touch of lavender, sky blue, and a little flower power for texture.

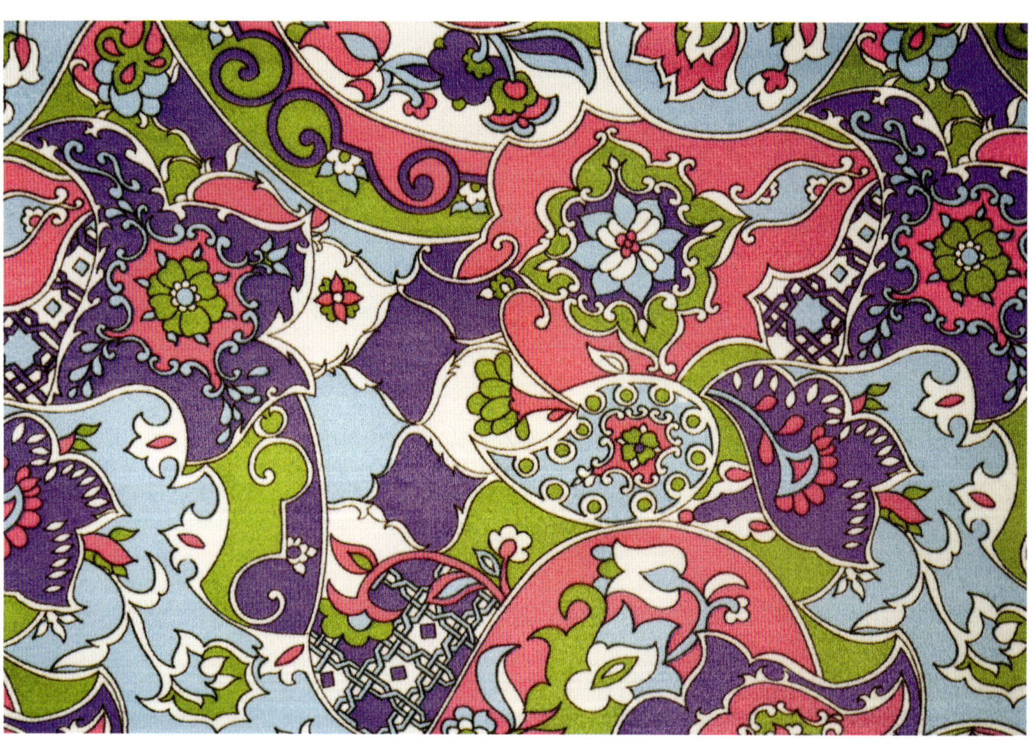

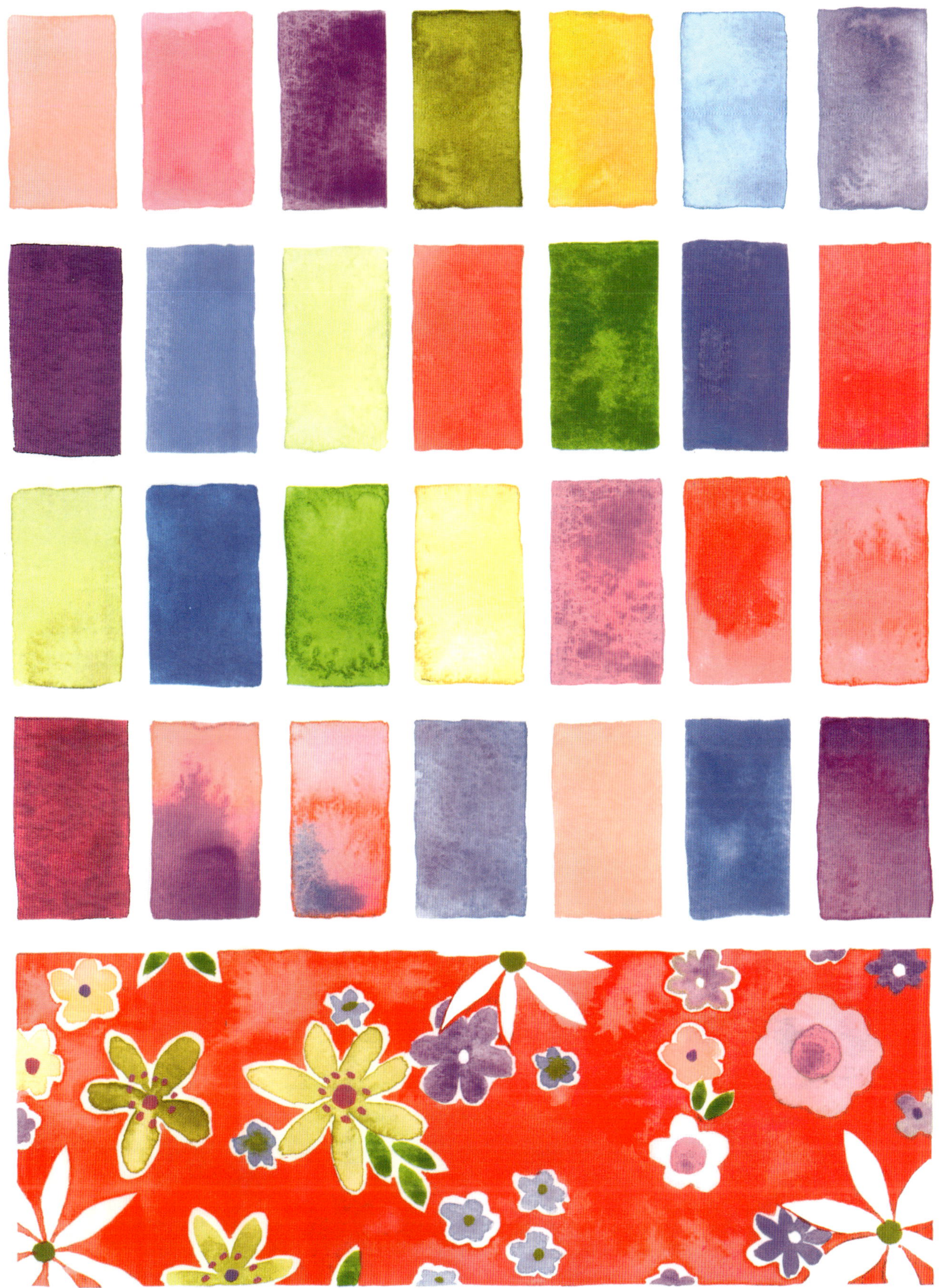

Ancient Egypt

On a trip to Egypt with my family when I was a teenager, I was overcome by seeing hundreds of spaces and walls covered in hieroglyphics and paintings representing stories and everyday life. The impact has never left me. What I remember is similar to this painting of Egyptian workers that was found on a tomb in Thebes, Egypt. As with most ancient art, the palette is muted and revolves around natural colors because earth pigments were used exclusively.

I enjoy this type of palette quite a bit. There's a certain elegance and timelessness to earthy colors and it inspires me to use these themes in my work.

I created a simple composition by using the vase elements from the painting to test different colors in a single work.

TECHNIQUE NOTES I mixed varieties of browns, ochres, oranges, and blacks in different values for the basic neutrals and made a few creamy hues by adding a touch of white gouache into some of the neutral color combinations I already made. This creates a chalky texture that makes paint more opaque for pastels and light neutrals. There are also very subtle hints of green and blue within the composition.

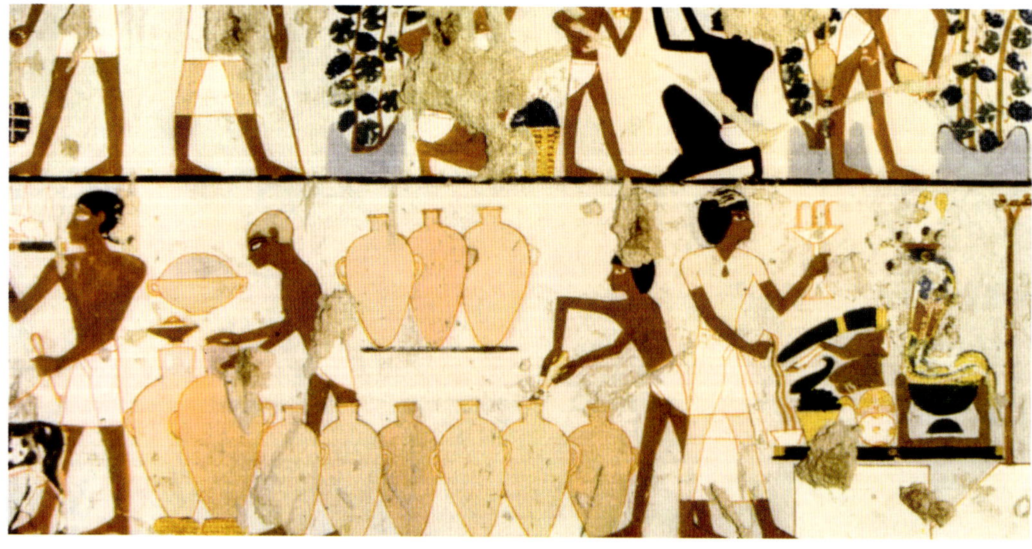

COLOR HARMONY FOR ARTISTS

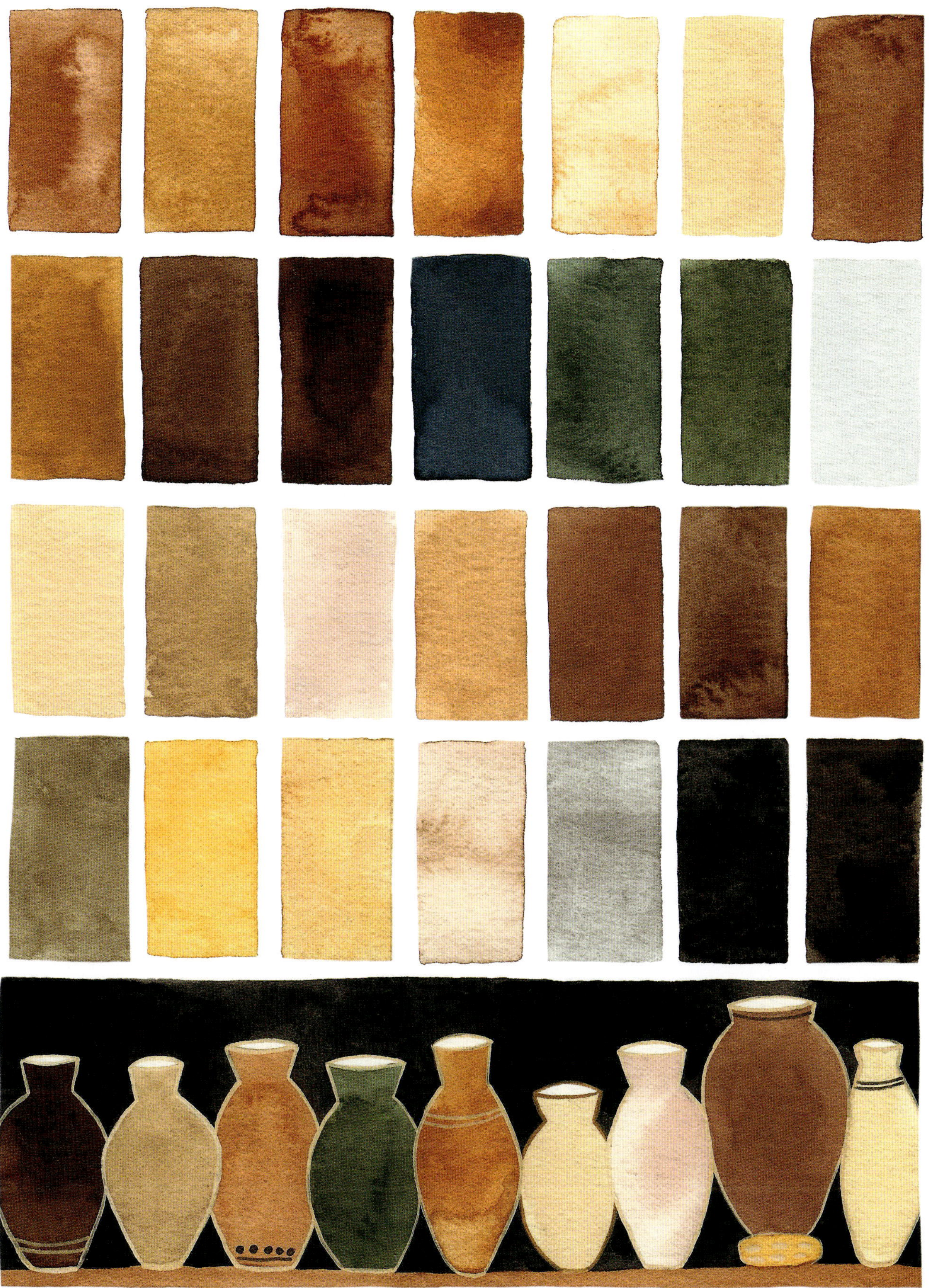

101

Mystical Jungle

Jungles are lush, humid, and predominantly green, with mostly layered warm greens ranging from mossy shades to darker shadow greens.

This photo inspired me to play around with a mini landscape with thick layers of plants and foggy sky. The greens gradually become brighter and more yellowish and move to the foreground.

COLOR NOTES To create warm greens, I suggest adding to your green mixes a variety of yellows, as well as ochre. The ochre will desaturate bright greens because of its orange undertone and will make your colors look more organic and closer to nature.

To darken greens, add a touch of indigo and a small bit of red (green's complementary color). This will tone down the green's vibrancy without adding black or brown paint.

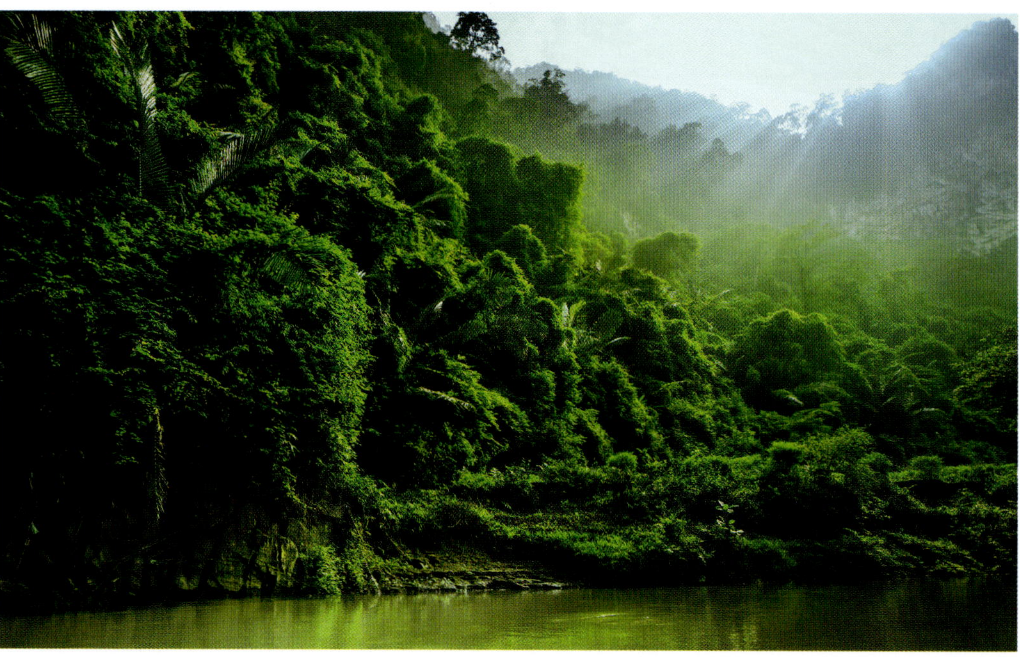

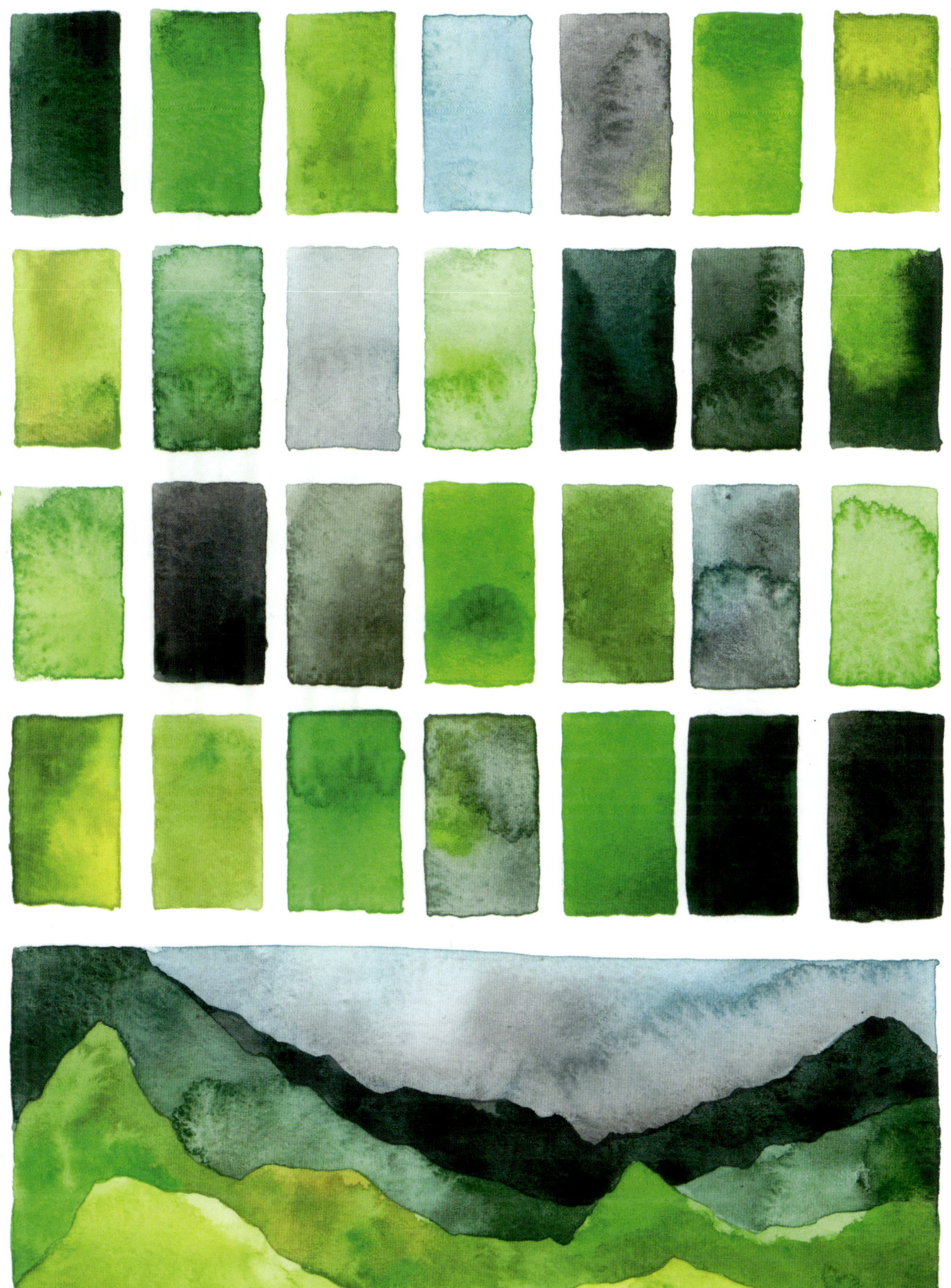

103

Tropical Paradise

This beautiful scenery is from the Mayan Riviera of Mexico, the area where I spent my entire childhood and am proud to call my hometown. In all the places I've traveled, I have never found water quite like the Caribbean Sea.

We described Cancun's palette as neon pastel, which I still think is exactly right! The peaceful turquoise water is in perfect harmony with the white sand and bright green palm trees. It really is paradise on Earth. From blue to turquoise, to green and yellow green, this is also a great example of an analogous color harmony.

TECHNIQUE NOTES To make these bright turquoise hues, I used Dr. Ph. Martin's Juniper Green and Ice Blue as my base colors, then mixed in a variety of blues from my pan set to create all the different colors in the sea and sky. For the sandy color, mix white gouache with a touch of yellow and peach. You can also add a bit of brown for the deeper colors found in wet sand.

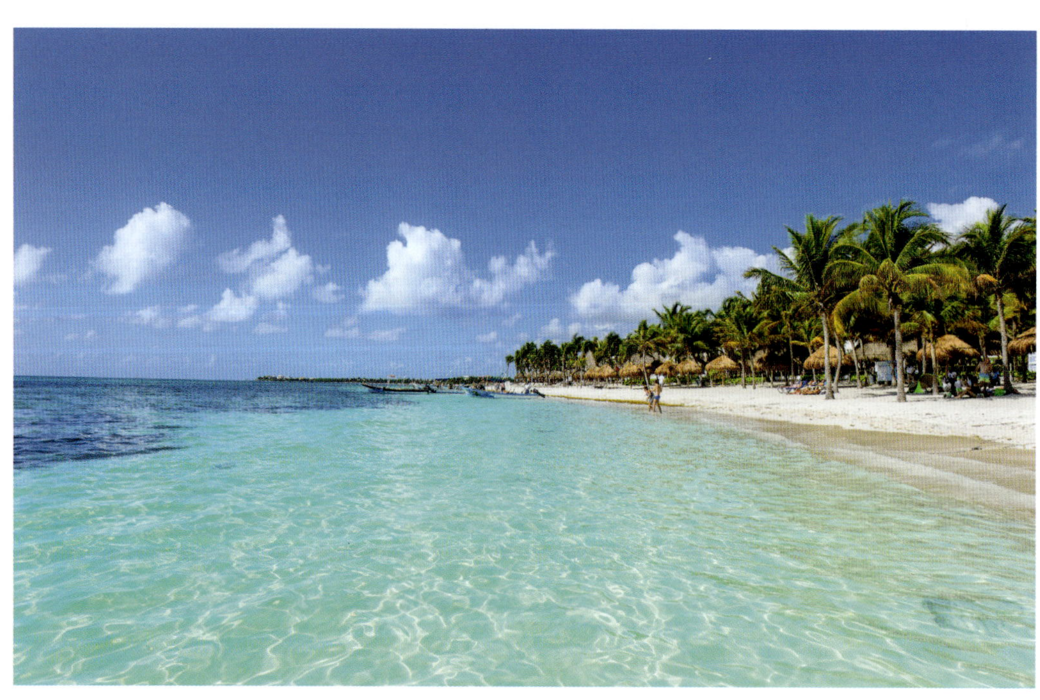

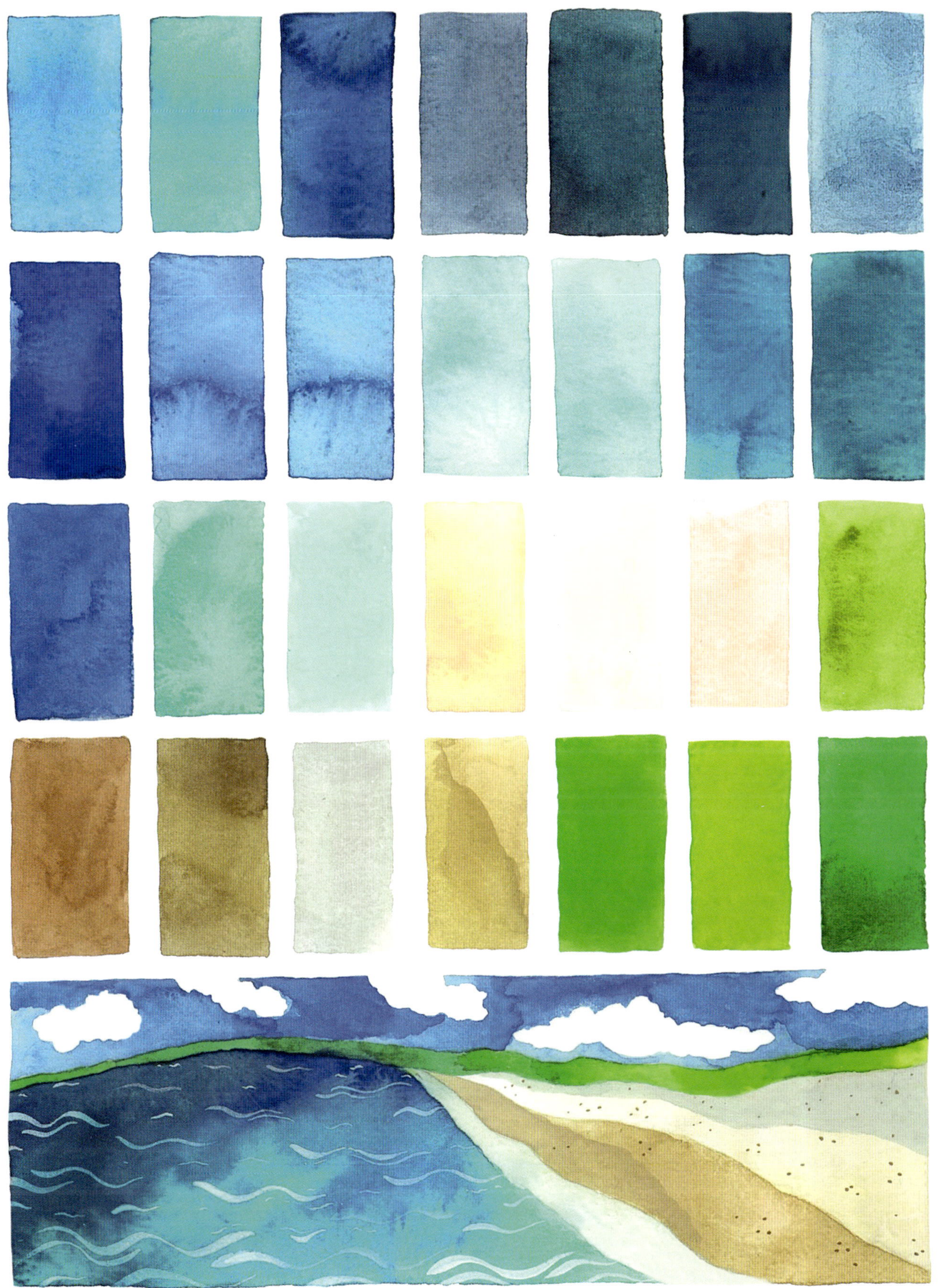

Majestic Canyon

Arizona's Antelope Canyon is one of the most visited spots in the United States . . . and it's easy to see why! This majestic canyon almost glows with its bright warm colors and sandstone texture. The vibrant oranges and sky blue are perfect complementaries.

The abstract image for my texture board is inspired by the opening of the canyon, which almost feels like a door into a new dimension. I'm hopeful this will inspire a larger painting along the same concept.

COLOR NOTES The range in warm tones is analogous; it begins at violet and navigates around the color wheel until it reaches yellow orange. Burgundy, brick red, rusty orange, and neutrals like clay and ochre create a beautiful scheme of deep, warm hues. I enjoy colors like Winsor & Newton's Mauve and hints of Dr. Ph. Martin's Persimmon mixed with purples, reds, and oranges from my pan set.

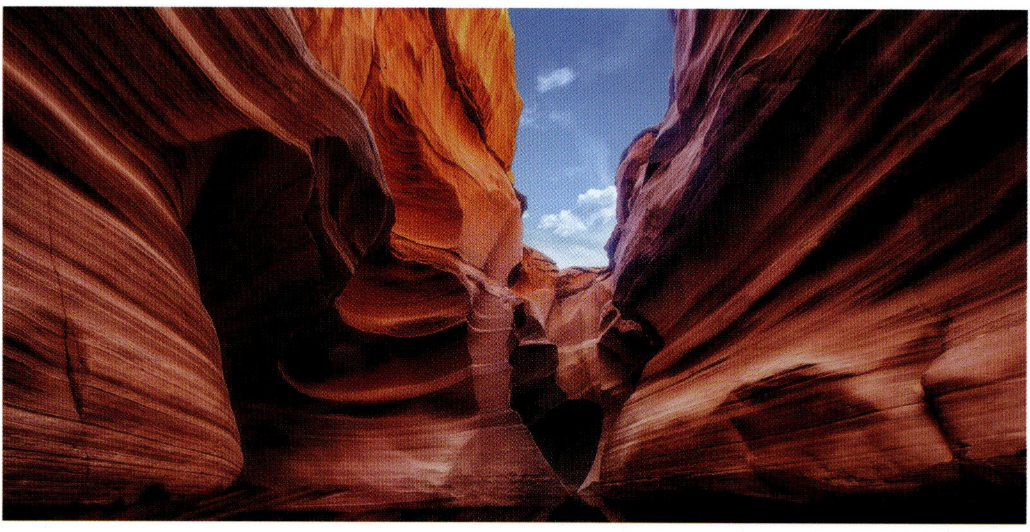

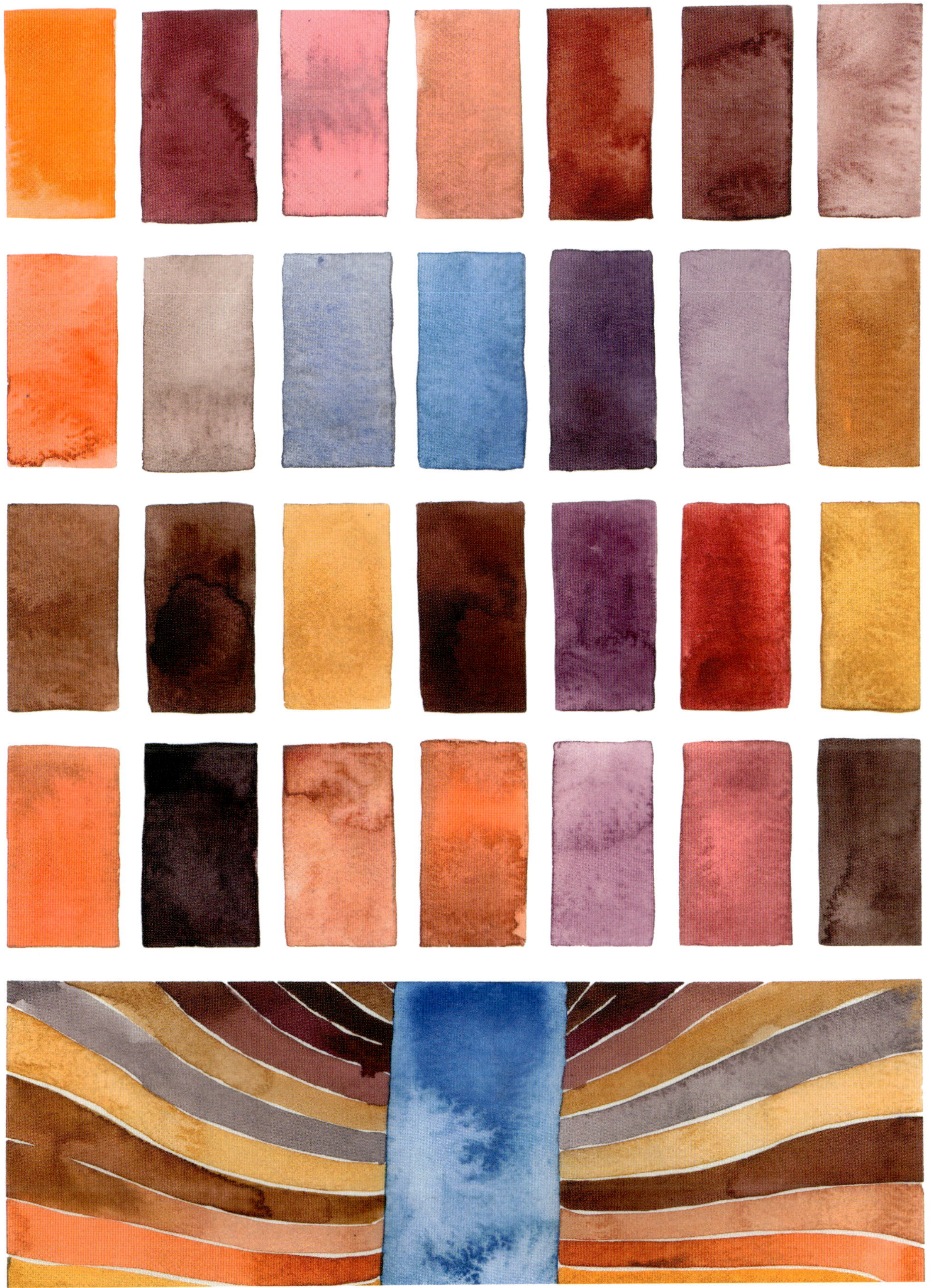

Underwater Fantasy

If you've ever been snorkeling or scuba diving through a magical coral reef, you might feel like you're floating through another planet! The vibrance of corals and fish, plus new and interesting textures, are so inspiring.

For the inspiration board I created a simple wet-on-wet wash with bright blues and some corals. While the paint was still wet, I added a sprinkle of salt to get a fun texture that reminds me of the shapes found in coral.

COLOR NOTES The palette is vibrant, bold, and fluorescent, so bright that I immediately knew my Dr. Ph. Martin's Radiant watercolors would do the trick. I swatched this palette with Turquoise Blue, Ultra, Persimmon, and my favorite, Juniper Green.

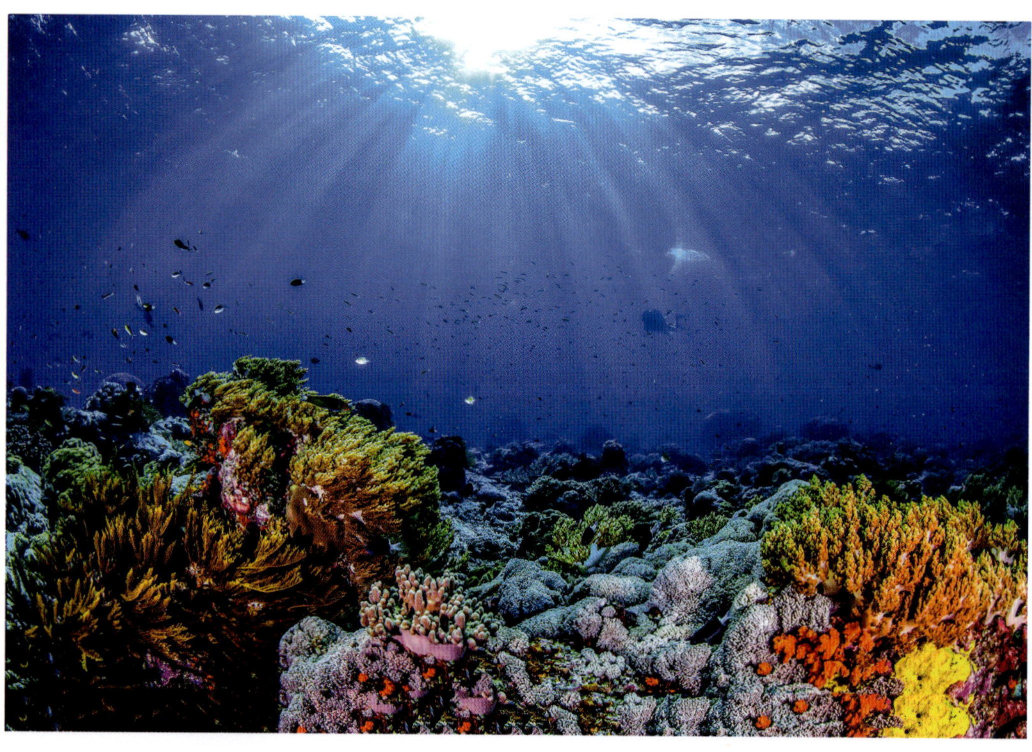

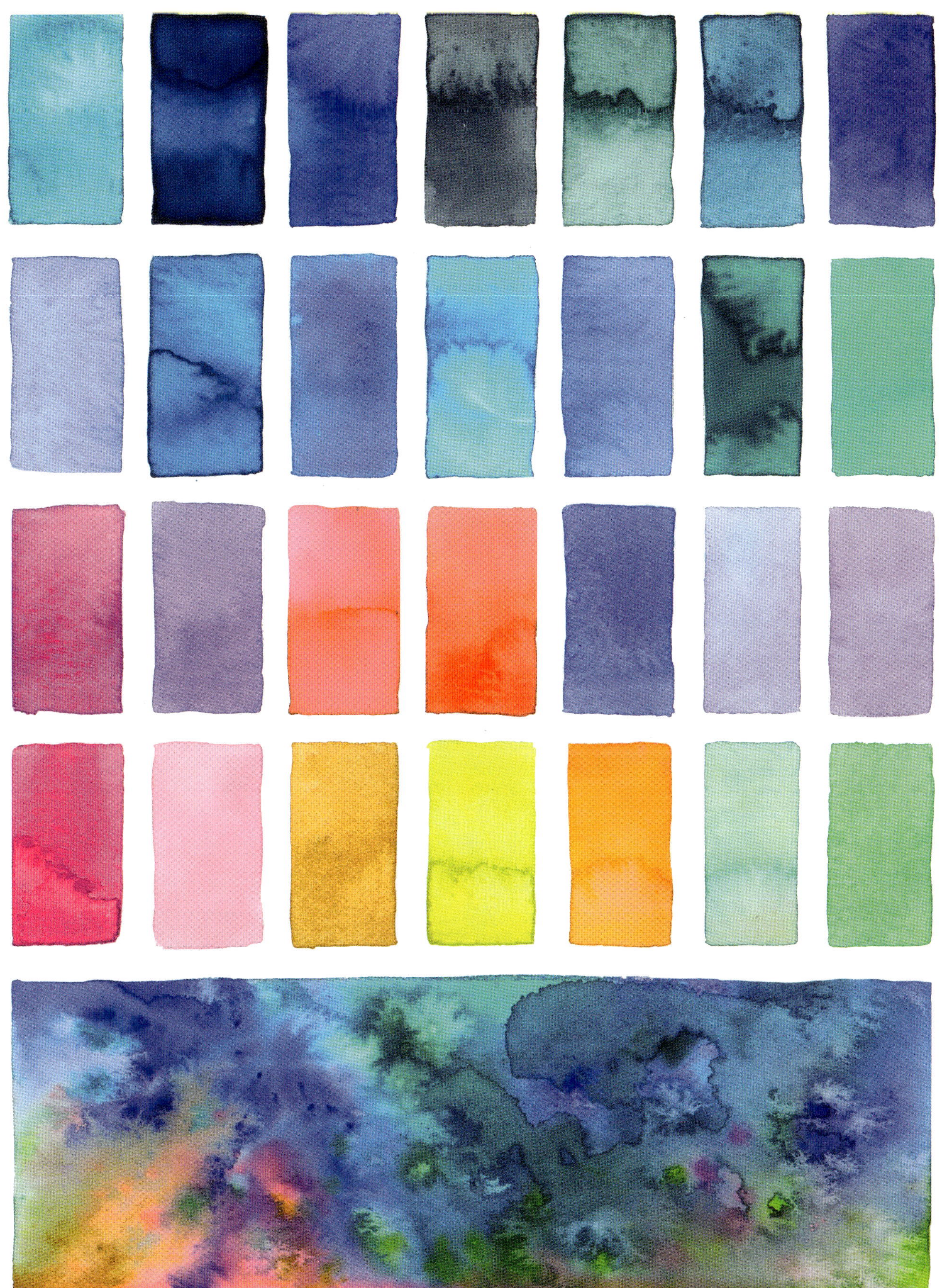

Rippling Dunes

I love searching for photography of Middle Eastern deserts to inspire my landscapes. The way the wind ripples the sand to create texture, the different levels, layers, and movement of each dune . . . it's completely mesmerizing!

Although there's no drastic color variation within desert sand, bright sun hitting each dune creates a wide range of color in shadows and highlights.

I really enjoyed playing with my Schmincke pan set to swatch this palette, especially experimenting with oranges and blues to create such a variety of colors. I also added touches of my favorite Winsor & Newton ochre to mix up the color range within the dunes.

TECHNIQUE NOTES In this case, sand is a warm neutral color composed of ochres with undertones of orange. To desaturate orange and make it a more neutral hue, simply add a light touch of blue to the mix. We see numerous times throughout this book that complementaries are a huge part of color harmony and mixing. In this case, the use of complementary doubles: First, to desaturate oranges to create shadows and organic colors; second, the contrast between the blue sky and ochre-orange sand is a complementary harmony scheme of its own.

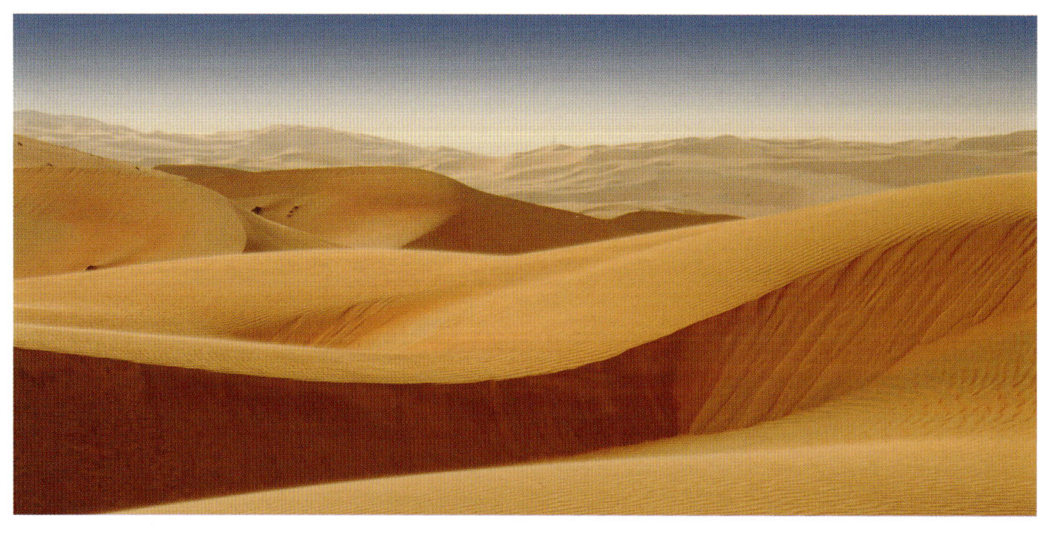

COLOR HARMONY FOR ARTISTS

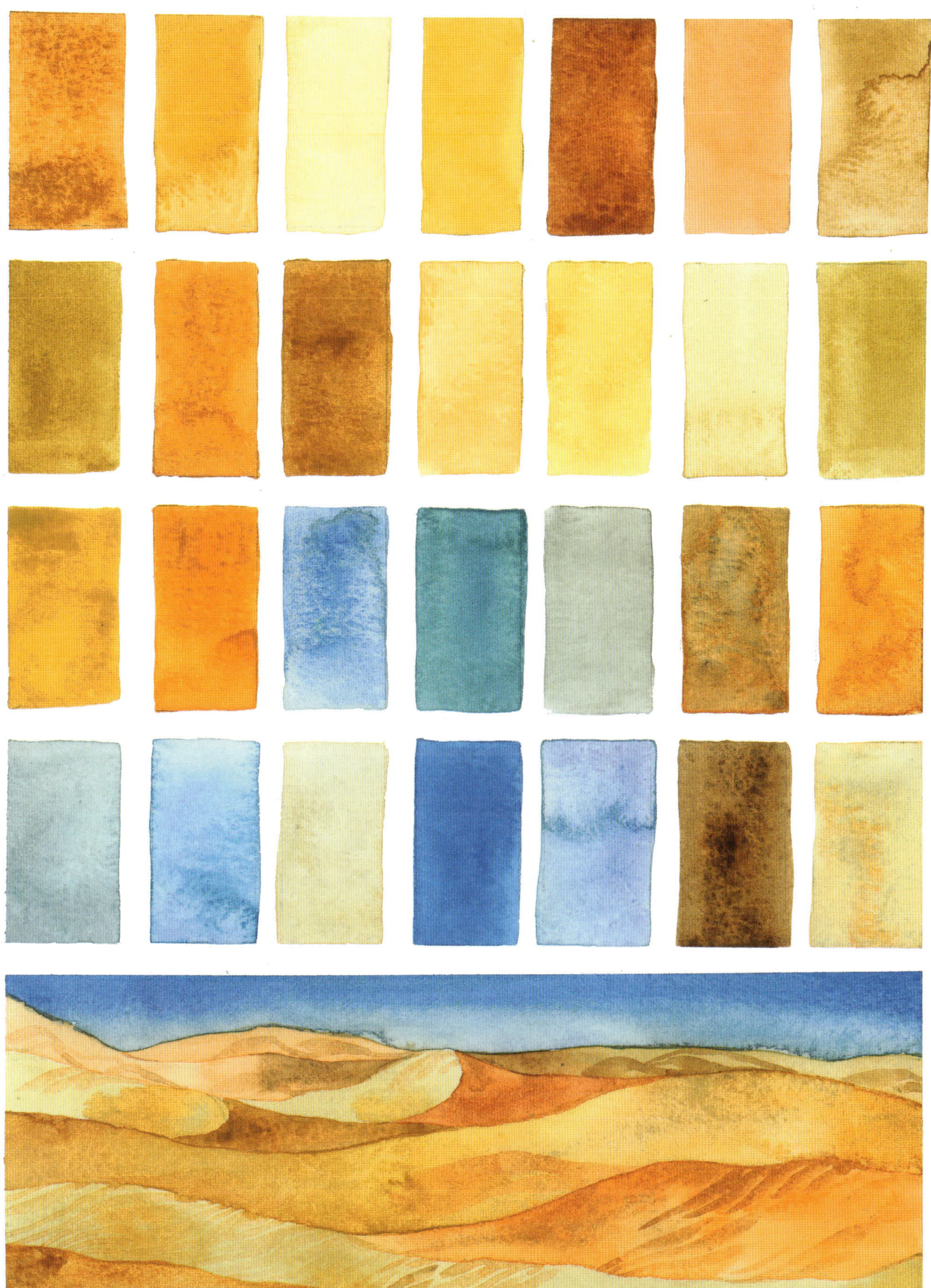

Swiss Alps

You might imagine this scene of snowy mountains in the Swiss Alps if you're asked to picture a peaceful landscape in your mind. It makes me think of crisp, clean air. The beautiful, cool palette consists of crisp blues and greens, with touches of warm green represented in the sunlight hitting the green fields.

Cool tones conjure feelings of freshness and vastness. The image is comforting to the eye simply because analogous color schemes are harmonious and pleasing to look at.

COLOR NOTES Blue is dominant, from navy to prussian and sky blue, and greens are secondaries, paired with neutrals from the mountains. I enjoy using cerulean blue, indigo, and turquoise from my pan sets. Like greens, blues tend to darken in the palette, so it's important to test them on a scrap sheet before painting.

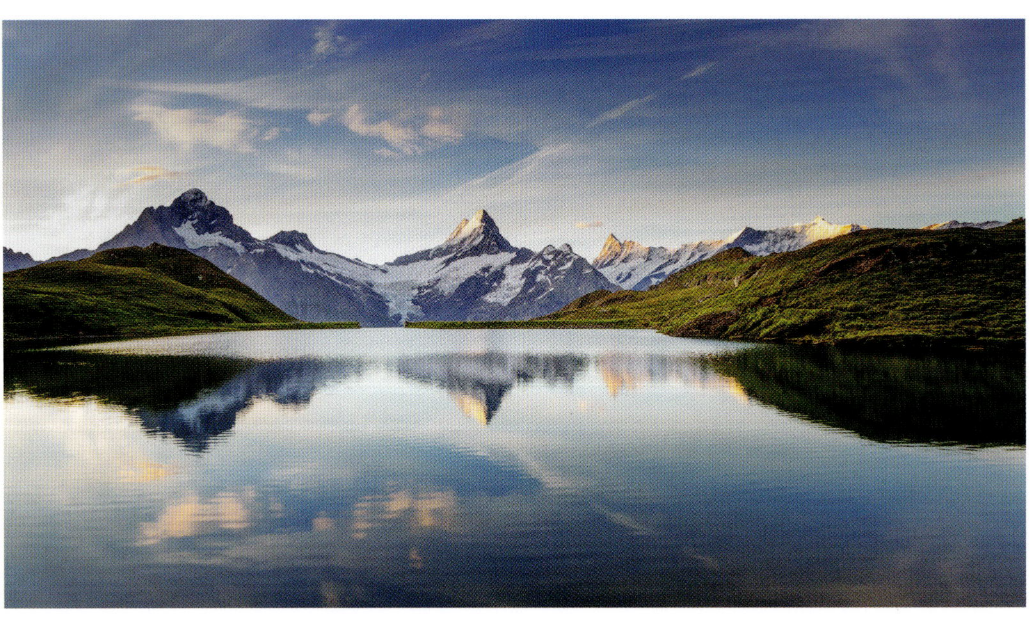

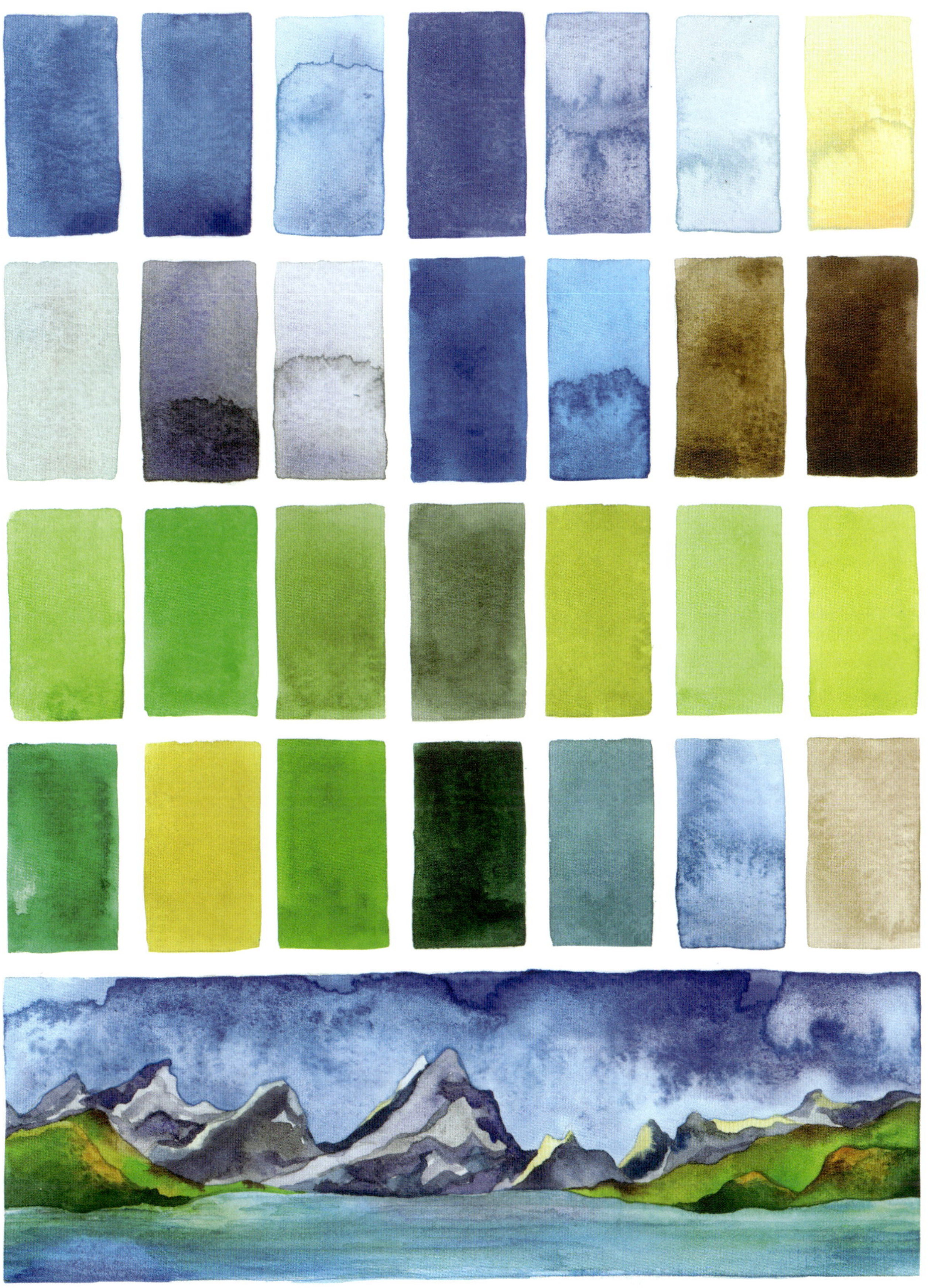

113

Lupine Field

This peaceful meadow of blooming lupines is extremely pleasing to the eye, with different plays on color harmony represented.

I enjoyed using Sennelier's Dioxazine Purple, Holbein's Lavender, and Dr. Ph. Martin's Mahogany and Violet for this palette.

COLOR NOTES This is almost a monochromatic harmony, with violet as the dominant color, but there's tremendous range with purples and lilacs and variants in warmth and value. I spot lavender, violet, magenta, mauve, lilac, pastel pink, and fuchsia. So it's really analogous harmony—the magenta and blue-violet that enable the different purple tones are adjacent to violet on the color wheel. Because the field is a yellowish ochre, which contrasts with the lupines (violet and yellow are opposites on the color wheel), we also have a touch of complementary colors.

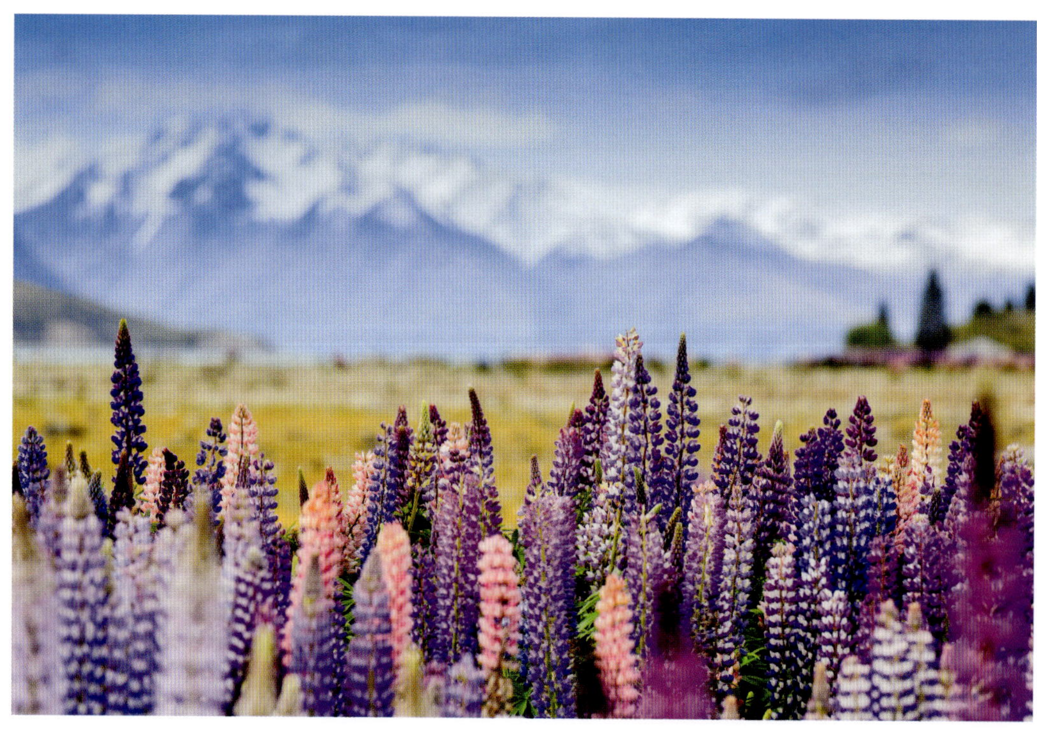

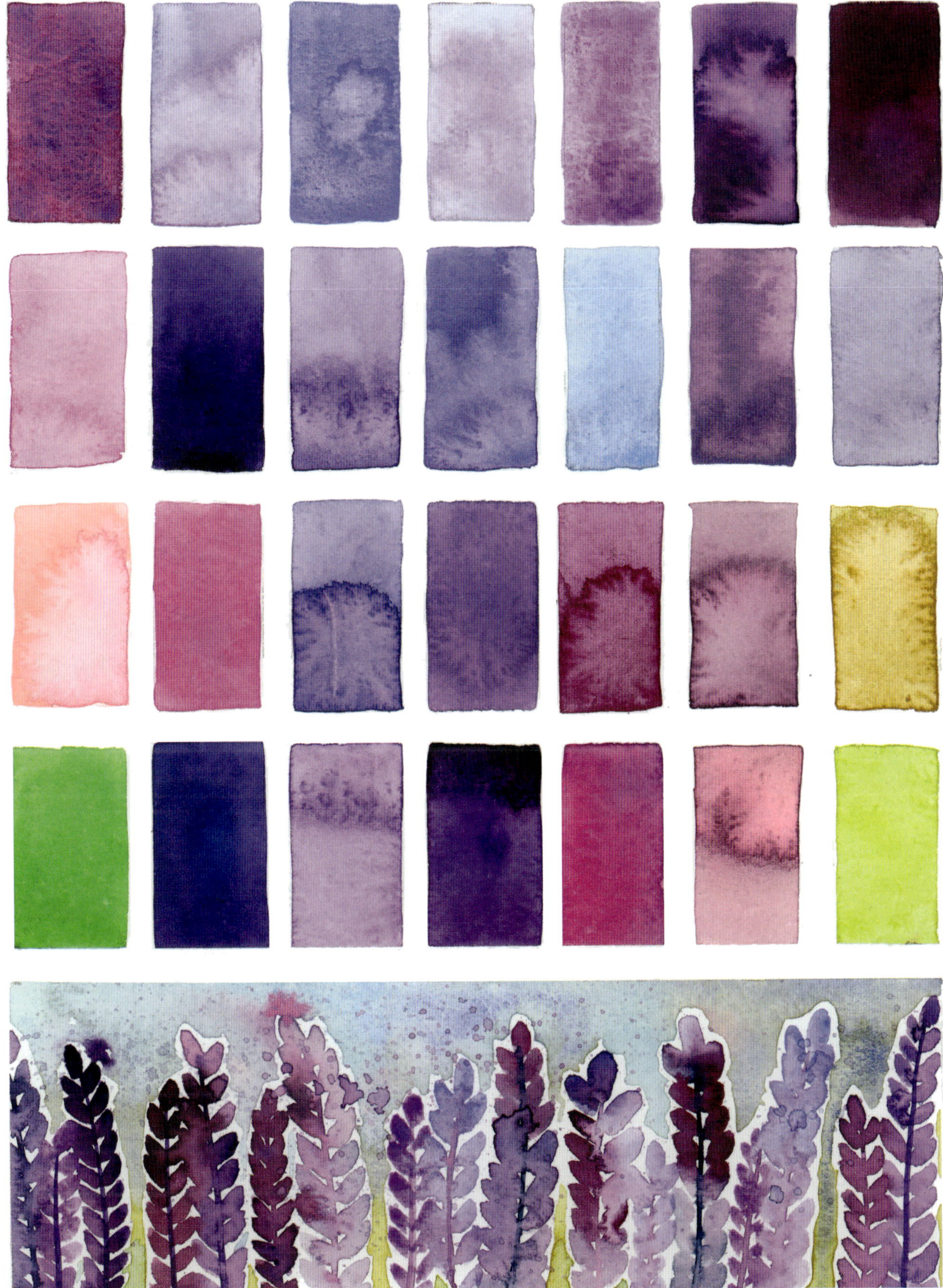

Colorful Succulents

Because succulent plants store water in their roots and leaves, giving them a thick, fleshy appearance, they can survive in arid climates. They're also one of the easiest houseplants to keep alive.

All sorts of greens infuse this image—vibrant grass green, soft sage, jade, lime green, and pickle green—complemented by touches of violet reds at the tip of each leaf, and in some cases a slight gradient of orange.

I really like experimenting with the greens in my pan sets for color schemes like this. Remember that green pans tend to appear darker in cake form, so test them before going straight to your painting.

COLOR NOTES This composition has nice variation in shapes and a gorgeous range of greens. Notice that succulents tend to have split-complementary harmonies that branch out from the green hues. To create a split-complementary, choose a main color (green in this case), find its complementary (red), then use the two colors on each side (orange and warm violet).

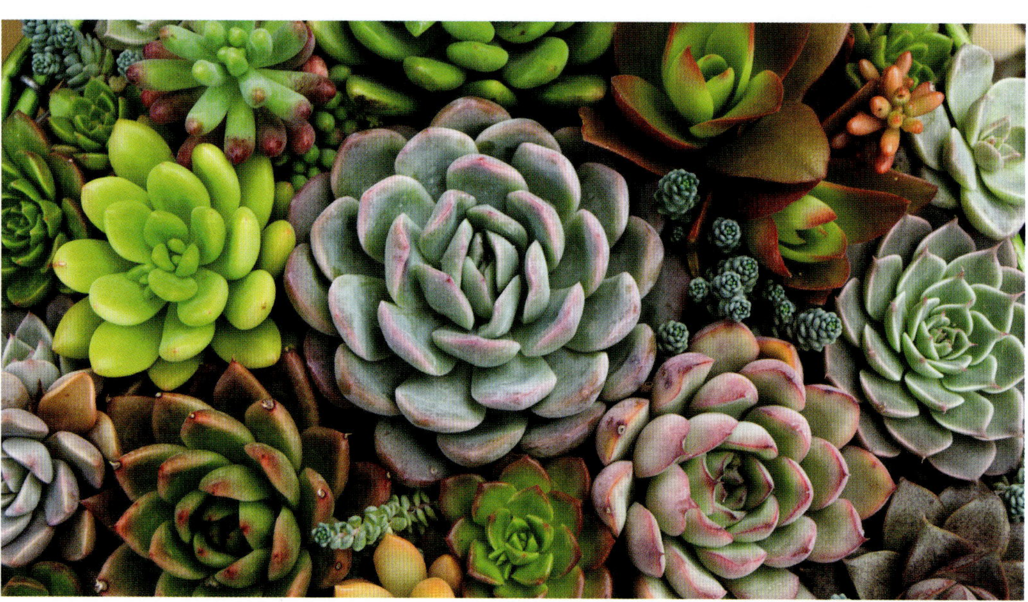

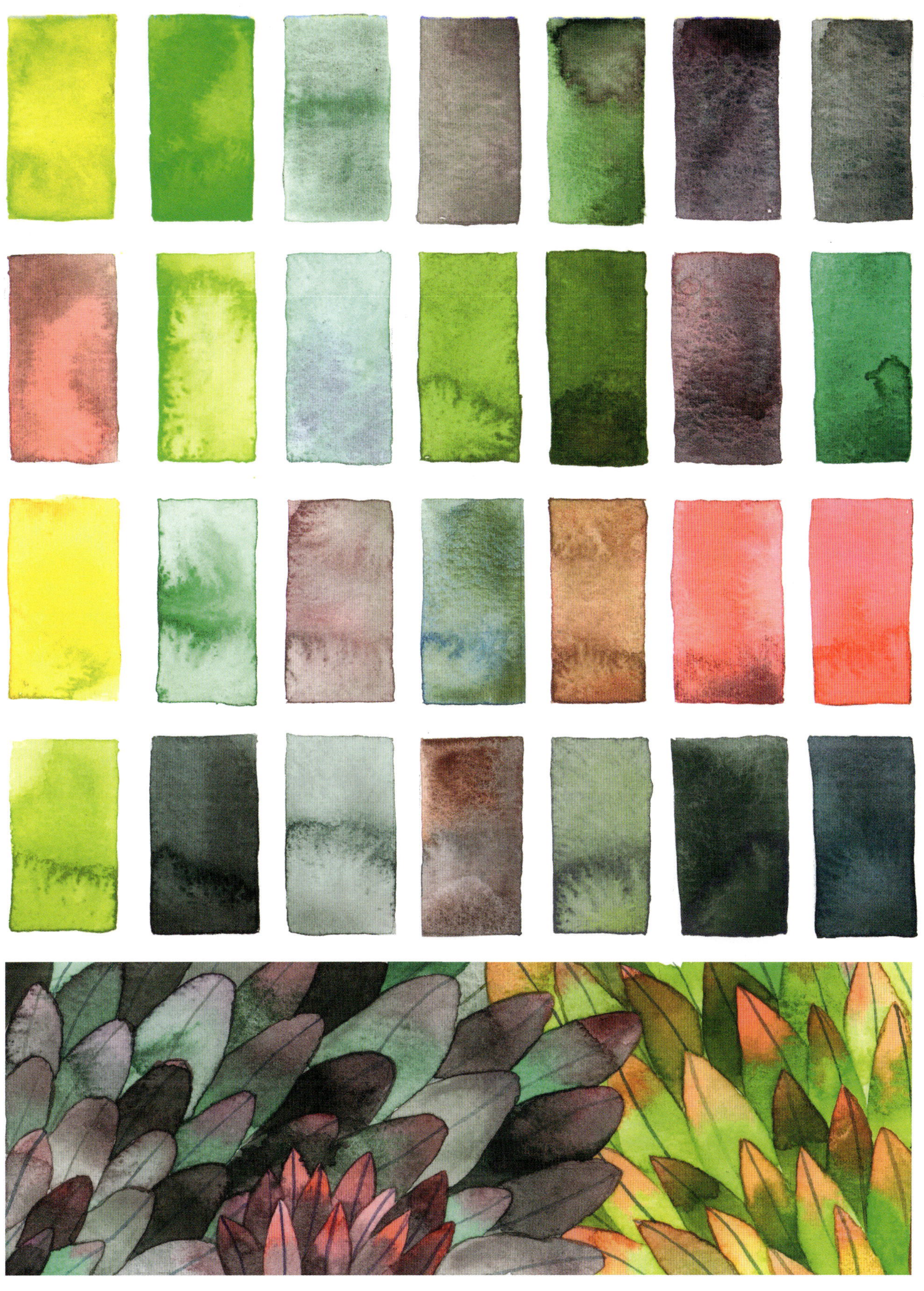

Rustic Farmhouse

This warm flower arrangement, with orange berries, green leaves, and cheerful sunflowers, is a great centerpiece for fall occasions such as Thanksgiving. The neutral wood backdrop and pumpkin vase give it an extra rustic touch. This perfectly warm color palette inspires feelings of coziness and friendliness and reminds me of joyful occasions.

I find it helpful to describe your feelings when observing color. You also gain insight. Color has a lot of theory behind it, but it's also deeply connected to emotions. Because color mixing is an extremely intuitive process, being aware of and in touch with how colors make you feel—and actually describing your emotions—will bring life and energy to your color swatching.

COLOR NOTES This image is pleasing to the eye because of the warm feelings it generates, but also because it's a perfect analogous harmony. Red-orange, orange, gold yellow, lemon yellow, lime green, and green hues in this palette are complemented by neutral textures in the wooden base.

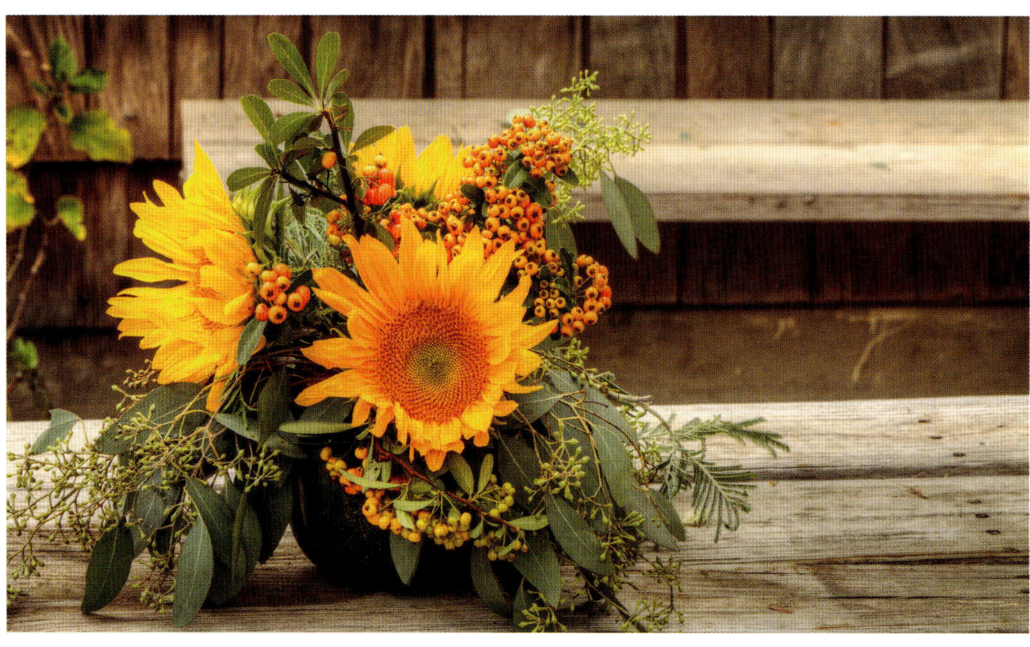

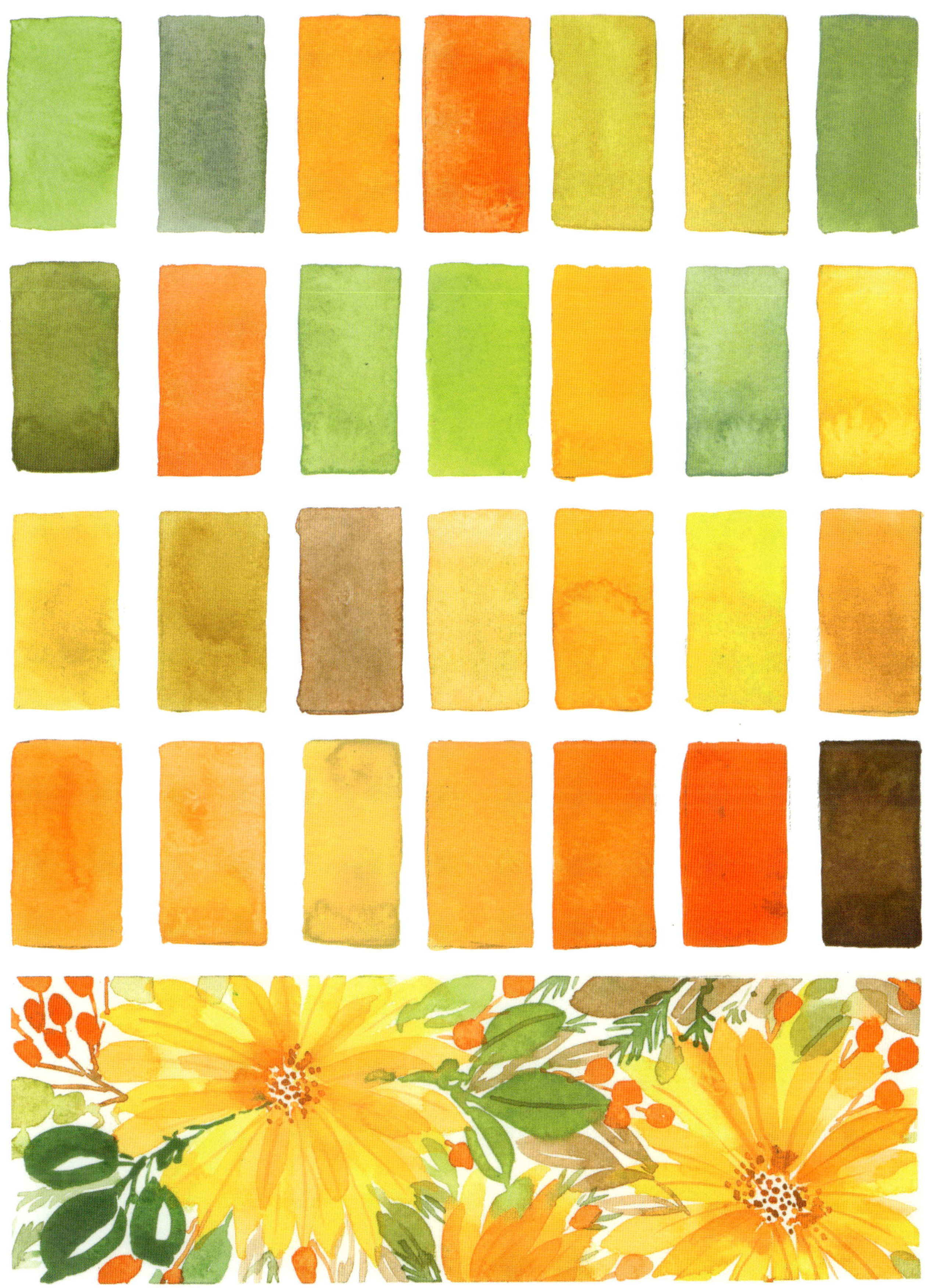

Tropical Brights

Anthurium flowers are sometimes referred to as laceleaf or flamingo lily. The open heart shape symbolizes hospitality and openness. They are brilliant and exotic with a high-gloss texture.

The beautiful anthuriums in this image are bright with touches of soft pastels to complement the overall vibrance. The palette is warm and tropical, ranging from shiny sunset orange, to sorbet pink and peach, with soft lizard green and bright canary yellow.

TECHNIQUE NOTES I used Dr. Ph. Martin's Persimmon for that bright orange base, which can also be watered down drastically and mixed with a bit of yellow to create peachy sorbet hues. I also mixed in touches of magenta and sap green with emerald green.

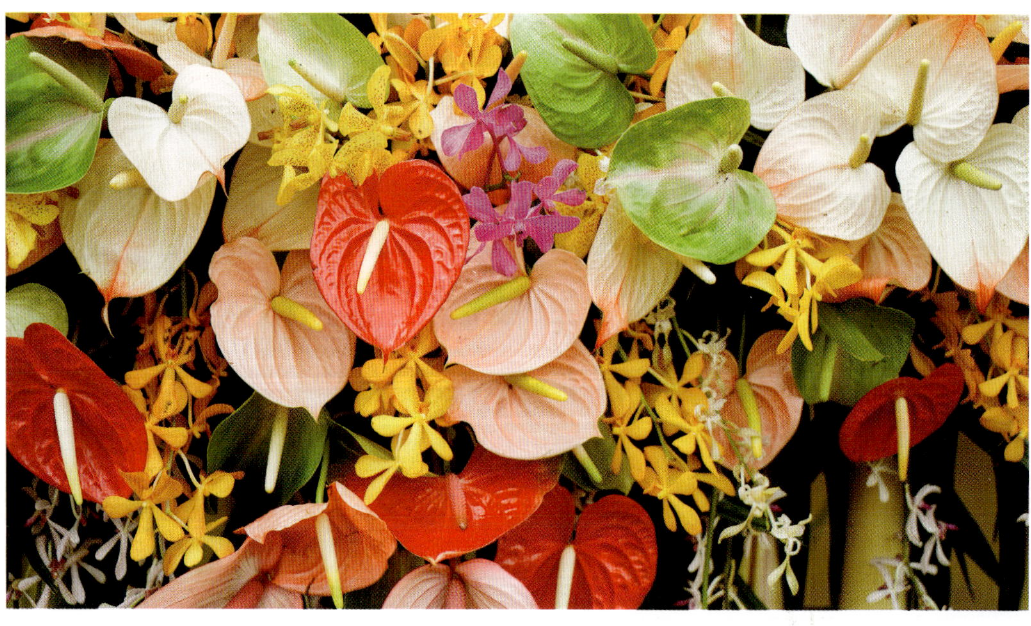

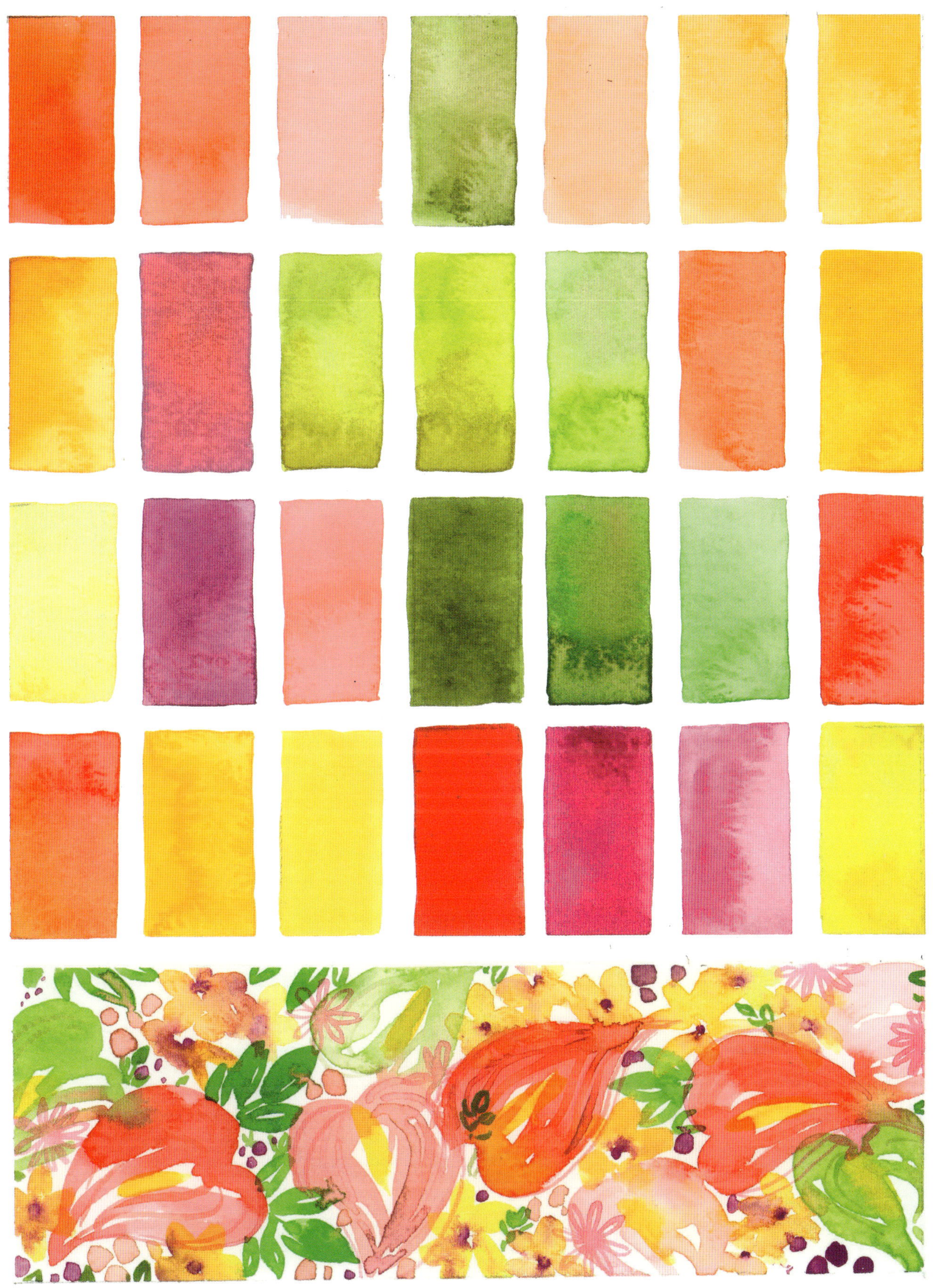

Romantic Bouquet

This soft and romantic rose bouquet of muted pinks and light greens inspires sweetness and innocence. Colors in this desaturated palette will generally be watered down to achieve light values. The few instances of deeper colors are actually the same base colors as the rest of the palette but with less water to make the paint more opaque and create darker shades.

Dusty rose and sage green are romantic, soft, and sweet in this mostly cool palette, with hints of warm greens, neutrals, and a lot of water. I think of this palette as cool because even though pink comes from watered-down reds, the undertone is cooler and leans toward violet (not orange) and the main green is sage, which is inclined toward blue (instead of yellow).

TECHNIQUE NOTES To make a beautiful dusty pink, mix watered-down Opera Pink with hints of green. You can also add a hint of violet to cool it down.

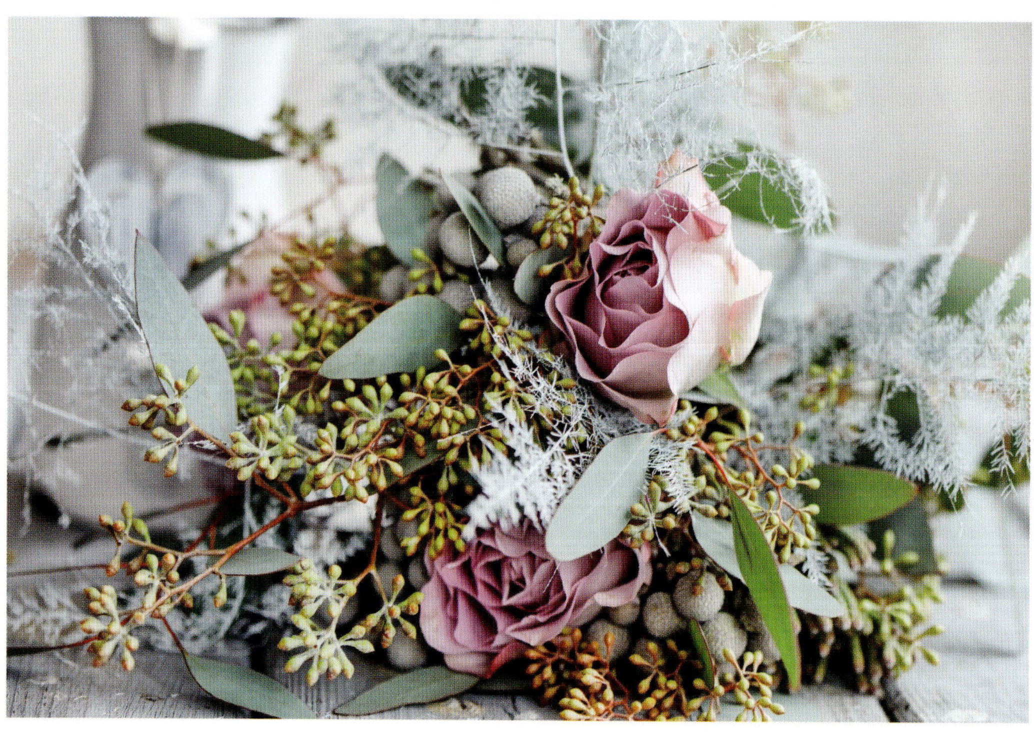

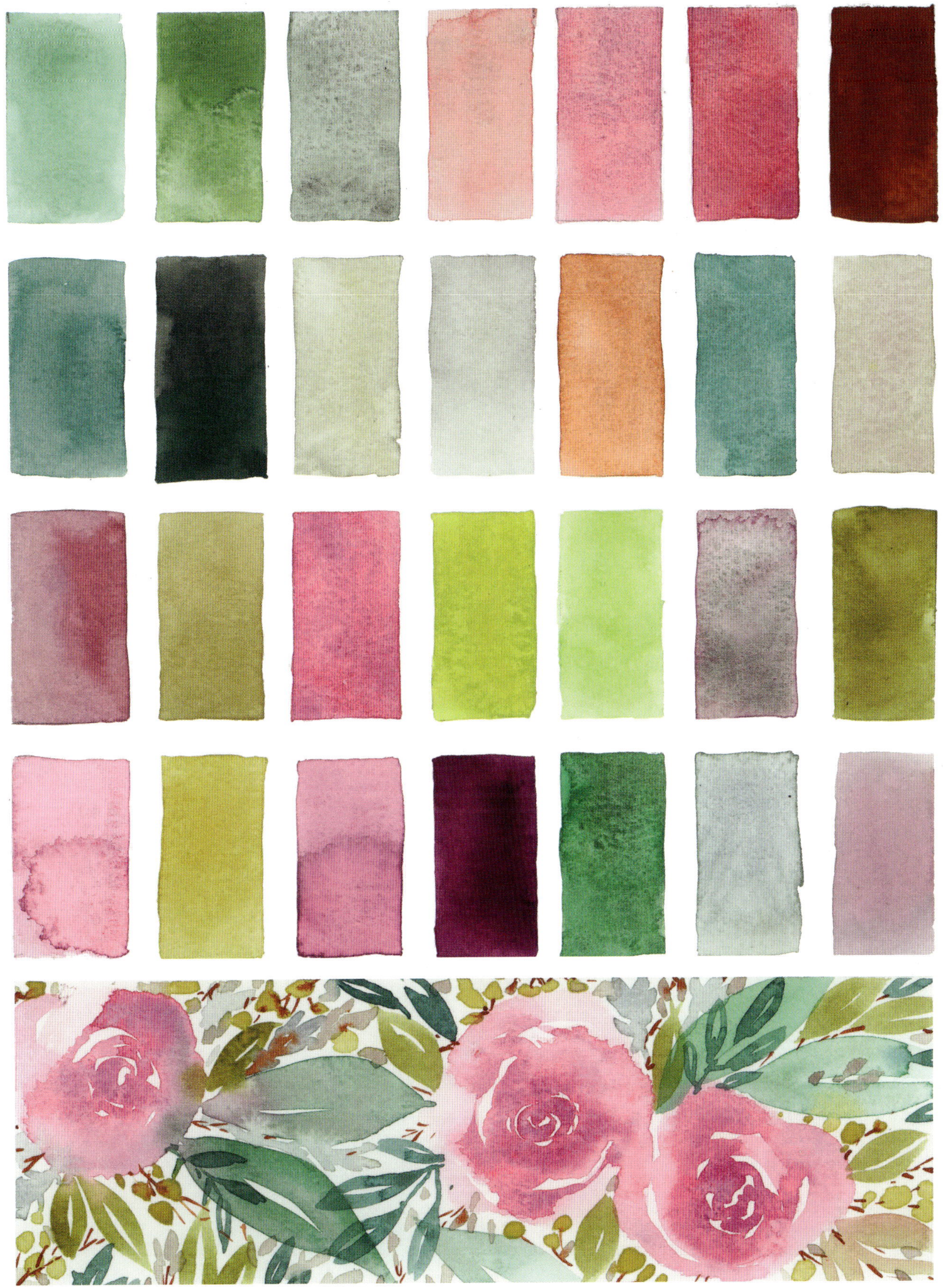

Marsala Blooms

This floral composition of peonies, protea, roses, and greenery is a great swatching exercise: The bouquet's overpowering color is violet-red, but there are still plenty of colors to observe and paint. Mauve, ruby wine, brick, maroon, magenta, beet red, burgundy, and berry are just some of the names that describe the incredible variety of violets, reds, and pinks in this image.

Once again, nature does a beautiful job at naturally combining complementary colors. The deep green leaves create perfect contrast with the dark reds in this floral arrangement. There are also soft touches of warm and neutral peach accents, which brighten this otherwise dark image.

COLOR NOTES   Mahogany by Dr. Ph. Martin's is always a favorite base color of mine to create deep reds and violets. I use it with Crimson Red to create cool and deep reds. The amount of water creates the variety in value throughout the palette.

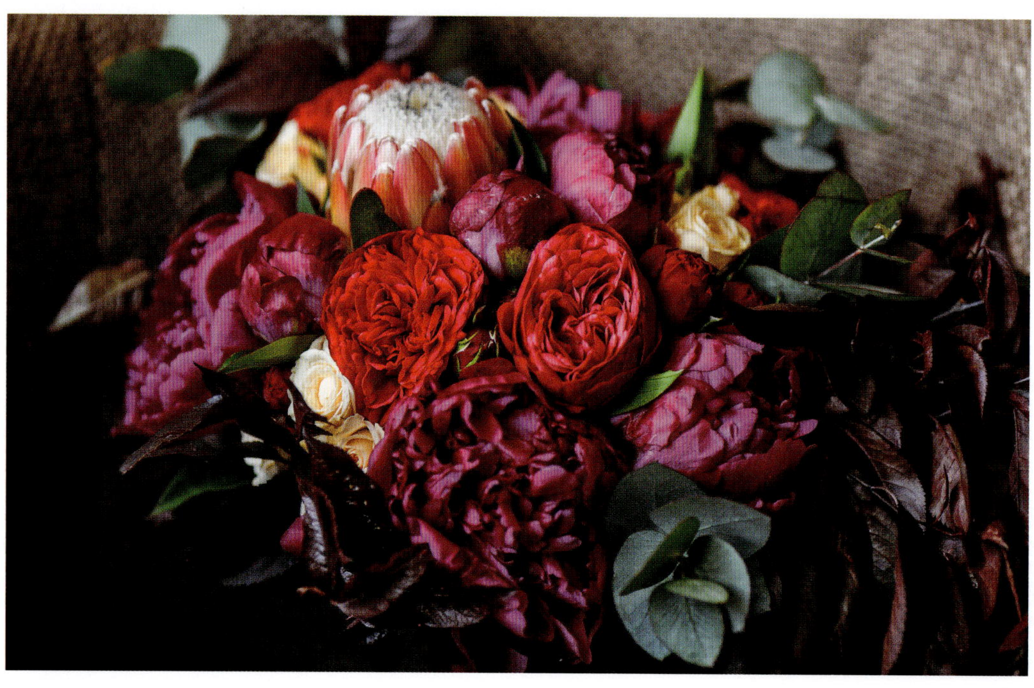

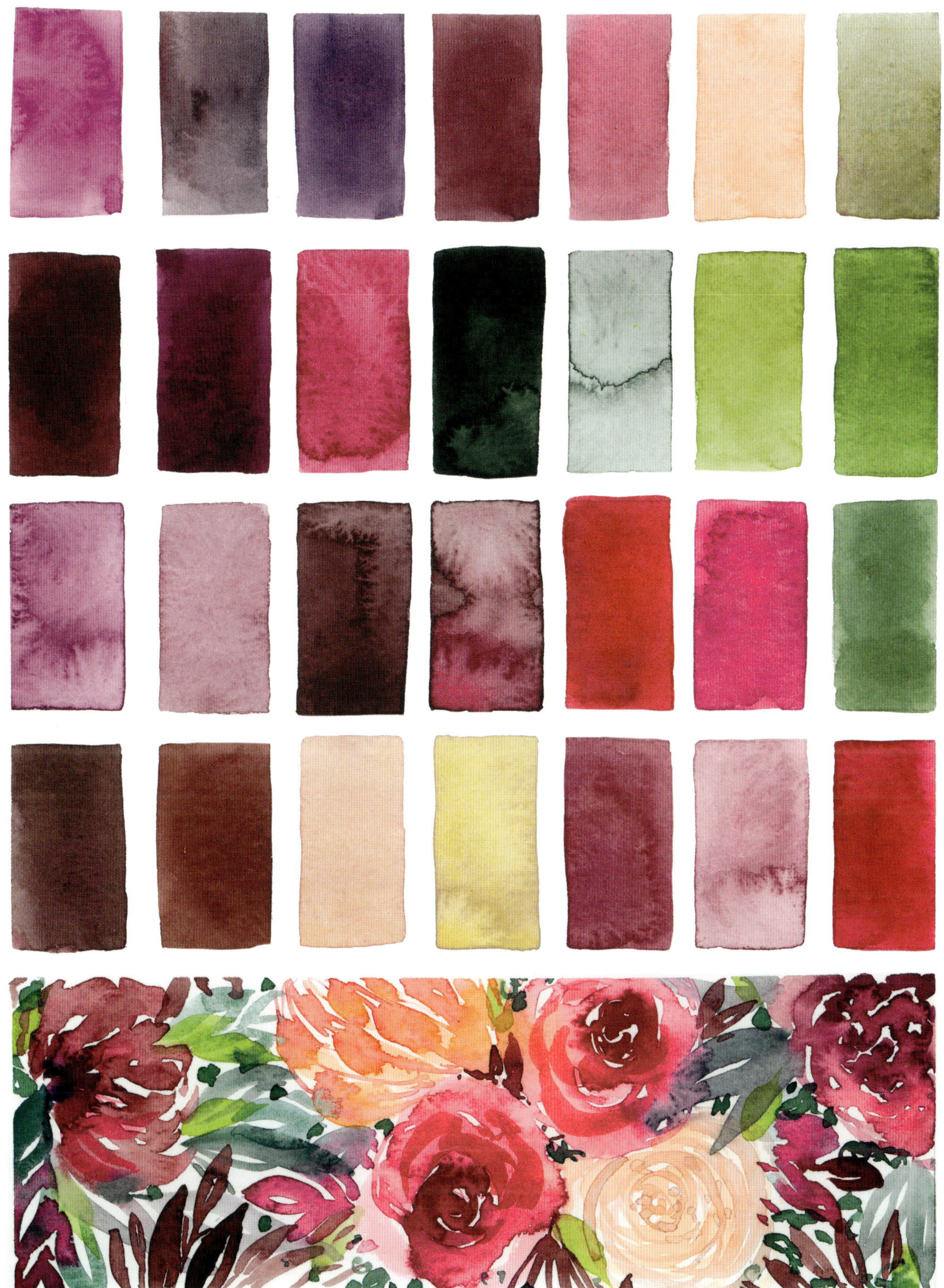

Still Life with Fruit

This is a classic example of still-life photography with cheese, nuts, fruit, and wine. The composition and contrast between light and shadow makes swatching these color schemes so interesting.

Sometimes I simply like to see what colors look like together, so I make color bars in a gradient order. Here I began with green and transitioned to reds, passing through all the ranges of brown to make the red, then analogous oranges and yellows, and finally, warm greens.

TECHNIQUE NOTES Creating shadows with watercolors, and paints in general, is best achieved by adding touches of complement to each color. In this palette, for example, you can create shades of moss green, army green, and pine green similar to the hues in the backdrop that are also reflected in the pitcher. These greens help you make shadow tones for the reds in the apples. I mention complementary mixing once again because it's such an important tool in color mixing. It's essential to understand how complementaries work with each other to create contrast while also mixing new ones.

The same goes for the shadows in the cheese. To desaturate bright yellows, add the smallest bit of purple and test it until it feels right. For a yellow-orange, the violet will need to be a blue-violet instead of a warm violet. Once the color wheel is embedded into your painting brain, these steps will be easy and intuitive.

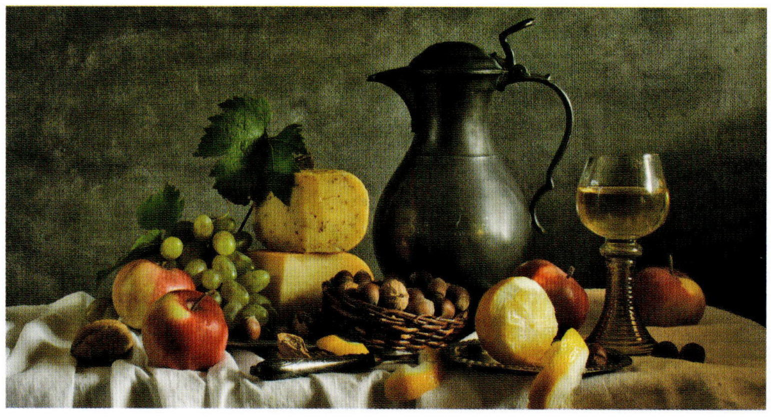

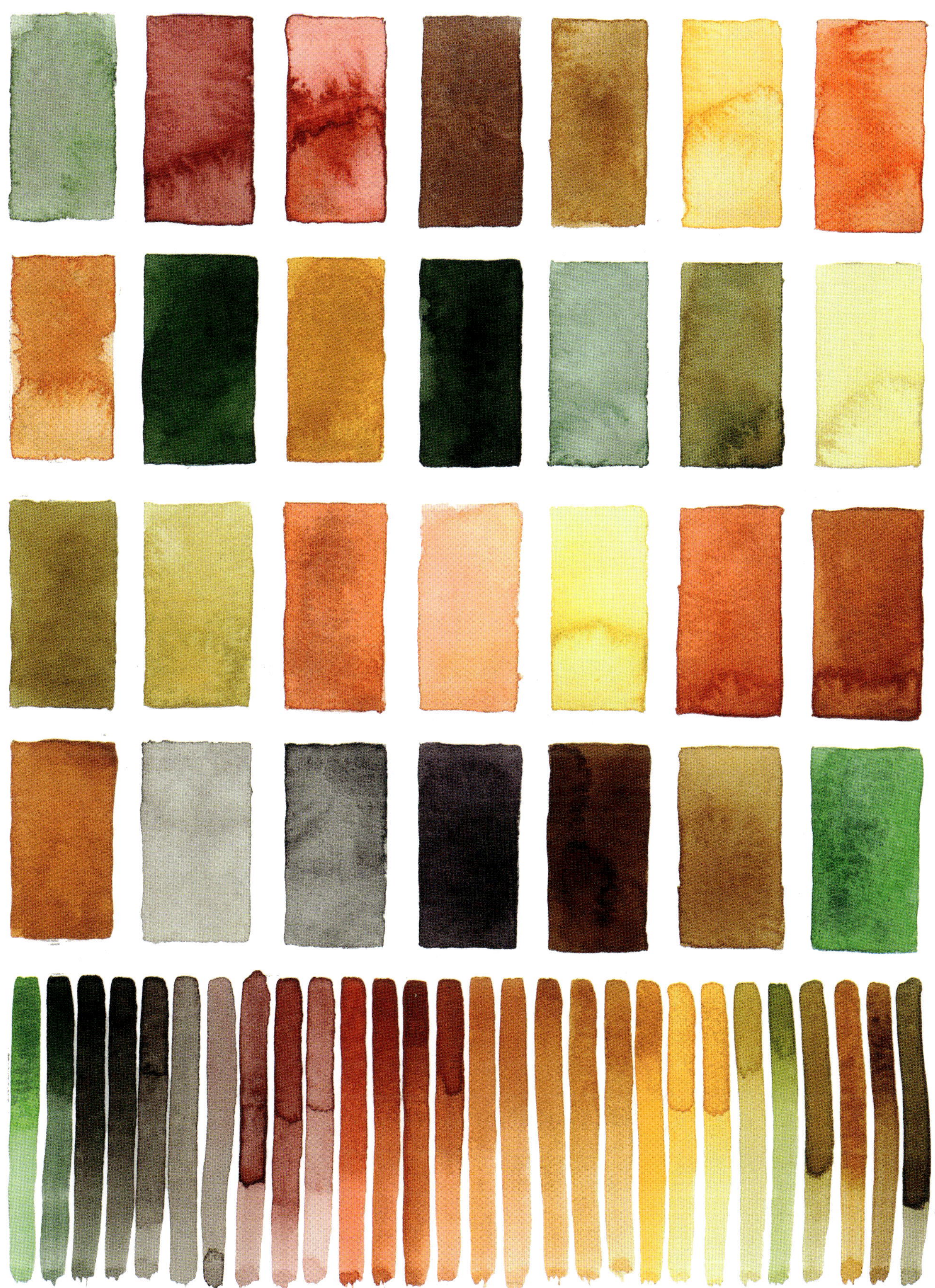

Abundant Harvest

Rich and warm color palettes suggest a fall harvest concept that represents abundance and gathering. When we think of autumn, we imagine falling leaves, spices, and pumpkins like the ones in this picture.

Painting still-life photography is interesting because the contrast in light and shadows is a great way to play with color variety. The palette is inviting and warm with its analogous harmony and also creates contrast with green being the complement (opposite) of red.

The analogous harmony includes mauve, brick, deep red, red-orange, orange, and highlights of yellow. The neutral hues in the wood table and butternut squash encourage the analogous harmony because they don't disrupt the scheme.

Swatching these colors is fun and relaxing: I like to play with my reds and yellows and see what varieties in shades emerge. It's also nice to add a touch of ochre to lessen the vibrance and get that earthy, seasonal feel.

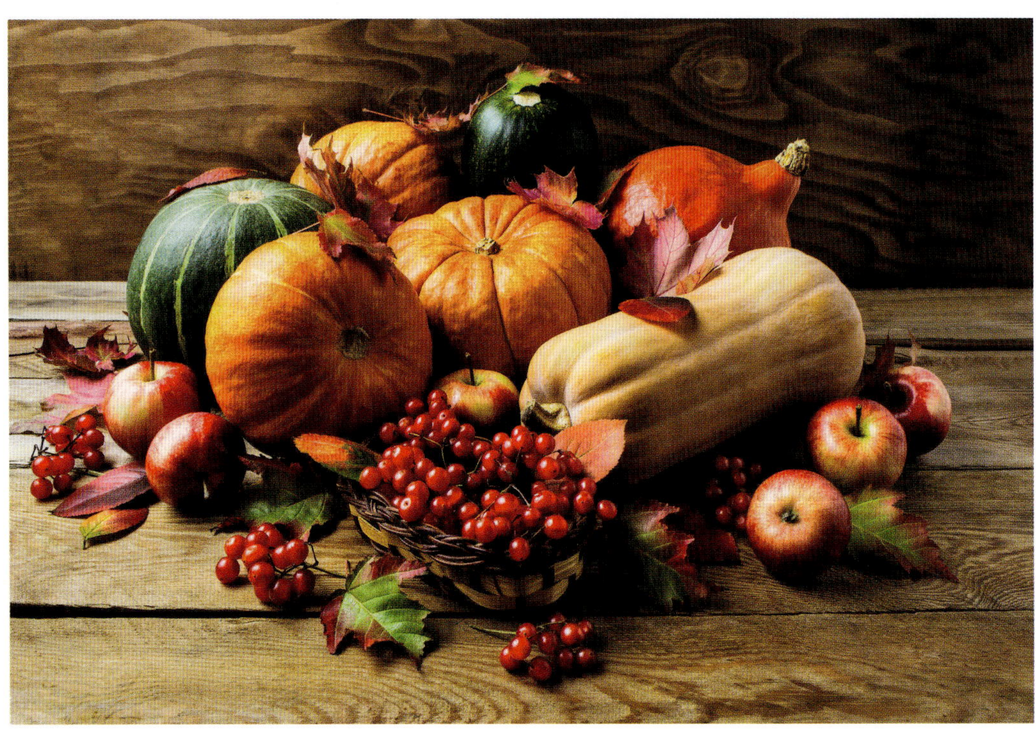

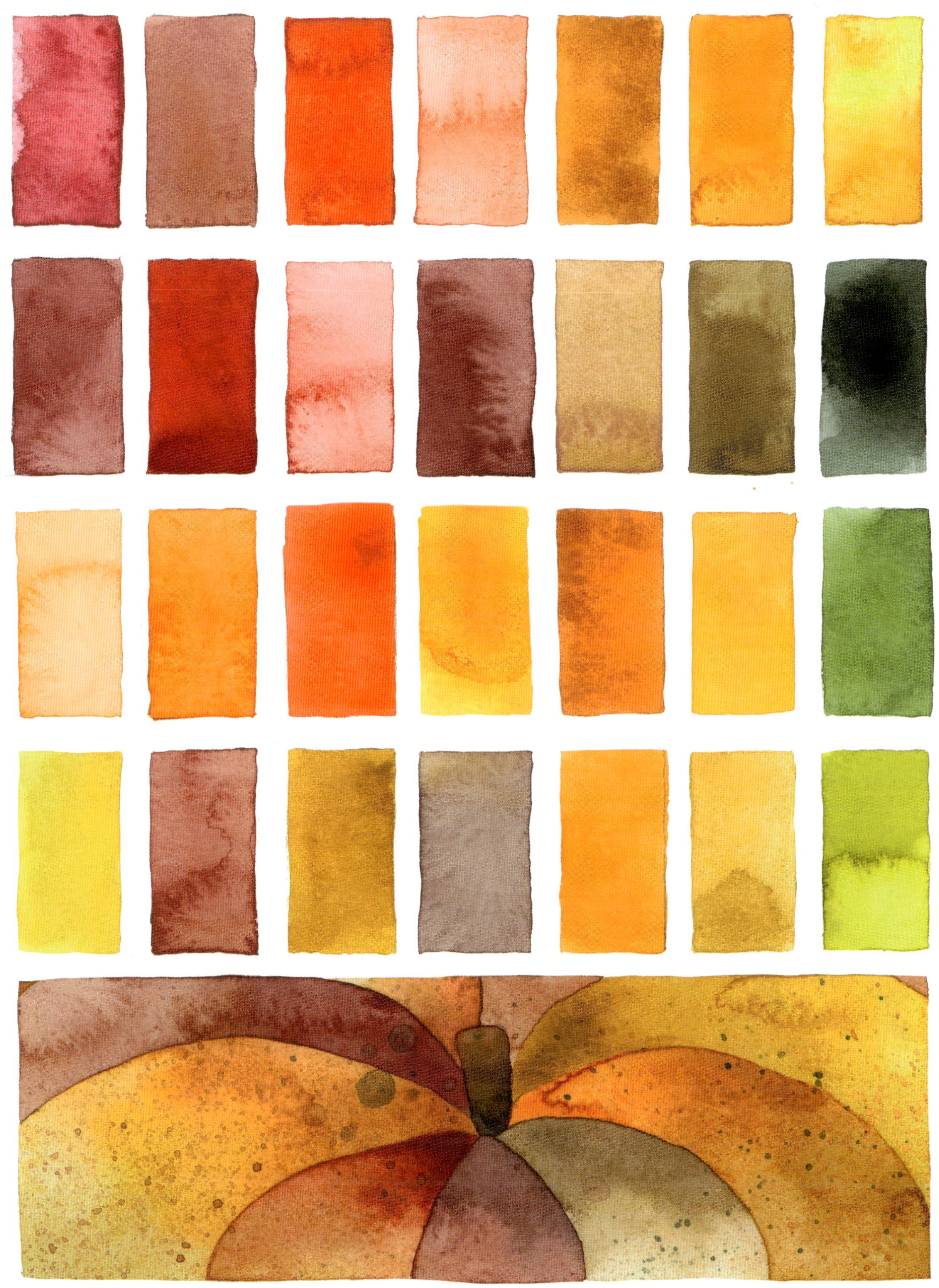

Monochromatic Amethyst

This is the only palette in the book that is one-hundred-percent monochromatic. I was eager to share this swatching example because I'm always amazed by watercolors and their beauty in transparencies. I painted the entire board using a single mix of color and different amounts of water to create a large range of values.

Painting crystals and gems is a recurring theme in my personal artwork, and I was excited to share how the light reflecting and refracting within the stone creates a fractal design and texture.

TECHNIQUE NOTES First, I had to create the perfect base purple and work from there with different amounts of water and opacity. I like to use a few different types and brands when I mix colors. I think that produces the best results for making unique and organic hues. For the purple base, I mixed Dr. Ph. Martin's Violet with some Schmincke Cobalt Violet Hue in my pan set, plus a touch of an amazing pigment from Daniel Smith in tube form called Amethyst Genuine. This type of watercolor is quite special—it's a granulated color with actual specks of crushed gemstone, and it sparkles a bit. What a perfect opportunity to use a bit of this paint! Keep in mind that you don't need to use my exact type of paint. I'm simply sharing my mixing process to reveal how complex it can be to find the right hue and texture. I rarely use just one color out of the tube or pan.

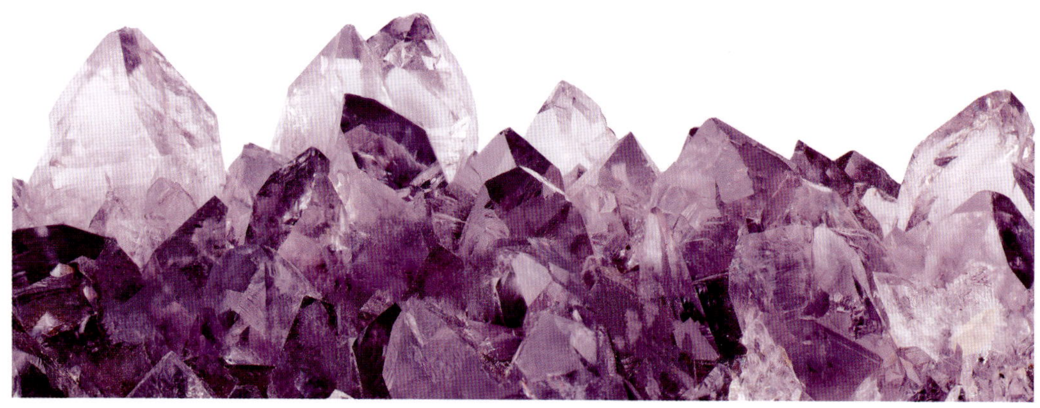

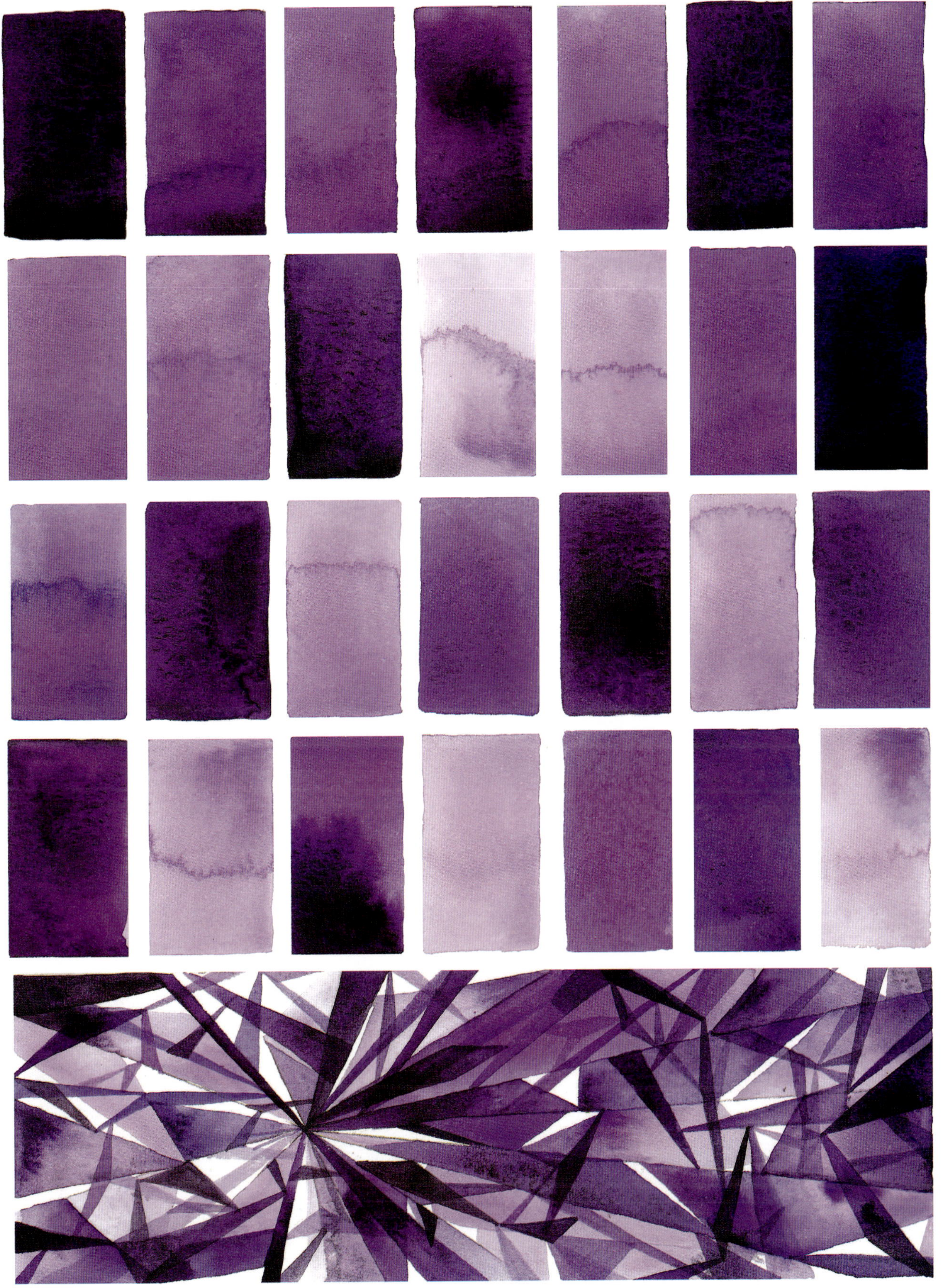

131

Smoky Quartz

I felt really comfortable creating this palette because I tend to gravitate toward dark, earthy tones highlighted with bright jewel tones. I think this is the darkest palette in the book! I used a variety of black watercolors, including a handmade Furnace Black by Kremer Pigments that's a bit cool. I also used a lot of Holbein's Ivory Black and Burnt Umber mixed with some of the browns and ochres in my Schmincke pan set, plus a bit of Holbein's Brilliant Orange.

I felt compelled to sketch a few floating crystals to create a texture board that honors this smoky quartz photograph. Each of the three centered crystals goes with a theme of one of the quartz crystals in the image. The common color theme is black, but the one on the left has hints of burnt umber and brown, the middle crystal has touches of ochre, and the one on the far right has higher contrast with touches of brilliant orange. I often find inspiration in earth minerals, and if I re-create a larger painting inspired by this image, I'll add gold-leaf flakes for dramatic embellishment!

COLOR NOTES I truly appreciate the variety of warm neutrals in this palette. There are a few other neutral palettes in this book, but they're softer neutrals centered around beige. This one has much more black and dark browns. The palette is similar to a monochromatic one because the black and dark browns tend to mesh into each other, but it's complemented by a variety of warm orange, yellow-orange, and ochre hues.

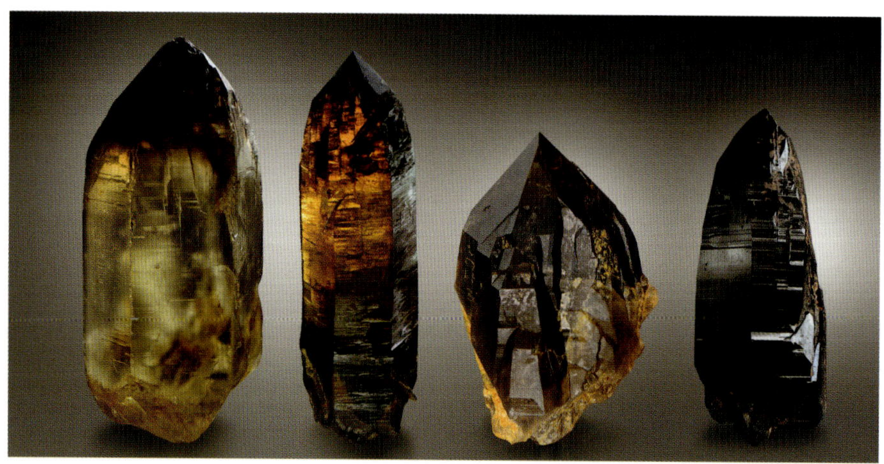

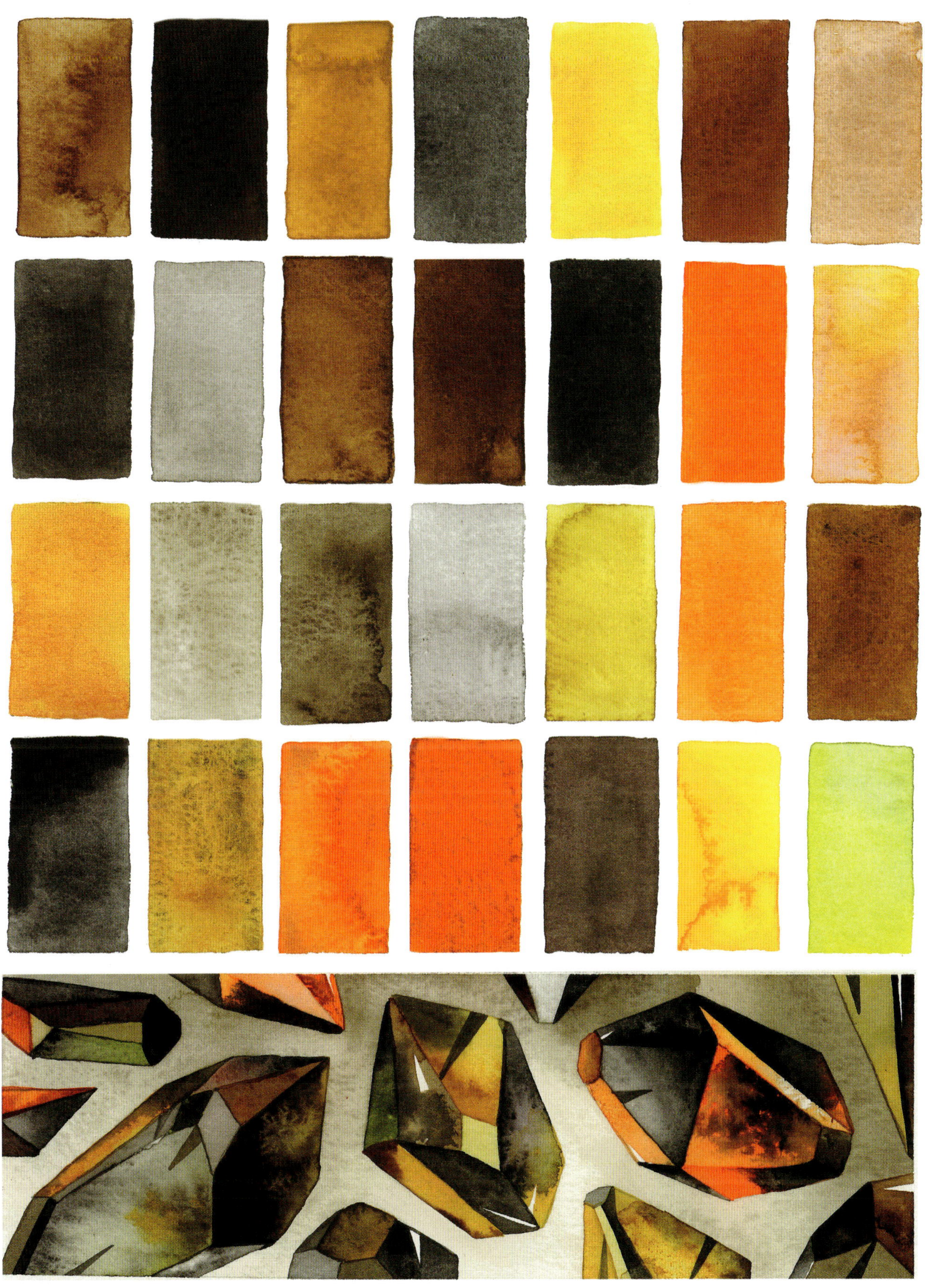

133

Orange Agate

This analogous harmony color scheme is pleasing to the eye and comforting because it comprises colors on the same side of the color wheel. The scheme is usually a primary color, secondary color, and tertiary color; or in this case, yellow, yellow-orange, orange, red-orange, and everything in between. There's a touch of light blue (also a complement to orange) in the agate that acts as a small accent color.

I was inspired by this warm palette and the mineral's amazing interior cut to recreate the shape in the picture. I painted the interior round shape with a pointed top, and then created rims in various widths, one after the other. If you're using watercolors, wait for the paint to dry between layers!

COLOR NOTES A few of the standout colors are by Holbein in tube form, including Brilliant, a bit of Shell Pink for those small pastel details, and Permanent Yellow. I also had a smidge of Dr. Ph. Martin's Persimmon on my pan set palette and added it to a few mixes of yellow to create a variety of oranges. Be mindful when using Dr. Ph. Martin's colors because they're extremely vibrant.

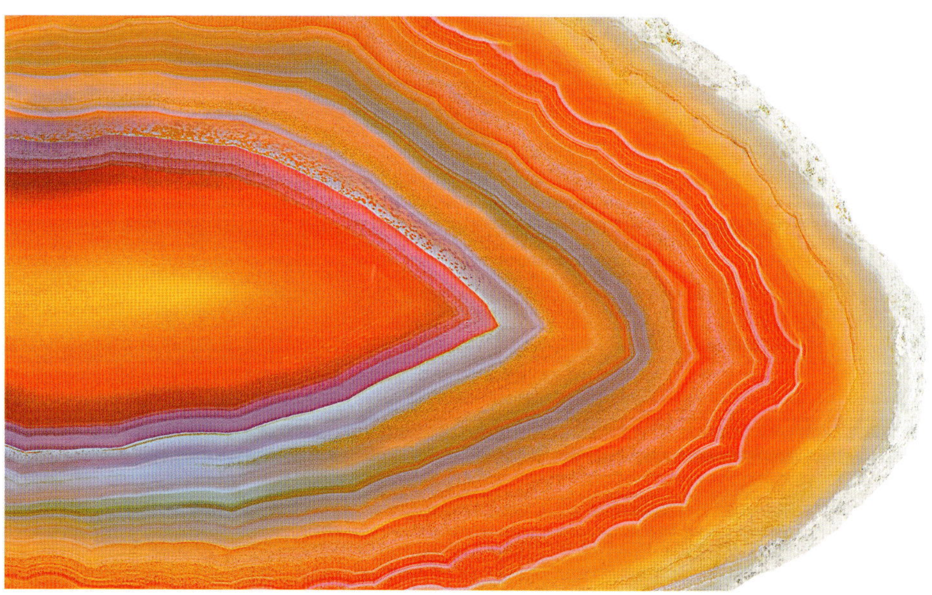

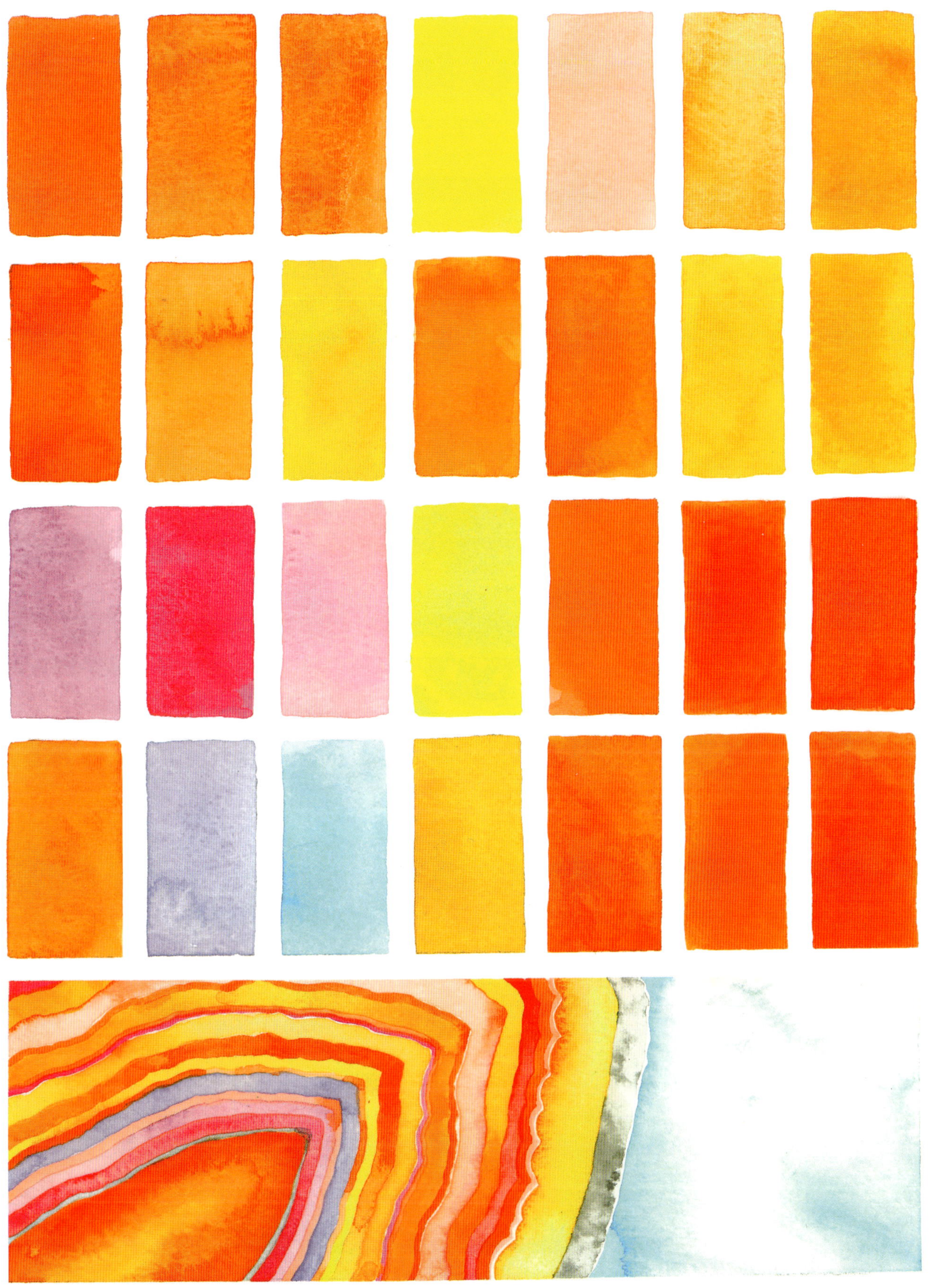

Stunning Skin Tones

At a quick glance, this picture represents four different skin tones—until you look closer. The colors range from base skin, to rosy cheek tints, lip color, freckles, spots, hair, and eyebrows.

The neutral color palette has warm undertones, with pigments such as ochre, orange, and cream. You might be surprised to learn that I created most of this palette by mixing shades of orange and blue. Because blue is orange's complement, this is a great way to create warm neutrals that are muted. To the base I added a variety of browns (which you can make with red and green for darker skin tones), and mixed in beige for fair skin.

I created what looks like a landscape in this palette, but I was actually inspired by close-up photography of skin texture. This palette is so harmonious that it relaxes me to see the colors all together.

TECHNIQUE NOTES Schmincke's Jaune Brilliant Dark and Naples Yellow are a couple of nice watercolor paints I like to use for creamy bases. Both these watercolor cakes are opaque and have white pigment in them, so they work wonderfully to lighten watercolor mixes in a neutral and warm way. I mixed my watercolors here very freely, with a large, blank, fresh palette, using bits of one tone to create another, and so on, with just a touch of one color in the next. To create the rosy cheek color, for example, I mixed a dab of red and water to my skin tone base colors.

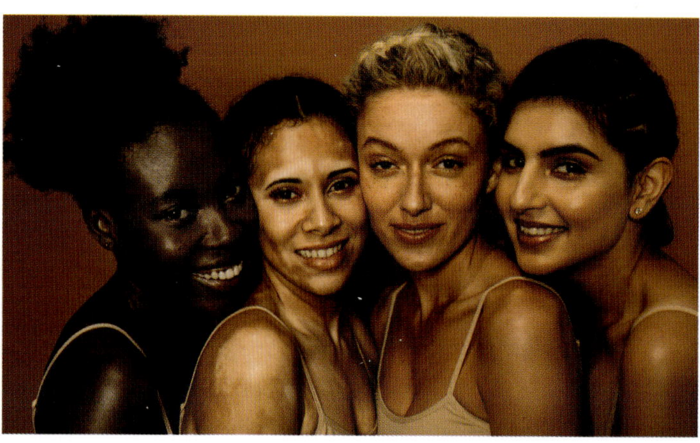

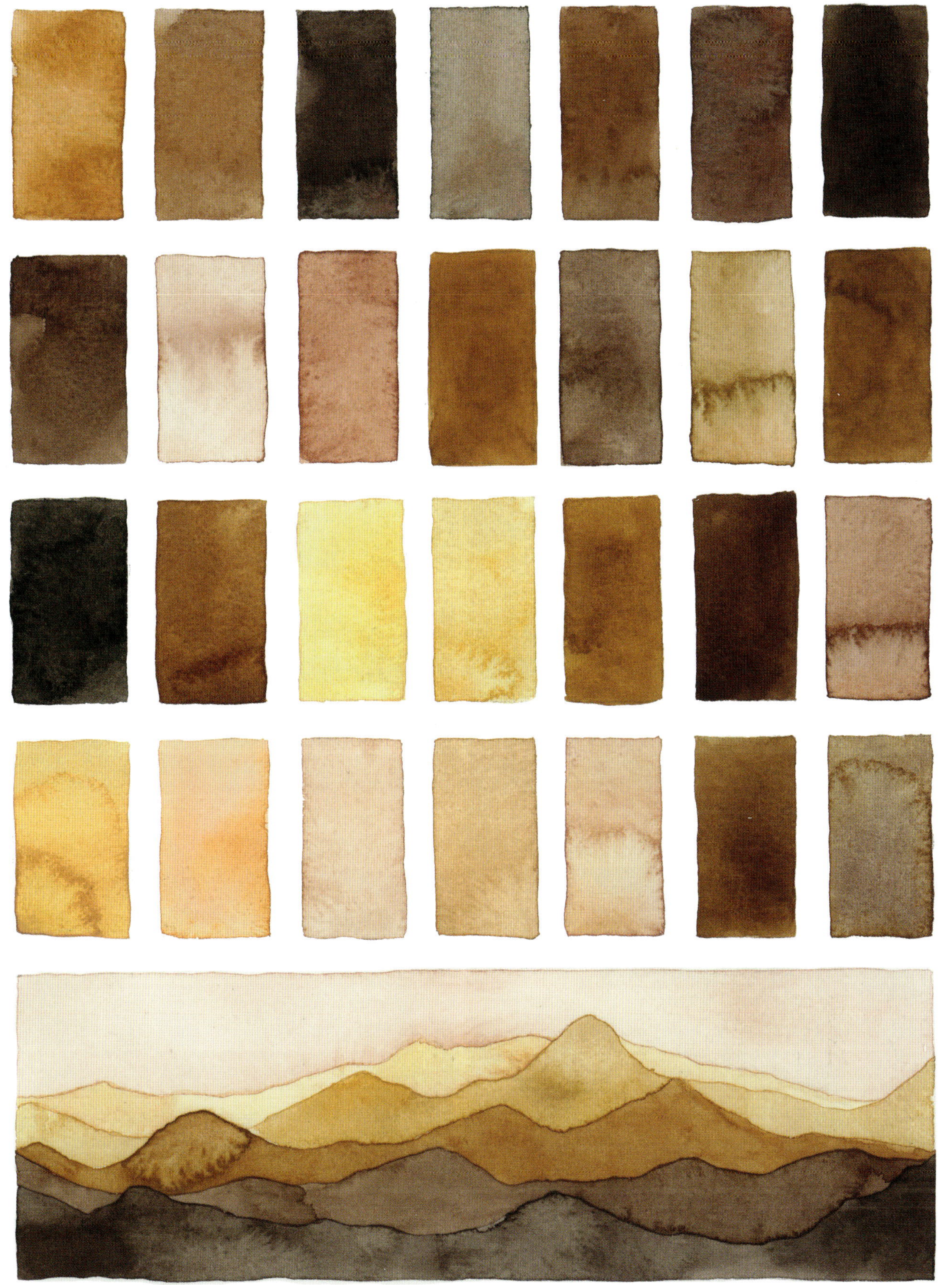

Lavish Locks

This collection of hair colors and textures is also an overall warm and neutral palette. If you've ever dyed your hair blond or are a natural blond, you will have experimented with complementary color theory in real life. Violet shampoos and tints are used on bleached and blond hair to remove yellow brassiness, especially from platinum hair. That's exactly how I swatched blond hair colors here!

The texture board inspired me to create thin long lines with a tiny brush to represent individual hair strands for all the colors I swatched.

> **TECHNIQUE NOTES** The color-mixing process is similar to the skin tone palette (see page 136), with a few additions. To your creamy base of yellow and browns, simply add black in different amounts and more red and orange tones for redheads.

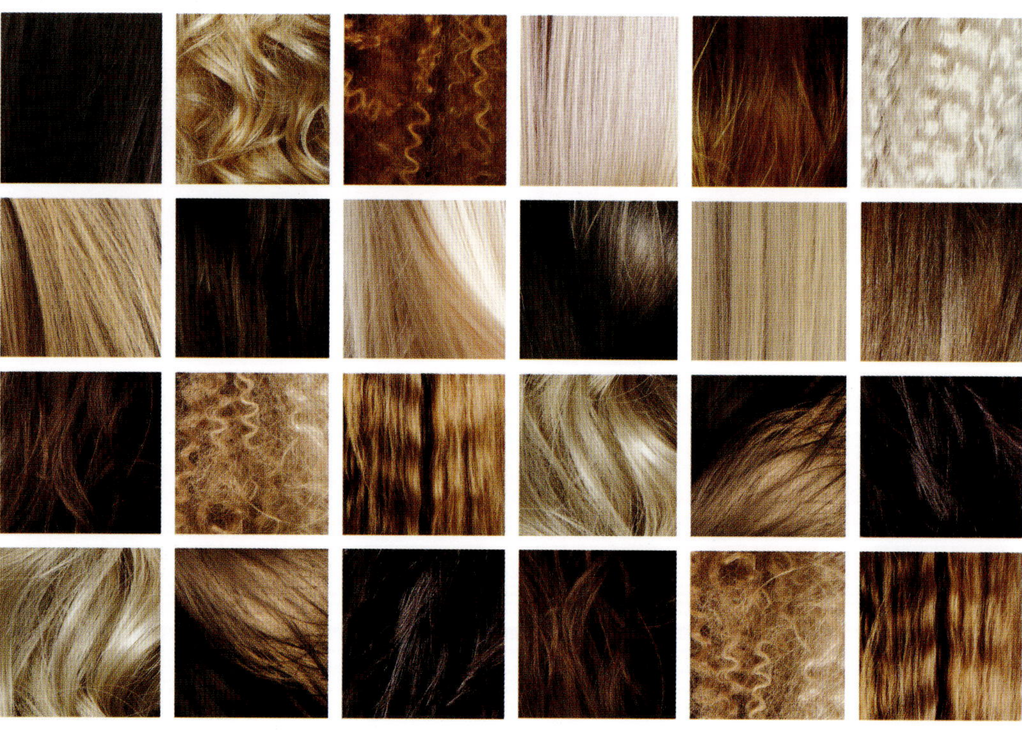

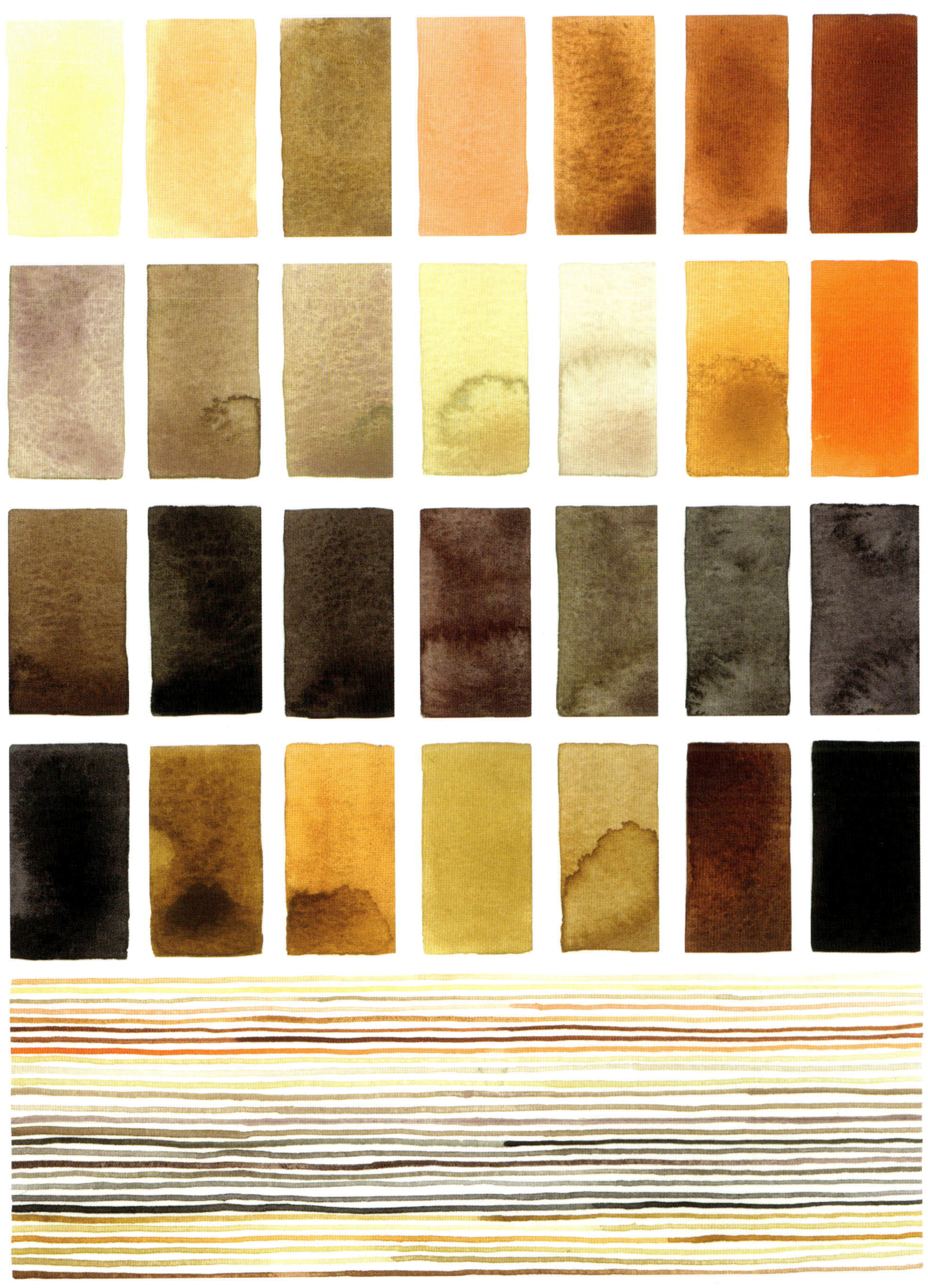

139

Template

You can use the template below to experiment with how warm and cool palettes evoke different emotions; see pages 20 and 21 for my examples. You can also use it to explore these kinds of differences between bright and neutral palettes, or two monochromatic ones.

To transfer the template to watercolor paper, photocopy this page at 100% (the same size). Scribble over the back with a softer or B pencil, making it dark enough so that it will transfer well. Place the photocopied template right side up on your watercolor paper, tape down the edges with washi tape or another removable tape, and draw over the outlines with a ballpoint or gel pen. Before removing the photocopy, pick up a corner to see if you've missed transferring any elements of the template.

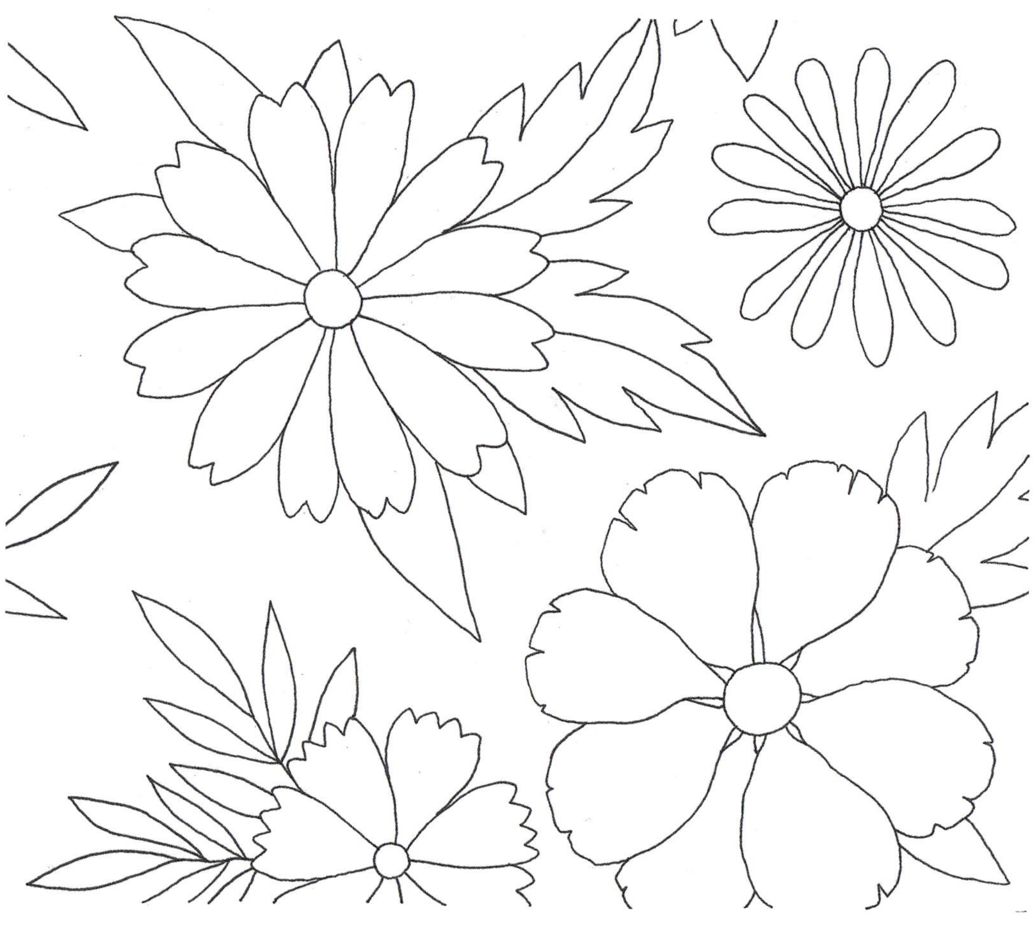

Resources

FOR BEGINNER WATERCOLOR INSTRUCTION

For more information, please refer to *Creative Watercolor: A Step-by-Step Guide for Beginners.*

FOR FURTHER WATERCOLOR INSTRUCTIONS

I highly recommend taking online lessons on Skillshare, or Domestika for Spanish speakers.

www.skillshare.com

www.domestika.org

FOR MORE INFORMATION ON SUPPLIES

I used Canson XL cold press watercolor paper for the color boards in this book.
en.canson.com/xl-series-pads/xl-watercolor

Basic color wheel · www.colorwheelco.com

PAINT BRANDS MENTIONED IN THIS BOOK

Daniel Smith · www.danielsmith.com

Dr. Ph. Martins · www.docmartins.com

Holbein · www.holbeinartistmaterials.com

Kremer Pigmente · shop.kremerpigments.com/en

Schmincke · www.schmincke.de/en.html

Sennelier · www.sennelier-colors.com

Winsor & Newton · hwww.winsornewton.com/row

Acknowledgments

I am incredibly grateful for all the circumstances that allowed me to pursue a creative life.

As an adult I now realize how special it was to have been raised in an environment that fomented expression and art through freedom and travel. What a gift it was to receive a wide vision of the world at a young age. Understanding since childhood that there are different countries, climates, and cultures all around the globe is something I truly can appreciate today. Witnessing true diversity and knowing that things are done differently in countries that look nothing like the one I grew up in planted a seed within me, and I am now seeing the flower bloom.

While writing this book I came across many themes I was delighted to remember having experienced in real life, such as cities on different continents, artisanal textures, and life experiences like scuba diving. As I grow older and approach the age of having my own family, I can now see what a gift it was to have had grandparents who prioritized showing their grandchildren the world as opposed to materialism. I will never forget the family trips we took every summer from ages 6 to 19. Although I was too young to remember everything during some of the travel experiences, I know my inner artist began to develop during this tender age.

I can only hope to someday give the gift of travel to a family of my own and plant seeds in young minds. Our planet is exquisitely diverse, and I can't think of a better way to pay homage to this world than making art.

¡Gracias Mamá Guille y Papá Memo!

About the Author

The author of *Creative Watercolor* (Quarry Books, 2018), **Ana Victoria Calderón** is a Mexican/American watercolor artist and teacher with a bachelor's degree in information design and continued studies in fine arts. Her licensed artwork can be seen in retail outlets throughout the United States and Europe, on a wide variety of products. Ana teaches in-person workshops and hosts creative retreats in Tulum, Mexico, as well as summer watercolor retreats throughout Europe. She has had over 60,000 students on Skillshare, where she is a Top Teacher, and she also teaches thousands of Spanish-speaking students on Domestika. See more of Ana's work on Instagram (@anavictoriana), YouTube (Ana Victoria Calderon), and Facebook (Ana Victoria Calderon Illustration). She lives in Mexico City, Mexico, with her husband and three cats.

Index

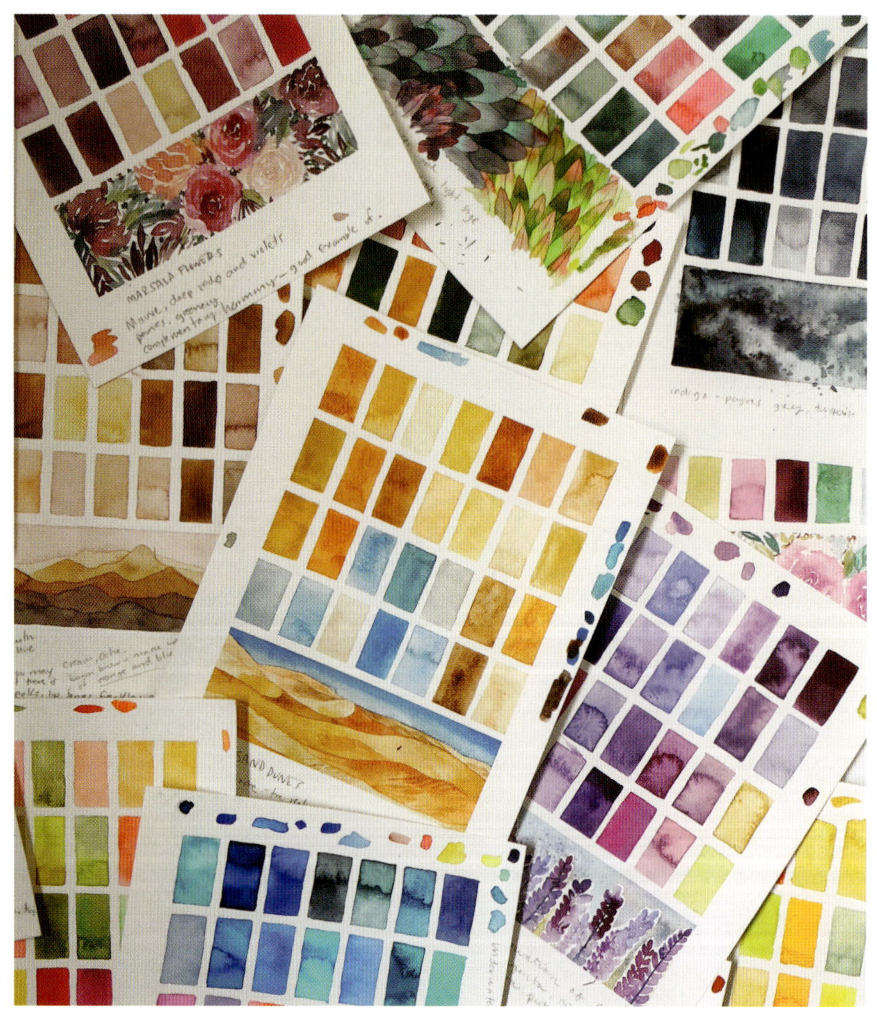